SPIRITUALITY
of
LIBERATION

Jon Sobrino

SPIRITUALITY
of
LIBERATION

Toward Political Holiness

Translated from the Spanish by
Robert R. Barr

ORBIS BOOKS

Maryknoll, New York 10545

Third Printing, November 1990

Originally published as *Liberación con espíritu,* © 1985 by Jon Sobrino, San Salvador, and © 1985 by Editorial Sal Terrae, Santander

English translation © 1988 by Orbis Books, Maryknoll, NY 10545
Manufactured in the United States of America

Bible quotations are from *The New American Bible*

Manuscript editor and indexer: William E. Jerman

LIBRARY OF CONGRESS
Library of Congress Cataloging-in-Publication Data

Sobrino, Jon.
    [Liberación con espíritu. English]
    Spirituality of liberation: toward political holiness / Jon
Sobrino; translated from the Spanish by Robert R. Barr.
      p. cm.
    Translation of: Liberación con espíritu.
    Bibliography: p.
    Includes index.
    ISBN 0-88344-617-0.   ISBN 0-88344-616-2 (pbk.)
    1. Spiritual life—Catholic authors.   2. Liberation theology.
3. Catholic Church—Latin America—History—20th century.   4. Latin
America—Church history—20th century.   I. Title.
BX2350.2.S575413   1988
248—dc19   87-34578
                                                  CIP

Contents

PART THREE
SOURCES OF SPIRITUALITY

Presentation

The chapters in this book are articles I have had published on spirituality from 1980 to 1984. And yet, strictly speaking, this is not a book on spirituality. Still less is it a book on particular spiritualities. Rather it is an attempt to cut through to the heart of what *any* spirituality must be. It is, further, an attempt to demonstrate the necessity of spirituality in today's world—the crucial importance of living with a particular "spirit" in order to be truly a believer, or indeed a human being. In a world like ours today, a world of such change, such crisis, such pitfalls—and such promise—doctrines and ideologies are not enough. We shall need "spirit" if we hope to control and direct life and history; if that life and that history are to be, when all is said and done, not absurdity, or sheer becoming, but promise; if life and history are to generate hope, not despair or resignation; if life and history are to radiate liberative transformation rather than passivity or selfishness.

The thematic of these articles, it seems to me, answers a genuine need. In Latin America this need is concretized in the urgency of giving the practice of liberation "spirit." Surely liberation practice provides us with a necessary, just, and good channel for our energies. But that channel must flow with "spirit." What else will remedy the limitations of those engaged in the various liberation practices? After all, they are human beings. But the correct "spirit" will raise to a new power not only the practice of liberation ("squaring" it, "cubing" it, so to say), but the agent of that practice as well. In Europe, Johannes B. Metz has long since called attention to the need for a marriage of spirituality and politics. In Latin America we hear of a need for "contemplation in liberation" (Leonardo Boff). We hear of the importance of "contemplation in action for justice" (Ignacio Ellacuría). In the present volume I shall be speaking of "political holiness," of "liberation with spirit." The intuition is the same. Spirit and practice must join hands. Without spirit, practice can always degenerate. Without practice, spirit will remain vague, sidelined, even alienating.

The Spanish original of this book forms part of a series of works in Latin American theology (*Colección "Presencia Teológica,"* no. 23). Taken together, the volumes of this series ought to be sufficient to allay suspicions concerning this theology, especially as expressed in the Vatican "Instruction on Certain Aspects of the Theology of Liberation." My apologia may achieve its desired effect, or it may not. But at all events there can be no honest denial that Latin American theology is concerned with spirituality. For Latin American theology, spirituality is a basic dimension of theology. It is precisely the application

ix

of theory to practice. Gustavo Gutiérrez made this point years ago, and my present concern is to concretize his assertion. Theology is based, above all else, on a practice and a spirituality. The practice is purely and simply the following of Jesus in our history. The spirituality is purely and simply the actualization of the spirit of Jesus in our own times. This is what the following pages seek to demonstrate.

Finally, I should like to state that whatever the reader may find enlightening here has been drawn from those wells from which Gustavo Gutiérrez invites us all to drink (*Beber en su propio pozo*, 1983; *We Drink from Our Own Wells*, 1984), those wells filled to overflowing by the poor of Latin America, along with those others who walk with them, with all their dedication, love, and self-sacrifice—the wells that they have filled to the brim with the spirit of Jesus.

We shall catch a glimpse of this in part 3 of this volume, when we contemplate the love that fills our martyrs and the hope that fills our poor. There we shall see what "liberation with spirit" really is. Parts 1 and 2 are but the attempt to provide a verbal explanation of this reality.

I wish to express my gratitude to all of those who, by their life and their death, have filled the wells from which the rest of us now drink in order to follow Jesus down the road that leads to God.

San Salvador
September 1985

Introduction

The Importance of the Spiritual Life Today[1]

The spiritual life is a time-honored tradition in the church and in the religious life—that of men and women under the vows of poverty, chastity, and obedience. Whatever its ultimate essence, and whatever its practices, the spiritual life is "traditional" first of all in the etymological sense of the word: it has been handed down from generation to generation. And the very fact of this transmission attests its importance and necessity.

We should scarcely be surprised, then, if from time to time we hear of the importance and necessity of the spiritual life. The late Jesuit Superior General, Father Pedro Arrupe, for example, never tired of insisting on the crucial importance of maintaining and fostering the *vitality of faith*—a new name for the spiritual life. When all is said and done, without the spiritual life, apostolic work would be threatened from within. It would be cut off from its deepest roots.

The age-old tradition of the spiritual life, and the frequency with which we hear of its importance, ought to incline us to take it seriously. The cumulative experience of centuries is not usually deceived in matters of this nature, particularly when the issues at stake are realities that touch on the very constitution of the person and groups of persons. The human person embodies elements that remain constant throughout the course of history, however much that history may change. As I see it, all of us—whatever our conception of the spiritual life, whatever our spiritual practices, and whatever our criticisms of particular ideas and practices—know almost instinctively that we are dealing here with a subject of extreme importance, a decisive issue for the Christian life.

By the same token, the mere reassertion of the importance and necessity of the spiritual life and its practices does not of itself generate a vigorous spiritual life. So often, general truths become real only in the act of being historicized, inserted into history. So it is with the general truth of the spiritual life. And in order for this truth to be historicized, the element of eternal truth in the importance and necessity of the spiritual life must come to light, again and again, and ever new, in each particular historical situation. In other words, the spiritual life must demonstrate its effectiveness for our life as Christians and religious. When all is said and done, the spiritual life must be efficacious for the transformation of the secular reality around us, helping us steer that reality in the direction of the reign of God.

It seems to me that something like this is happening right now. We see a new interest in the spiritual life all around us. We see a new insistence on its importance. We are witnesses to new ways of bringing it to realization. But this new enthusiasm for the spiritual life does not come primarily from some kind of wooden fidelity to the tradition of the ages. To be sure, a profound truth is (re)emerging in this revival. But the renewal of the spiritual life all around us arises primarily from our de facto situation. It is the concrete reality of our existence that poses the problem of the spiritual life once more.

It is significant, for example, that the theology of liberation, which is interested primarily and per se in the practice of the faith, emphasizes spiritual themes like prayer, contemplation, and generally what we might call a spirituality of liberation.

What I hope to offer in the following pages, rather than a theoretical consideration of the abstract nature of the spiritual life, is a reflexive description of what has actually taken place in recent years. My aim will be to discover the historical roots of this renascence of the reality of the spiritual life—the historical roots of its concrete shape in our Christian and human lives today.

Before embarking on this reflection, however, I must clarify what I understand by "spiritual life," but not by an academic definition or description. I might begin by saying that "spiritual life" simply means life with a certain spirit, life lived in a particular spirit—specifically, in the case of the Christian spiritual life, life lived in the spirit of Jesus. This assertion may appear to be oversimple. It may seem purely nominalistic or even tautological. But if we do not take it for granted that we already know what it is to live as a Christian, and what "spirit" is (and the relationship between them), then, as we explore these two elements in greater depth, we shall be able to make some progress in our historical understanding of the Christian life.

The importance of this focus lies in the fact that the spiritual life cannot be understood from a point of departure in its specific practices, important and necessary as these may be. The spiritual life can be understood only from the perspective of something more comprehensive, something of which spiritual practices are but the expression, their enlightenment and motivation.

1. The Lesson of the 1970s: The Relationship between Spiritual Life and Historical Life

If we compare Christian and religious life in the late 1980s with Christian and religious life ten or fifteen years earlier, it cannot be denied that a great change has taken place, and that the change has been in the spiritual life itself. The decade of the 1970s was the decisive one. The crucial thing then, in my opinion, was the discussion about whether there are automatic, autonomous channels of the spiritual life, or whether these channels ought to form part of a larger whole, a more basic and primary channel called life, historical life, Christian life. In other words, in order to have a "spiritual life," must you not first have *life*?

1.1. The Christians and religious who most felt the impact of Vatican II and Medellín, and who allowed this impact to have factual consequences in their lives, generally tended to be suspicious of the mechanical conceptualization of the spiritual life that we form when we begin our thinking with specific mechanisms of that life. They began to search for new spiritual forms and practices that would be more in keeping with the new situation around them. At the same time they began to abandon, to a greater or lesser extent—sometimes reaching the point of contempt for—old practices with their underlying theology. But in any case, Christians and religious began to insist that the spiritual life must include real life, historical life. As a result, the ultimate meaning of the Christian life and its basic structure now came in for serious review and revision.

I have no wish to belabor the obvious. But it will be helpful to remind ourselves of the modern rediscovery of the basic characteristics of the Christian life. We in Central America are witnessing a reemphasis of the indispensability of *incarnation* in the reality of our countries. There is a new emphasis on the importance of incarnation not merely in our culture, but in our society as well, where we have a clearer picture today of the misery, oppression, injustice, and repression to which the Central American majorities are subjected. This incarnation placed Christians and religious in more or less immediate contact with the poor, and—*mirabile dictu*—the poor were transformed into the locus, the place, of the Christian life.

Then we made a preferential option for the poor—using different language, perhaps, but making that option. Christian life, now understood as a *practice of service* to the poor, gradually came to be seen as a practice *in the midst of the poor*. The practice of love, especially love expressed in justice—accompanied, then, by a denunciation of structural sin and a search for structural transformations—was once again the fundamental content of the Christian life.

Finally, this form of incarnation and practice has been the object of *persecution*, in various degrees. This phenomenon has constituted at one and the same time (1) a sign of our solidarity with an oppressed people, (2) the criterion of the authenticity of our incarnation and practice of love, and (3) a historically necessary ingredient of the Christian life.

The important thing about the decade of the 1970s, then, was our rediscovery of the real life of the impoverished majorities, together with our evangelical rediscovery that it is to them that the good news of the gospel is addressed. In this perspective, the poor become the locus, the place, of the Christian life, and hence of any Christian religious life whatsoever. And so—the most important thing of all for our topic—the poor were now the locus of the spiritual life as well. The content of the qualifier "spiritual," as attached to the noun "life," can no longer be understood or actualized in any other locus than that of historical life. In a word, the intuition that has gradually forced itself upon our perceptions is that without historical, real *life* there can be no such thing as *spiritual* life.

Light was shed on this conviction by a new reading of the scriptures, as well as by numerous statements in official documents of the church. The intuition of the Old Testament prophets that "to know God is to practice justice," the intuition of the gospels that the ultimate scope of Jesus' self-understanding and practice was the reign of God as inchoate in history and not merely eschatological and transcendent, together with the power of chapter 25 of Matthew bequeathed to us as a reminder of the ultimate criterion of Christian faith, had an enormous impact on us. Then Medellín formulated the same basic thesis, recalling the declaration by Pope Paul VI that "in order to know God we must know the human being." And the Thirty-Third General Congregation of the Jesuits has reminded us that our basic mission is "the service of faith and the promotion of justice."

All these formulations, like others developed by theology, have two things in common. First, they all acknowledge the bipolarity of Christian existence taken as a whole. That existence contains a historical element—the reign of God, justice, knowledge, and service to human beings—and a transcendent element—God, the knowledge of God, faith in God. Secondly, all these formulations recognize that the transcendent element is not directly accessible—that it must be reached through its historical mediation.

It seems to me that this intuition contains something absolutely essential to our faith. Further, I think that, for many Christians and religious, this intuition will prove to be historically irreversible, at least for the foreseeable future. Whatever theoretical and practical problems may arise out of this new comprehension and practice of the totality of the faith, one thing is perfectly clear: it is impossible to profess God without working for God's reign. One cannot profess Christ without following Jesus in history. In terms of my concerns in this book, there is no *spiritual* life without actual, historical *life*. It is impossible to live *with spirit* unless that spirit *becomes flesh*.

1.2. The mere fact of opting for historical life as I have described it, and really, actually living that life, is itself the expression of a spirit. Historical life is never purely historical. It is always in some sense intrinsically a *spiritual* life. Let us not forget that, for Christian faith, the giver of life is the Spirit. The Spirit sends messengers to proclaim the good news to the poor, the Spirit stirs the word of prophecy, the Spirit bestows fortitude in persecution, and so on. An incarnate historical life, lived in behalf of the poor, and steadfast in persecution, is a *spiritual* life in and of itself.

And yet—as the pioneers of the theology of liberation recognized—the practice of a new historical life does not automatically resolve the problem of the content of the adjective "spiritual." A life immersed in history may well shape a structural channel for one's spirituality, but it will not be a spiritual life as such. There are, in my opinion, two kinds of experiences and historical observations that have motivated a return to the indispensable "spiritual" element in the historical life, and our immersion in that element. First there is the honest admission that even Christians and religious who have opted for a new type of historical life remain subject to temptation and sin. Secondly, even within the indispensable channel of a new historical life, the Spirit of God continues to pronounce new words and make new demands. We can set no a priori limits to the will of the Spirit. There is no arbitrary silencing of the "more" that never ceases to arise in history.

I personally believe that those who have most honestly experienced the process of the 1970s have also recognized that they are still subject to human frailty. They know that the very channel they have chosen, necessary and correct though it be, generates its own brand of concupiscence. One can be tempted to swagger a bit, to vaunt one's ethical superiority, to believe in one's immunity to temptation and sin. And then too the very channel we have selected bears with it structural difficulties, such as that of reconciling and harmonizing effectiveness and generosity, struggle and magnanimity, justice and compassion, fairness and forgiveness.

None of this, in my view, militates against the validity and urgency of our basic option. The intuition that there is no spiritual life without historical life remains intact. But both our own frailty and the autonomy of the Spirit make it clear to us that there is no avoiding the question of the spirit with which we must live and bestow life. Here, it seems to me, three important points call for our attention.

1. In the first place, it now becomes especially important to analyze not only Jesus' practice, but the spirit of his practice. We have them both in his programatic proclamation in the Sermon on the Mount. The Lucan version of the first Beatitude—"Blest are you poor; the reign of God is yours"(6:20)— makes it clear that the material principle of spirituality is real poverty. We must not, however, overlook Matthew's version, with its poverty of spirit ("How blest are the poor in spirit; the reign of God is theirs"[5:3])—*not* in order to neglect the primary importance of material poverty for identifying those addressed by the Beatitude. The meaning of the Matthean version is that we must be, to borrow Ignacio Ellacuría's telling expression, "poor with spirit." And again in the last Beatitude—"Blest are you when they insult you and persecute you . . . " (Matt. 5:11)—it is clear that the historical verification of the spiritual life is precisely the persecution that rages when justice is practiced.

These two Beatitudes, the first and the last, proclaim the indispensability of the material element of poverty, so evidently present in our situation. But they also stress the special element, contained in other Beatitudes as well, of the interior Christian attitude that finds expression in the imparting of mercy and the building of peace.

To me personally, this atmosphere, this interior attitude, is formulated in an especially beautiful way in the Beatitude that speaks to us of the pure of heart, of those who "see God." They are the ones who are not attached to themselves (or even self-seekingly attached to the causes for which they struggle), those whose eyes are pure, those who seek the truth, the "chaste" in the deepest sense of the word. They are the ones who, within history, ever and again place themselves before God, in order to hear the word of a God whose word is greater than any we can pronounce, however correct it may be. Taken together, the Beatitudes paint a picture of the person who not only has made a correct option and a correct commitment to history, but has made that option and that commitment "with spirit."

2. We experience a growing conviction of what I might term the "efficacy of holiness." Obviously, any commitment to the poor will call for, and seek out, historical efficacy. Hence our insistence on liberation, on the promotion of justice, on participation in liberative processes—in extraordinary cases, even in revolutionary processes. But without denying any of this, we have also gradually come to see that life with spirit—holiness—has an efficacy of its own. And we have made this discovery not by way of any a priori speculation, but by way of historical observation.

To take just one meaningful example, we might recall the case of Archbishop Oscar Romero. Surely there can be no doubt about his historical commitment. But his immense social influence, and the effectiveness of his practice, cannot be understood apart from his personal holiness. The inescapable fact is: not only does a historical life "with spirit" not alienate Christians from real problems, it actually lends them more effectiveness in the liberation of the poor.

3. I believe that we have recovered the conviction that our "life with spirit" must be expressed in spiritual practices. Once more we have seen the need for these practices, but this time not merely on the strength of a priori considerations, but on account of the demands of real life, and because real life becomes less Christian when spiritual practices are missing. We might say that we have become aware of the demand of reality for expression at the level of meaning—and conversely, we now realize that when the expression is missing, one may doubt the existence of the reality. In our own specific case in Latin America, we perceive the need precisely of a spiritual expression, both for our enlightenment in historical life and for our motivation in that life.

This is not the moment to enter into a theoretical discussion of what has priority in Christian faith—life or its explicitation. We need not take sides in the controversy surrounding the *contemplativus in actione* model and the *contemplata aliis tradere* model. I personally hold for the ultimate priority of life over its explicitation. At the same time there is no denying that there is at least a dialectic between life with spirit and an expression of spirit in life. Thus the practices of spirituality, though enjoying no priority over those of historical life, are necessary. They enable us to live life with more spirit.

I can only conclude from all this that, although certain practices may or should be abandoned, and others modified, the need for spiritual practices as such is clear, especially those that touch on the deepest roots of the Christian life, such as the eucharist, prayer, spiritual exercises or retreats, discernment, and the like.

In sum, I personally believe that the great lesson of the decade of the 1970s for the spiritual life is twofold. (1) We now see the absolute necessity of historical life (life in unfolding history) for spiritual life. This is the more novel datum. But it is also a basic demand of our Christian faith itself. It is therefore indispensable. And for many Christians and religious there is no turning back. (2) We now see the need to live history with a Christian spirit—with a spirit that continually judges us even as we flow in the correct channel of historical life, and above all, with a spirit that continues to demand, ever more insistently, that we immerse ourselves in history in more and more of a Christian spirit.

It all comes down to (1) committing ourselves to the building of the reign of God in the very midst of history, and thus drawing near to God, and (2) being women and men of pure heart, a heart that sees God, and thus building the reign of God. Or to put it another way, it is a matter of doing *what* Jesus did, and of doing it ever more *as* Jesus did it (but this is not to be understood as fundamentalism might have it). After all, it is of the utmost importance that we live in conformity with the inspirations of the Spirit of Jesus, who both bids us look at Jesus, reminding us of his concrete, dangerous memory, and opens up to us new routes, new challenges, new historical mediations.

2. Importance of the Spiritual Life Today

As was said at the beginning, we are witnessing today a new concern for, and a rebirth of, the "spiritual" element in the life of Christians and religious. The religious life has demands of its own that are not automatically met simply by choosing a new channel for our historical life. True, this new channel bestows profound meaning on our religious life. But the question of the specific problematic of the religious life remains the problematic of responsiveness in the spirit of obedience, of the total self-dedication of celibacy, of the self-emptying of poverty, of the conditions required for life in community, and so on. All of these realities, each with its own potentialities and its own difficulties, call for spirit if we are to overcome the difficulties and activate the potentialities.

For my present purposes, however, I shall concentrate on those historical realities in which faith and the religious life are lived in Central America, and which can be lived in Christian fashion only if they are lived with spirit. I want to mention those that seem to me more important generally, although of course their importance will vary from situation to situation.

2.1. None of us is entirely exempt from persecution today. This calls for a *spirit of fortitude*. We are all aware of the ongoing repression suffered by the people in so many of our lands. When Christians and religious enter into genuine solidarity with the people, persecution bursts upon their heads as well. Persecution is one of the most effective instruments for bringing religious and religious communities face to face with ultimate, hazardous, and difficult options.

Acceptance of persecution, and especially the strength to stand firm under it, is not an easy thing. It is not something that goes without saying for us. It is not simply part and parcel of the momentum of the religious life as such, or something that flows from the general principles of that life. It means going back to what is deepest in the Christian life, going back to the fundamental principle of Christian love, going back to a readiness to give of one's own life, indeed to give one's very life.

What is needed in persecution—in our situation today, then—is spirit: the spirit of Jesus in the garden, the spirit of the good shepherd who will not abandon his sheep at a time of danger. If we are to have the strength to stand steadfast in persecution, and to be of support to those who work with us or depend on us, we shall need a special spirit of fortitude, a strength of spirit that will be mightier than our fears and terrors. We need to hear, in our frailty, Jesus' comforting, strengthening word: "Take courage! I have overcome the world" (John 16:33). And we must cling to the end to that final word of Jesus that "says it all": "There is no greater love than this: to lay down one's life for one's friends" (John 15:13). "Spiritual" life today, then, means life with a spirit of fortitude.

2.2. New conditions in our countries call for deep discernment. They demand a *spirit of quest for truth*. This quest will be of paramount theological importance. The new processes of liberation, the revolutionary struggles that we perceive about us, the new noncapitalist societies springing up, or soon to spring up, the reconstruction of nations, constitute "virgin territory" for religious as well. We must learn to live in the "new land," as human beings, as Christians, and as religious. Serious questions arise, then. What is the correct form of incarnation in these liberative and revolutionary processes? How can we support what is just and good in these processes? What should be our most important and specific contribution? How may we maintain a sound autonomy and identification of our own? What "we've always known" is no longer enough to answer all these questions—not even what we have known as Christians, not even the knowledge we have from our charisms. We find ourselves simply facing a new history, and therefore facing a new word from God.

Lest we overlook, or eviscerate, the novelty of history, and above all lest we fail to discern the will of God in that novelty, we must have a pure spirit, pure eyes, a pure heart, which will not cling to truth "we've always known," but will seek in truth the will of God. The "spiritual" life, then, means life with a spirit of passion for the truth.

2.3. The historical situation of our countries is changing, and changing basically. This phenomenon demands a *spirit of fidelity*. History marches on, and brings novelty. We must of course embrace incarnation in each historical situation, as was said above, but we must just as surely accept the fact that an incarnation is never effectuated once and for all. We must be ever ready to accept a new conversion.

Recent years in Central America have seen precisely the sort of change in society and the church that calls for successive conversions. Even when a revolutionary process has triumphed, as in Nicaragua, history does not stop dead. New problems and demands arise. And if we turn to future history, no one can predict what will happen over the next ten or twenty years.

Readiness for continued incarnation, for honest confrontation with history, whatever that history may be, calls for the open-mindedness and availability demanded of us by St. Ignatius Loyola. It calls for fidelity to God, as we make our way through the unknown in history. It requires of us a readiness to "leave our father's house," as Abraham was called to do. And it demands of us that we "walk humbly with [our] God," as the prophet Micah enjoins us (6:8). The "spiritual" life, then, means living history with a spirit of openness, availability, and fidelity.

2.4. Finally, I should like to call attention to a widespread phenomenon within the church and religious life—the divisioning into various groups, with each group claiming to have the monopoly on what it is to be the true church or the authentic form of the religious life. I think this is a problem that attacks the very basis of Christian life, and that therefore its solution calls for a *spirit of holiness*.

There are those who, often enough, attempt to vindicate their exclusive claim to the truth by an appeal to pure orthodoxy. Others—more correctly, in my view—appeal to the gospel, and to a theology more in accord with that gospel. The former attempt to solve problems with an appeal to authority. The latter appeal to the power of theological reasoning. Thus the former insist that the true church is the institutional church, with its hierarchy, its doctrine, and so on. The latter, although in no way denying what the former have to say, are concerned to stress that the true church is the church of the poor.

I have no wish to deny the importance of theological argumentation for an elucidation of the problem of the identity of the true church. I should only like to add an additional element—namely, that, when all is said and done, the stamp of approval of any ecclesial group claiming to be the true church can only be the holiness of that group. In the long run, only holiness will win the battle of the true church—though sometimes losing it in the short run—as we see from the lives of so many saints and founders of religious orders.

Those who truly love the church today—those who desire its renewal, those who would like to come to its aid in its present situation of confusion and division—must be ready to bear the witness of holiness. It would be an error to confuse love for the church with an outrageously exaggerated defense of institution and orthodoxy. But it would likewise be insufficient—not wrong, but insufficient—to wish to demonstrate one's love for the church only by way of correct theological argumentation.

And what has been said of the church applies also to the religious life, inasmuch as confusion and division also abound here. Ultimately, only holiness counts. And only holiness sheds the light of credibility on the truth of argument. In the current situation of the church, then, the "spiritual" life implies a spirit of holiness.

2.5. These are some current realities that call us to a "spiritual" life. In theory, their demands can be formulated universally. They call for fortitude, discernment, fidelity, and holiness. But it is the current situation that points up their necessity, or points it up more trenchantly, and this enables us to see that they must be invested with a concrete content.

Hence the importance of living "with spirit." We are forced to this by necessity, as well as encouraged to undertake it in the name of a quest for historical efficacy. On the level of argumentation, there may not be a great deal more to say. At all events, this is not the moment for a theoretical development of that necessity and that efficacy. The necessity of the spiritual life is clear enough. Thus our conviction of the need to "live with spirit" must necessarily become clearer too, precisely in proportion to the depth of our immersion in historical life.

It is sometimes difficult to express in words what we mean by the "spirit" we speak of. Perhaps it would be easier to indicate what it is not. But neither, on the other hand, can it be denied that, in the presence of men and women of spirit, we are struck by something novel, regardless of whether we are able to compose an adequate definition of the spirit. We are struck by the fact that the historical life of these men and women, their option for the poor, their struggle for justice, their commitment to liberative and revolutionary processes, have something special about them, something that, far from separating them from history, imbues their life with a special quality and depth. And so, although it is difficult to define "life with spirit," it is by no means difficult to point to concrete persons of religious groups who live and demonstrate that life, that spirit. Archbishop Romero was a person "with spirit." Communities of religious women living among *campesinos*, members of base communities, women and men toiling unselfishly for the good of others, with great commitment and generosity, with humility and eagerness to be of service to others, tell us better than words ever will what it means to live history with spirit.

Part One

LIBERATION
with
SPIRIT

Chapter 1

Presuppositions and Foundations of Spirituality[2]

In this chapter I propose simply to sketch the structure of a spirituality of liberation, leaving an examination of the more concrete content of that spirituality for another time.

I must begin with the fact that there is such a thing as a Christian practice of liberation, and that therefore there must be a spirituality underlying this practice. True, the theology of liberation has dealt more explicitly with the practice of liberation than with its spirituality. Implicitly, however, a great deal has already been said. When we speak of following Jesus, of listening to God's word and putting it into practice, of embracing the situation, the cause, and the lot of the poor, we have already made important assertions about the Christian spirituality that "informs" the practice of liberation. But we may not yet have explicitated the structure of spirituality as such.

Let me turn to that task, then, and let me begin by stating what spirituality is. Spirituality is simply the spirit of a subject—an individual or a group—in its relationship with the whole of reality. This proposition is formal in the extreme, of course. But it contains two important bits of information. First, it reminds us that spirituality is not something absolutely autonomous on the part of the subject; it stands in relationship with reality. Secondly, my descriptive definition implies that this relationship with reality is not a "regional" (restricted) relationship, or a relationship with other spiritual realities only, but a relationship with the totality of the real.

I think it important to underscore the "relational" character of spirit vis-à-vis the sum total of reality. First, this is an underlying intuition of the practice of liberation, and so it will have to underlie its spirituality, as well. Secondly, we must take care to avoid the temptation (frequent enough when it comes to the framing of a spirituality, as history shows) to "leave reality to itself"—to avoid the historical. To succumb to this temptation is to welcome into our lives an alienating parallelism in which the spiritual life and historical activity never meet. Here we shall be caught either in a subtle accommodation to whatever history will happen to offer "on its own"—and history will leave us behind—or in a no less subtle flight to a simple anticipation of the eschatological—leaving history behind.

Lest we fall victim to these temptations, and fail to make any progress in our understanding of spirituality, let us ask ourselves: What is the correct relationship between the spirit of the subject and the reality surrounding that subject? What would constitute the minimum demands of this relationship? What would be the prerequisites for spirituality as such, and thus for any and every concrete spirituality? We are looking for prerequisites that, once fulfilled, will become the foundations on which a spirituality will be built, if only the spirit of the subject remains faithful to the internal dynamics of these presuppositions.

There are three such prerequisites, it seems to me. Any genuine spirituality will demand, in the concrete: (1) honesty about the real, (2) fidelity to the real, and (3) a certain "correspondence" by which we permit ourselves to be carried along by the "more" of the real. These three basic attitudes can be converted into mediations of our relationship with God, so that these presuppositions and foundations are also objectively theological.*

In Latin America, we have rediscovered these presuppositions, or at least we have clarified them for ourselves, in the practice of liberation. And this rediscovery has facilitated their rediscovery by us in the life, practice, and destiny of Jesus. Accordingly, in the following exposition I shall be alluding both to Jesus and to the practice of liberation, although references to Jesus and to liberation will be more by way of illustration than by way of strict argumentation.

1. Honesty about the Real

What I seek to convey by the expression "honesty about the real" is admirably (if negatively) expressed in a passage from the Letter to the Romans: "The wrath of God is being revealed from heaven against the irreligious and perverse spirit of [those] who, in this perversity of theirs, hinder the truth" (Rom. 1:18). God condemns the negation of reality implicit in the denial of the truth of reality. Before all else, God condemns dishonesty about the real.

This dishonesty is not simply a noetic error with regard to the truth of things. Rather it consists in doing things an injustice—violating them in their very being, refusing to be honest with them, refusing to deal with them honorably. From this dishonesty flows a threefold perversion. (1) Things are deprived of their proper meaning, their capacity to function as sacraments of transcendence, and their capacity to release history. (2) The subject or agent of this dishonesty is deprived of the capacity for an adequate knowledge of reality. His

---

* Sobrino distinguishes between "theological," *teológico*, and "theologal," *teologal*. "Theological" refers to the study of theology; "theologal" means "related to God." —Ed.

or her heart is "beclouded." (3) This dishonesty issues in a practical denial of God, inasmuch as God is no longer recognized as the foundation both of the real and of the very spirit of the subject. And so, because this dishonesty precludes the absolutely basic "right relationship" between subject and object, between agent and reality, spirituality itself is precluded. Spirituality, then, must begin with exactly the opposite attitude: with an act of profound honesty about the real, the recognition of things as they actually are.

I am well aware that what has been said so far is very abstract. I may have left myself open to the allegation that, at this level, spirituality does not seem to involve any particular difficulty. But this is not the case. Let me cite a particularly significant example. How do we deal with the truth about human beings, historically and theologically? Very often, especially in the First World, the truth about human beings in their historical contexts is spoken of in universalizing language: "humankind"—or worse still, "modern humankind." The implication is that these expressions apply to the reality of all human beings; the achievements and problems of all human beings today are those of "modern humankind."

Theologically, human beings are usually treated as products of divine creation. This they are, to be sure, and here we have an important datum for both theology and anthropology. The creation of human beings is rightly regarded as the commencement of God's salvific plan, which is to continue to unfold throughout the whole course of history until it reaches its plenitude.

But to understand human beings today simply in terms of "humanity" or "modern humankind" is to mask their deeper reality. How can "humanity" be essentially distinct from the vast *majority* of human beings? How much does the vast human majority today hold in common with "modern humankind"? Theology, if precipitous in its approach here, can miss the primary meaning of God's creation: the *life* of human beings.

In order to recognize the truth of creation today, one must take another tack in this first, basic moment, a moment of honesty. The data, the statistics, may seem cold. They may seem to have precious little to do with theology. But we must take account of them. This is where we have to start. "Humanity" today is the victim of poverty and institutionalized violence. Often enough this means death, slow or sudden. In theological terms: God's creation is being assaulted and vitiated. The main problem continues to be "protology," not eschatology. Further: because this reality is not simply natural, but historical—being the result of action taken by some human beings against others—this reality is sinful. As absolute negation of God's will, this sinfulness is very serious and fundamental.

To recognize that this is "the way things are" is an act of intelligence, to be sure. But it is an act of correct, converted intelligence, intelligence that identifies as its primary interest the objective service of reality, not the service of the thinking subject. Knowledge of things is translated into thought systems, of course. But this translation is not done for the benefit of the agent of the knowledge. It is done for the benefit of the reality known by the agent. What

dialectical theologians, especially Karl Barth, have asserted of human cognition, to the effect that it can be (and for Barth, is) a way of defending oneself
against God, must also be asserted of cognition of reality. There is a manner of
knowing that is shaped out of a concern to defend oneself against the real. The
correct manner of knowing defends the real, defends the objective interests of
the real. This is why it must know the real objectively. And this is what I mean
by honesty about the real.

But now this primary honesty reaches out beyond the first moment, the
noetic moment, to embrace the moment of correspondence with the exigencies
of the reality that has come to be known. Unless it is "hindered in perversity,"
as Paul puts it, reality itself utters an unconditional no and an unconditional
yes. The no of reality is no to its own negation, absence, lack, annihilation. In
biblical terms, this unconditional no is no to Cain and fratricide, no to
oppression in Egypt, the prophets' no to the sale of the just one for a pair of
sandals. No theology or theodicy can silence or relativize this primordial no
uttered by reality, regardless of any other exigencies of this reality. In the world
of today the nonlife of the majorities can in no way be condoned.

The yes demanded by reality is yes to life. And inasmuch as the greater
portion of human creation lies prostrate in the death of subjection, this yes to
life becomes a yes to the restoration of life: a yes, then, not only to life, but to
the bestowal of life. Thus reality itself demands what we might define generally
as love. But let it be noted that honesty with the real demands a prioritization of
love as practice—a practice directed to the bestowal of life on the majorities, a
practice that can be denominated justice. Hence it follows that a spirituality
based on honesty with the real cannot be an alienating spirituality—which
would be a self-contradiction. Nor would it be well simply to equate spirituality
with love. In the abstract, this might not be wrong. But in the concrete,
spirituality will have to establish and maintain that form of love for which the
greater part of reality calls out: justice.

All of this is exemplified in Jesus. Jesus was honest with the primary datum
of prevailing reality in his own day. He recognized that the creation of God his
Father was vitiated. He could see that the majority of his contemporaries did
not epitomize the "human being alive, the glory of the living God"—*homo
vivens, gloria Dei.* He could see this because he was honest with reality. This is
the honesty that dictates so many of the words and deeds of liberation
theology—words that are ignored as seemingly not profound enough to be able
to say anything important about Jesus as the Christ. Jesus took pity on the
crowds in their real need and called on his disciples to feed them. Jesus prayed
for "daily bread." Jesus defended those who, in their hunger, ate of the grain
growing in someone else's field. Jesus unhesitatingly healed the sick even if it
meant ignoring prescriptions that looked to areas of human life that seemed
more exalted, such as the area of religious worship. To be sure, Jesus did not
restrict his salvific attitude to the domain of the lowly. But neither did he turn
his back on it. On the contrary, he cultivated it explicitly. Nor did he ignore or
depreciate it even when offering the fullness of salvation that extends to other
spheres of life.

Medellín (like the theology of liberation in general, together with its practice) begins with this same act of honesty about reality—in this case, Latin American reality. Our theological explicitation of the key importance of being honest about reality tends to be in terms of the following of Jesus, and we generally refer to passages like Matthew 25, or Luke 4:18-21, or to the exodus of the people of God from the land of Egypt. But deep down, there is an even more profound logic in our insistence on active solidarity with the poor of this world. We do not derive the importance of this solidarity only from the exigencies of the following of Jesus—at least not in the sense that if Jesus had not made the demand it would cease to be a demand. No, the imperative of active solidarity with the poor of this world proceeds, at bottom, from a profound honesty about Latin American reality. On a deeper level, then, this imperative coincides with Jesus' demand, so that each of the two demands, that of Jesus and that of our reality, sheds light on the other.

This, then, is the first prerequisite of spirituality: honesty about the real. Without it, any attempt to build a spirituality will be in vain. True, the attempt to concretize this objective reality can sometimes be "hit-and-miss." But the attitude, the attempt, is basic—as basic as the disposition for conversion—when it comes to seeing reality as it really is. In Latin America we believe that we have this attitude, and that it is the poor who have enabled us to have it, both objectively (because the truth of things is better known from below and from the periphery than from above and from the center) and subjectively (because the poor have the gift of turning the gaze of others toward their world, and dislodging their interest from themselves so that now they "tune in" to the interests of reality instead).

2. Fidelity to the Real

Honesty about the real requires that one act upon the real along the twin lines already pointed out: denying its negation and fostering its positivity. But difficulties arise. There is a price to pay. Honesty with the real must be maintained through thick and thin. Honesty with the real may lead us where we did not expect to be led. We must be faithful to that reality, regardless of where it may lead. This fidelity is the second prerequisite for spirituality. In our historical experience, past and present, a correct response to the real—love in all its forms, above all in the form of justice—does not always succeed in its aim. Indeed, frequently those who seek to foster life must give up part or all of their own life. The giving of one's life by waging a struggle with sin will suddenly be transformed into the necessity of bearing the burden of sin. Suddenly sin destroys not only the human reality upon which one seeks to bestow life, but also the very one seeking to bestow it. Now the subject operating on this human reality begins to wonder whether it is possible to bestow life at all. Understandably, situations arise in which the temptation to abandon the direction of one's first, honest response to reality, or to consider that response illusory, is strong indeed. This is the temptation of infidelity to the real.

The act of keeping faith with reality, in the basic dimension now under analysis, is exemplified by the servant of Yahweh of Second Isaiah. Taking the four servant songs together, we see, first, their initial judgment, that reality is oppressed; and then their first, honest, response to this reality—the demand for right and justice. But the special lesson the servant has to teach us is the perseverance of this honesty through thick and thin. The servant never swerves from his path, not even in the face of the tragic surprise of negativity, which annihilates not only him, but worse, his righteous cause. Still he is faithful. He is faithful to the end, toiling within reality come what may. There is no anthropology here, and no positive theology. But how effective is the negative theology with which we are confronted! One thing, and one thing alone, can the servant never permit himself to do: cease to be honest about reality.

Jesus is the archetype of this steadfast honesty toward the real—and not only, or even principally, in view of subsequent theologizations in which Jesus is proclaimed servant of Yahweh par excellence, but because of the sheer factual testimony of his historical life. Jesus opens his mission on a positive note. "The reign of God is near," he cries, and he places all that he is and all that he has in the service of that reign. But then comes the tragic surprise. What is good news for the poor is bad news for the mighty. Instead of enthusiasm and gratitude, it encounters resistance and opposition. Grace is seen as menace, threat. Still Jesus stands firm. His cause is under attack, his very person is assaulted, but still he keeps faith with reality. This fidelity on Jesus' part is admirably described in the Letter to the Hebrews: obedient, amidst groans and tears, Jesus is faithful to the end, despite the sinister night that engulfs his cause, despite the mortal peril to his person. Triumphantly Hebrews proclaims Jesus "the faithful one."

We see the same fidelity in the practice of liberation. It has been said that although, properly speaking, there cannot be a theology *of* captivity, theology can be done *from* captivity (Leonardo Boff). After all, captivity is a fact. It is a part of reality, and within captivity one must be honest about it. Martyrs are not lacking in Latin America to serve as examples of this fidelity. They seek, they strive for, liberation. But they do not turn their back on this goal of theirs when it is negated. They are faithful to it wherever it may lead them.

Fidelity to the real, the second prerequisite of any spirituality, is simply and solely perseverance in our original honesty, however we may be burdened with, yes, engulfed in, the negative element in history. Our first knowing is shrouded in obscurity by a certain not-knowing, and the power of negativity will challenge that first hope of ours. We shall know only that we must stay faithful, keep moving ahead in history, striving ever to transform that history from negative to positive.

This fidelity to the real is exemplified in Jesus' cross. Even when Jesus no longer perceives the coming of the reign of God, but sees only everything imaginable to the contrary, even when he hears only silence on the part of his Father, Jesus never wavers in his fidelity. He continues his incarnation in the history he seeks to transform, though that history now be his cross. The silence of the cross is the silence of God and history. The silence of Jesus is the only honest, honorable response. To force an articulate word would be dishonest. In accepting the silence of God and history, the silence of the cross, and in accepting the burden of this silence, Jesus keeps faith with the real.

3. Willingness to Be Swept along by the "More" of Reality

History is not sheer negativity. Obscurity and the heavy price of fidelity are not "the whole story." As Paul tells us, creation lives by the hope of its own liberation from all servitude and corruption. Reality contains something of promise, something of a hope unquenched by long ages of misery. Reality itself, despite its long history of failure and suffering, challenges us ever and again, and instills in us the hope of plenitude. The possibility of a new exodus, a new return from exile, a liberation from captivity, reappears again and again. None of these liberations is definitive, of course. But there will always be a new herald, another Moses, to announce a new heaven and a new earth, a more human life, *homo vivens*.

Honesty about the real, then, is hope. Whatever direction reality takes, it calls on us to have hope. But the hope it calls for is an active impulse, not the passive hope of mere expectation. It is a hope bent upon helping reality become what it seeks to be. This is love. Hope and love are but two sides of the same coin: the conviction, put into practice, of the possibilities of reality. Hope and love foster one another, nurture one another. We may hope for the earth to become hearth and home to the human being (Ernst Bloch) only to the extent that we set our hand to the construction of this home. We truly hope for the life of the world only if we are willing to bestow life on the world. The task of humanizing the human being, of bringing it about that human beings live, is not some arbitrary demand, nor even the loftiest of the commandments, whether issued by Jesus or anyone else. It would bind even if it had never been mandated. It is consummate harmony with reality. The humanization of the human being—love—is the supreme, self-justifying task, the task without internal limits.

Hope and love are the ways we correspond to the "more" that is inherent in reality. In this way we do justice to that reality. In this way we are being honest with reality and faithful to it. Our enterprise will have to be concretized in various ways, and Jesus and the practice of liberation have concretized it in various ways. But the variety of concretions must not conceal the heart of the matter: hope and love are the way we correspond to the "more" of reality in its ceaseless quest for plenitude.

The most profound element in the person and practice of Jesus now becomes clear. In the shadow of the sublime christological formulations elaborated by church councils, some New Testament statements can seem shallow—the ones that refer to him, for instance, as compassionate, or as the one who simply "went about doing good." And yet it is here that we touch the very marrow of Jesus' personal spirituality. In systematic terms, Jesus devoted himself to the humanizing of human beings, to the realization of the *homo vivens, gloria Dei*, as Christians would later say. His point of departure was the *pauper vivens*, the living indigent, and the life that he offered flowed from this starting point to all other human beings as well (in the case of oppressors, by calling them to conversion), and to all—including the poor—Jesus offered true life, asking of them all that they be poor *with spirit*.

Thus we correspond to the "more"of creation by going about doing good. But we quickly discover, as Jesus did, that in order for history to give more of itself, the subjects , the agents of the correspondence with this "more," must now give more of themselves. The commandment of love, proclaimed and supremely illustrated by Jesus himself, and its demand to be "for" others, dare not be understood merely as a wise axiom ("do unto others as you would have them do unto you"), or in terms of "human success" (as the path to self-achievement). The commandment of love must be interpreted as correspondence to what is most profound in the reality around us, by way of assisting it in becoming more. The "for" with which Jesus' life is suffused is not only the sine qua non of all future Christian soteriologies. Before all else, the "for" of Jesus' life is the affirmation of what it actually means to be alive, what it means to be attuned to God's creation.

This same hope, with which reality trembles, and our praxic response in rushing to its aid, that there indeed be life, is what underlies the practice of liberation, at least in its best intentions. This is why there can be an authentic spirituality of liberation. It will not be something ideologically superimposed on the raw fact of liberative practice. It will be the very spirit of the giving of life. The practice of liberation is attuned to reality, and therefore, despite the grave difficulties liberation faces, the hope of the poor does not fade away. If, with this sky and earth of ours as our reference, we can speak of a new heaven and a new earth, this is only because hope arises from the liberative process itself, although it can be understood and formulated only from within this same process, not out on its margins. In affecting reality by striving to give life, we deepen our conviction of the "more" of reality. We must be honest with the "more," despite the negativity that abides within it as well.

Correspondence with the "more" of reality, then, in hope and in love is the third prerequisite of a spirituality. As correspondence, it expresses the element in spirituality that is a response to the demand of reality. But this is not all. Reality itself makes it possible to meet that demand. Thus the subject is not only challenged by that reality, but borne along by it as well, and this sweep, this pull, is a gift from reality, a mediation of gratuity.

4. Experience of God

My reflections on spirituality thus far have sought neither to pose nor to resolve the casuistry of the various forms and methods of spirituality. Strictly speaking, I have made no attempt to develop a *Christian* spirituality. Indeed—

and this may shock some readers—I have made no mention of personal relationship with God.

I have been speaking only of the prerequisites for spirituality, spirituality as such, all human spirituality. I think it necessary to insist on these prerequisites, however, lest spirituality be relegated to the vicious circle of the "purely spiritual," without the involvement of a mediation on the part of reality, without passing by way of historical reality. Jesus revealed the pitfall of a detour around reality in his parable of the good Samaritan.

I have said nothing explicit, then, about spirituality as a relationship with the Christian God. But implicitly I have said a great deal. In the first place, the particular prerequisites singled out for consideration here correspond precisely to a Christian view of reality. Lest reality be sheer negativity, in order that reality be promise as well, we must adopt a particular view of God. But secondly, and more in depth, in enunciating my three prerequisites I have also spoken of the mediations of God's revelation and communication, and of the fundamental manner in which we are called to respond to and correspond with that revelation and communication. Honesty with and fidelity to reality is more than a prerequisite for a spiritual experience of God. It is its very material as well. Apart from, and independent of, this honesty and fidelity we neither grasp revelation nor respond to it. This honesty and fidelity is our positive response to the consistently historical structure of God's revelation.

Revelation is historical. It is historical in its origins, in the course of history, in the incarnation of the Son, and even in its eschatological consummation. And it is our negative answer to the Pauline admonition that, apart from honesty with the real, things are no longer what they are for us: they lose their revelatory, sacramental character, and one can no longer have an experience of God, either from the side of the object (God, who no longer is revealed in reality) or from the side of the subject (the beclouded heart of the human being who does violence to reality).

The question of spirituality is purely and simply the question of a correspondence to God's revelation in real history. True, dogma regards real history as "closed" in Christ. But this does not mean the closure of the spiritual experience of God, or that that experience is now to be had out on the margins of current history. On the contrary, it means that now God continues forever to give self-manifestation in real history. God's past revelation understood simply as "deposit" guarantees only a teaching *about* God; it guarantees no experience *of* God. An experience of God presupposes God's ongoing self-manifestation. But God's self-manifestation, today as all through the course of biblical revelation, is realized only in real history. Accordingly, honesty with and fidelity toward the real are not only prerequisites for a spirituality, they are the very foundations of that spirituality, and this is what is most basic about spirituality. They permit us to keep on hearing God in history, and they express the basic realization of our response to God's word.

Thus my prerequisites are more than prerequisites. They are the foundations of a radically anthropological spirituality. But they also found an objectively and radically theological spirituality. They set forth the correct mode of human relationship with history, and thereby with God and the personal aspect of God. This is the theological spirituality of Jesus. The Letter to the Hebrews is clear and forthright: Jesus' historical and theological experience, his mercy and his fidelity, are joined in one. In systematic terms, Jesus' fidelity to the reign of God and to the God of the reign, his historical practice and his experience of the Father, are but two sides of the same coin. In his practice of humanizing others, Jesus appears as the human being facing God: in his practice of making brothers and sisters of human beings, Jesus manifests himself as the Son who stands before the Father. Jesus is the spiritual human being. He calls God his Father, and thereby demonstrates his explicit relationship of obedience to and confidence in that Father. But "he invokes him as (Father) in a liberative historical action" (Christian Duquoc).

To paraphrase Paul: if the wrath of God has burst upon both gentiles and Jews who hinder the truth in their perversity, then upon Jesus has burst the grace of God, because Jesus has done justice to the truth, to reality. In Jesus, then, appears, first, God's truth—how God sees the world and what God wants of this world; and secondly, the truth of the human being—how men and women should view God, and how they ought to realize God's will in order to enter into relationship with God.

Honesty with the real, then, and with whatever this honesty leads us to, is necessary for spirituality and for the experience of God. Without entering upon a discussion of the theory of the anonymous Christian, I would say that anyone who enters into a correct relationship with this reality is corresponding to God objectively, and that God will bestow self-communication to this person, although this communication may not be in a thematically reflexive form. Of course, those who believe that grace and truth appeared in Jesus can and should thematize the correct relationship with reality as a relationship with God, as experience of God, as God's grace.

Honesty with Latin American reality; fidelity to that reality amid its taxing demands, in a hope and a practice of love steadfastly maintained, in order that these birth pangs may be transformed into the joy of new life; the experience of gratuity in the discovery that, once we accept the burden of this reality, we are then borne along by it—these seem to me to be the ultimate prerequisites of the spirituality of liberation. The particular ways in which Latin America explicitates them, in reference to Jesus and God, also constitute ultimate foundations of Christian spirituality. These practices of ours must ever be nurtured and fostered in the direction of Christian fullness, as will appear in other chapters of this book. But in the first place they are necessary as prerequisites. Without them there can be no Christian spirituality of liberation. And they are fruitful, for they give rise to the spiritual human being, and to peoples with a Christian spirit.

Chapter 2

Spirituality and Liberation[3]

The historical (in-history) liberation of the oppressed peoples of the earth, many Christians assert, is absolutely necessary and just. By that very fact, they continue, the practice of liberation is just and necessary. These Christians further assert that, in personal and community commitment to liberation, they grasp, and endow with altogether new dimensions, the meaning of their lives. Indeed, they claim, the practice of liberation has become the principal (if not the only) mediation of their personal experience of God. From the vantage of their immersion in that practice, they reread the scriptures. They reread them from cover to cover. There they find liberation to be the chief concern, and the manifestation both of God's will for the oppressed and of the duty of believers. Achieving liberation of the oppressed is now seen to be incumbent upon believers. Liberation is now seen to be the central reality, the merger of the historical and the personal, the blending of present exigency and scriptural norm. For these Christians, then, liberation poses no problem. Rather it seems to offer the solution to all problems, potential or actual, in their life as human beings, believers, and Christians.

But when it comes to *spirituality*, matters may take another turn. To be sure, for some Christians committed to liberation, spirituality is invested with the same urgency as is liberation itself. For others, however, this is not the case. They may even regard spirituality with mistrust and suspicion. It will be worth our while, then, to examine the reality, the importance, and the necessity of spirituality in the practice of liberation.

Before actually getting into this subject, however, let me make certain clarifications.

1. I propose to concentrate here on the spirituality of liberation rather than on the practice of that liberation. I shall take for granted the need for a historical liberation, along with the fact that this liberation will include, as a matter of highest priority, the structural transformation of oppressive societies. Thus I shall take for granted both the need for a struggle for justice, and the political forms that this struggle may assume. I likewise presuppose biblical and theological treatment of this practice.

2. Rather than examine spirituality in a merely general way, I propose to analyze it precisely in terms of the practice of liberation. In other words, I shall examine the spirituality demanded and fostered by a practice of liberation.

3. I shall treat spirituality in programmatic and synthetic fashion, in an attempt to uncover its ultimate roots and basic content—not its details, and not in its various manifestations as articulated in so-called spiritualities, in the plural.

4. Finally, let me observe that, though it will be expressed conceptually, my analysis of spirituality will be based on the deeds and words of Christians committed to liberation in Central America, especially in El Salvador, and that this spirituality has certain parallels in the deeds and words of nonbelievers.

Accordingly, I divide this chapter into the following parts:

1. Spirituality and its problematic.
2. The necessity and importance of the practice of liberation for spirituality.
3. The necessity and importance of spirituality for liberation.
4. The spirituality of liberation as an approach to God.

1. Spirituality and Its Problematic

1.1. *In Latin America, de facto and de jure, spirituality has been present in our liberation processes from the very outset. Later history has only shown the necessity and importance of this spirituality.*

Those engaged in the practice of liberation have insisted from the beginning that this practice calls for more than theoretical categories—categories of theology and science. It demands, as well, "a vital attitude—global and synthetic—calculated to inform our lives in their totality and in every detail" (Gustavo Gutiérrez). Years later, it was observed, with respect to liberation practice, that "at the basis of all innovative practice on the part of the church, at the root of all authentic, new theology, there lies, concealed and latent, a typical religious experience" (Leonardo Boff).

This attitude and this experience, then, are of course historically connected with liberation practice. But the connection is not a mechanical one. It complements, and respects, both dimensions. The element that historically had resulted in an emphasis on the urgency of something more than mere practice is, I believe, the fact that from the very outset this practice has never been a "general" practice of liberation. It has always been a practice of liberation *of the poor.* I further hold that this qualifier, "of the poor," far from being routine or secondary when it comes to the practice of liberation, is essential to it. It imposes upon it certain concrete conditions, sweeping it up and subsuming it into something more than mere practice.

The poor are not simply the beneficiaries of liberation. By the mere fact that they exist, for believers they are the historical locus of God, the "place" where God is found in history. In other words, "liberation practice and [theological] theory are sustained by a spiritual experience of encounter with the Lord in the poor" (Leonardo Boff). "Encounter . . . in the poor": liberation is historical. "Encounter with the Lord": in terms of the gospel, liberation pertains to the reign of God, which is a totality that absolutely requires socio-economic liberation. By the liberation of the poor, then, I mean a "totalizing," comprehensive liberation—in the language of the church, an "integral" liberation. In other words, liberation must be practiced in a variety of areas. This calls for a practice charged with spirit if we are to promote a variety of historical liberations leading in the direction of the fullness of the reign of God.

As the theology of liberation never tires of reminding us, the poor should be the agents of their own liberation. If we take this proposition absolutely seriously, we shall have to face the scandal of the servant of Yahweh: liberation comes by way of frailty as well. It is one thing to work for the poor; it is quite another to believe in their capacity to liberate themselves. The latter attitude demands a faith that liberation practice alone does not necessarily generate.

Finally, though it is absolutely necessary, it will not be enough that the poor be delivered from their unjust material poverty: they ought also to grow to the stature and status of "poor in spirit" (Ignacio Ellacuría). This is the systematic synthesis of the first Beatitude in its Matthean and Lucan presentations as worked out by liberation theology.

In Latin American theological theory, therefore, the practice of liberation not only does not exclude other dimensions of human existence, such as (besides the self-evident need for theoretical analyses) religious experience, vital attitude—in a word, spirit. It demands them. These realities do not worm their way into theology through some back door—by way of idealism or voluntarism. Nor do they enter theology merely in virtue of a formalistic loyalty to a tradition that has bequeathed us the realm of the spiritual. They take their place in liberation with full right and increasing necessity.

At bottom, I believe, spirit is part and parcel of theology because the poor constitute a reality that challenges and mobilizes the totality of human and Christian being, not only its praxic dimension. And this truth, this tenet of liberation theology, is lived in practice by the agents of liberation. It is they who need and produce spirituality—as we see in an Archbishop Romero, in the Christians of the base communities, in the Christians of the refugee hospices and the combat zones, even in Christians involved in armed combat.

1.2. *Other Christians, however, may still regard spirituality with suspicion. They will see no reason for concern with it other than to ensure that it not be used in an alienating way.*

Spirituality can be suspect in the Christian mind. This may be due to any of various causes. First, some Christians regard spirituality as nothing but subjective reflex of the de facto phenomena of the practice of liberation. For these persons, any good spirituality will emerge almost mechanically from the simple practice of liberation. Of course, they concede that a minimal spiritual decision will be required for a commitment to liberation. But spirituality does not seem to them to have any substantiality of its own. It is regarded as adventitious to liberation practice, and therefore as requiring no cultivation of its own. Such cultivation will therefore be viewed with suspicion.

Secondly, it must be admitted that spirituality has a tendency to acquire an autonomy of its own. It tends to declare its independence of practice—in this case, of the practice of liberation. This will lead to insurmountable dualisms, hence ultimately to alienation.

Thirdly, in more secularized milieus the facet of spirituality consisting in an explicit personal relationship with God can be difficult. To be sure, to toil for the reign of God is an act of response to God's will, and as such implicitly involves a relationship with God. But it may be more difficult, in the milieus in question, to acknowledge the value of an explicit acknowledgment of the God of the reign, who is something more than a mere ethical demand of justice or thrust toward utopia. But spirituality means confrontation with the reality of a God who, beside being an ethical demand or utopian thrust, is a person, too, and a Father—a God who is the architect of a reign for the benefit of all God's daughters and sons, yes, but who is also in dialogue with those daughters and sons.

1.3. *These difficulties vary in degree, depending on the milieu. They are present in different intensities in different persons, groups, and places. I am of the opinion that their solution is to be sought not on the level of a purely conceptual elucidation of the meaning of spirituality, but on the level of reality itself. That is to say, if a liberation practice is imbued with a spirituality, these difficulties can be met. If a spirituality invests the practice of liberation with dynamism, it will not be alienating but positive. If without a spirituality the practice of liberation degenerates, spirituality will be necessary.*

A minimal clarification of what I mean, and what I do not mean, by spirituality will be necessary to clear the field of any unnecessary difficulties.

By spirituality I do not mean the general substrate of "spiritualities" or "spiritual practices" so frequently regarded as mechanisms for holiness—as if "spirituality" were optional for the ordinary human being, the run-of-the-mill Christian, and necessary only for someone who has chosen the way of perfection. Nor do I mean an esoteric method of placing ourselves in direct contact with the spiritual world—as if such contact were possible on the outskirts of concrete history. Finally, I do not mean that a spirituality can be built up by some particular mechanisms that could then be applied to any and every situation or practice with which the Christian might be faced—as if these situations or practices themselves did not enter into the formation and basic content of the spirituality itself.

But with all this being said, it cannot be denied that the human being is spirit, too, and that human groups have their own spirit, analogically; that there exists a domain of the spirit; that spirituality is as much part and parcel of the human being as is corporality, sociality, or the praxic. True, the human spirit has indissoluble ties with the material, the historical, and this conditions one's spirituality. But these indissoluble ties exist in freedom and creativity. The material, the historical, must be shaped, in all creative freedom, by the human being. It does not mechanically dictate its own shape and configuration.

With reference to liberation, then: liberation offers the human spirit a material, a channel, which supplies the matter upon which it is to act. At the same time, however, the human spirit must "inform" liberation. It must give liberation a determinate direction, provide it with a particular content, and furnish it with certain values to further it—values that will be present in the liberation project.

1.4. *These a priori assertions are observed a posteriori in the concrete processes of liberation as they develop, and not only as contemplated in prospect. Spirit is necessary in the practice of liberation.*

1. The objective conditions for launching a practice of liberation have been present in Central America for some time. The subjective conditions have come into being only recently. It could be argued, therefore, that the decision in favor of liberation as an act of the spirit has come about almost mechanically. But this would be jumping to conclusions. The only legitimate conclusion is that the spirit operates in function of objective historical conditions—not that it is mechanically determined. After all, for one thing, not everyone in Central America has decided in favor of liberation. A decision for liberation is itself an act of the spirit, occasioned by a consciousness that has been enlightened, but not forced, by the possibility and necessity of liberation. It is likewise an act of the spirit to remain steadfast in the practice of liberation, with its exigencies of fortitude, creativity, hope, and the disposition to give life. The content of the practice aids in the development of these attitudes, but does not automatically guarantee them.

2. The practice of liberation, however just and good, is also creaturely. For all its positive possibilities (which I shall be analyzing below), liberation practice is subject to limitation and sinfulness too—and not merely to sinfulness as such, but to the sinfulness proper to the practice of liberation. Furthermore, the practice of liberation runs the risk of generating negative by-products, and indeed such by-products as are not remediable from within liberation practice itself. They must be dealt with separately and directly.

Among the more common temptations to befall this just practice, as Archbishop Romero warned, and as committed Christians recognize, are the following:

A. An exaggerated competitiveness, either among the several groups engaged in a liberation practice, or among liberation groups working in one manner and those working in another manner. This foments disunion and dulls effectiveness. It also gives rise to a sense of ethical superiority, so that now any action performed by "us" will tend to be regarded as commendable merely because it is being done by "us."

B. The gradual displacement of the popular element in the liberation struggle. Little by little, almost imperceptibly, the work of the popular majorities is taken over by their organizations, the role of the organizations is preempted by the leadership, and leadership dwindles to a few stalwart individuals. This phenomenon, however inevitable it may be historically, and however necessary for the effectiveness of the struggle, involves the threat of separation between the leaders and the people, the real needs and suffering of a people. Now a real people will be sacrificed to the concept of an imaginary, ideal "people."

C. The absolutization of some particular mechanism of liberative practice (which will vary with the social, political, or military situation). Now the totality of the life of the people will shrink until it becomes restricted to some one of its sectors. That sector will be absolutized, as if fullness in one area of life would automatically bring fullness in the others.

D. Abuse of the convergence of liberation and the gospel through a manipulation of the religious element so that it oversteps its legitimate bounds. This violates the historical religious dimension in the life of our peoples. And it deprives them of the important function of religion as a motivating force for liberation.

E. Dogmatism in the analysis, interpretation, and even observation of facts. As a result, a priori positions and interests will come to be automatically confirmed, because they will no longer be submitted to verification by the yardstick of reality.

F. Ambiguity in the use of power. Power tends innately to serve the interests of self-assertion. Instead of serving its original purpose as a necessary means, power will be transformed into a mystique. Now it can be abused.

If these negative by-products in the practice of liberation are to be avoided, spirit will be needed—abounding spirit.

3. Spirit will also be necessary if liberation is to have a specific direction, and specific personal and structural values. The specific direction in question is denominated—coldly enough, perhaps, with all the doctrinal resonances the term has in church documents—"integral liberation." Of its very nature, liberation necessarily tends toward its own totalization, both in its ultimate goal and in the partial liberations undertaken in the process of achieving that ultimate goal. At the ethico-religious level, this totalization involves such values as solidarity, reconciliation, and mercy. Such values go hand in hand with liberation, and magnify its dynamism. At the humano-cultural level, this totalization implies manifestations of spirit in the creativity of culture, art, celebration, friendship, and love.

Accordingly, the liberation process must become open to utopia and transcendence. Only in the utopian ideal do we glimpse, in the distance, the fulfilling reconciliation of all the disparate elements of historical liberations, elements so difficult to reconcile in history: the personal and the structural; a genuine struggle and the longing for peace; justice and forgiveness; triumph and reconciliation. Maintaining an openness to utopia in the practice of liberation is not something mechanical, but a thing of spirit. It is not easy to consistently choose one's position in the concrete reality of history *in the light of utopia*, that that utopia may judge us and animate us. And this is something we must do consciously, with great disinterestedness, and great hope.

1.5. *This systematic description of what occurs in the processes of liberation demonstrates the need of spirit, for both an initiation into the practice of liberation, and steadfast fidelity to the basic exigencies of that practice. Only spirit will overcome the otherwise inevitably negative by-products of even a just liberation. Only spirit will enable us to maintain an openness to utopia. Attention to spirit may, at first, appear to draw off some of the energies that otherwise could have been devoted directly to the practice calculated to achieve spiritual liberation. In fact, however, the cultivation of spirit will render the practice of liberation more effective.*

In saying this, I am not denying that liberation comports an absolute, urgent exigency of the liberation of the *poor*—understanding "poor" here in the sense of the socio-economic poor. I am not denying the absolute, urgent need to revolutionize socio-economic structures. And so of course I admit that liberation will necessarily entail a powerful element of political struggle. All I am saying is that the political is not everything, neither in the liberation project itself nor in the means thereto. In order to open liberation to its fullness— indeed, even to secure its socio-economic nucleus, or to give efficacy to the political struggle itself—spirit is indispensable.

Accordingly, a relationship obtains between practice and spirituality. Liberation has need of practice and of spirit. These two factors are not only not antagonistic, they are complementary. Their relationship can be stated negatively and positively. Negatively: spirituality today in the absence of the practice of liberation is purely generic, evangelically impossible, and historically alienating. Liberation practice without spirit is generically good, but concretely threatened with degeneration, diminution, and sin. Positively stated: spirituality has need of the practice of liberation in order to have the proper channel and appropriate material for its evangelical and relevant self-realization in current history. Practice has need of spirit in order to maintain itself precisely as a liberation of the poor, while becoming, ever more creatively and powerfully, a liberation that is truly comprehensive.

Now we can see the attitude and intent that should be ours as we undertake an examination of the problem of spirituality in relationship to liberation. An overcautious treatment of spirituality, one that would be on the defensive from the start, would be insufficient—however understandable that attitude might be in terms of long historical experience. Similarly, it would be inadequate to propose liberation as a remedy for the alienating tendency inherent in spirituality. No, we ought to approach our consideration of spirituality with a positive attitude and intent, in the belief that the evangelical spirit will heal, and invest with a special dynamism, the practice of liberation. This will be the object of my reflections in the two following sections, as I now begin to look at spirituality from an explicitly Christian viewpoint.

2. Necessity of Liberation Practice for Spirituality, and the Nature of Its Contribution: Basic Theologal Spirituality

The practice of liberation is *necessary* for Christian life, and therefore for the basic spirituality of that life. Bereft of a forthright option for the poor majorities, deprived of any commitment to the liberation precisely of these majorities, Christian love today would be impossible. To be sure, love, the quintessence of the Christian life, has other manifestations besides the practice of liberation. But if that practice is not included, and included in a central position, be it only analogically, it will be difficult indeed to speak of "love." I shall not insist, then, on the necessity of the practice of liberation for the Christian life. I shall assume it as self-evident.

Instead I shall concentrate on the precise *contribution* of the practice of liberation to the development of a basic Christian spirituality today. My thesis will be that, *by its very nature*, and not only in virtue of a concomitant intention, the practice of liberation today brings the Christian face to face with ultimate realities, to which the spirit must respond with ultimacy. The precise manner of this response cannot be programed. But it will obviously be in terms of a spirituality that *of its very nature* comes face to face with the ultimacy of reality. Hence I shall be speaking of a fundamental theologal spirituality. Only at the conclusion of this examination shall I mention God explicitly.

Ultimacy accrues to practice as a practice of liberation precisely of the poor. In and through this practice, men and women are called upon to define themselves with respect to truth, love, and hope. They are presented with the opportunity to confront the ultimate in a way that is ultimate, historical, and evangelical. If their response is positive, they cease to be followers of themselves and become followers of Jesus. They will cease to be carnal human beings, to become spiritual human beings.

2.1. *The poor and impoverished of the world, in virtue of their very reality, constitute the most radical question of the truth of this world, as well as the most correct response to this question.*

Of the poor of this world it can rightly be said that they have hope, and that they struggle for their liberation. Of course. But let us not be overhasty. First of all these are the poor. They are the trash and offal of humanity, crucified by the structures of this world. If they resist, they are crucified suddenly and violently. If they do not resist, they are crucified gradually and slowly. The poor show the reality of this world for what it is: sin. Sin is not the only reality in this world. But whatever else the reality of this world may be, unless we see flagrant sin, we shall miss the mark—if we really want to discover the truth of that reality. In theological terms, the poor demonstrate that God's creation is threatened and vitiated—that the lords of the world, its authentic gods, are idols of death. The truth of this fact leaps out at us all the more when we consider that, although the poor are quantitatively the majority of humankind, it is only from time to time that some of them manage to call public attention to their plight. And qualitatively the poverty of these persons reaches excruciating extremes of misery and agony as they undergo torture and death.

It is this reality in itself that brings women and men face to face with a question, a question they must answer with a profound act of honesty, which is an act of spirit. Human beings act first and foremost in terms of precisely how they see reality. The question posed by the reality of the poor, then, is no rhetorical question. Precisely as sin, this reality tends to conceal itself, to be relativized, to pass itself off as something secondary and provisional in the larger picture of human achievements. It is a reality that calls on men and women not only to recognize and acknowledge it, but to take a primary, basic position regarding it. Outwardly, this reality demands that it be stated for what it is, and denounced. This is the stage of prophetic denunciation. But inwardly, this same reality is a question for human beings as themselves participants in this sin of humankind. It is the call for their first great conversion. Men and women are being served notice here. They are being warned that the poor of this world are not the casual products of history. No, poverty results from the actions of other human beings. Peter's denunciation of the murderers of the Just One (Acts 2:23; 3:14-15), and the Genesis indictment, "Where is your brother . . . ? What have you done!" (4:9-10), are matters of the ultimate truth of our very being. A recognition of the truth of reality, and a willingness to acknowledge the truth of one's own being, constitute the first demand of spirit—and the poor mirror this demand with a clarity that defies subterfuge. This recognition of the truth is called conversion.

Human knowledge has a concupiscence of its own. It tends to reject things as they are, to take them captive, to dominate them in the interests of the knower (see Rom. 1:18).

2.2. *The poor and impoverished of this world set human beings squarely before the question of their place and position in this world, and suddenly the questioned find themselves face to face with themselves as persons.*

Our place and position in the world is not something secondary or accidental. It involves our whole capacity to know and to act correctly. To know reality, we must impinge upon it. But we human beings, alien from reality as we are, are incurable in our tendency to distort and manipulate that reality. In Christian language: to be in reality is not simply a matter of being in a particular place, or of wishing to be in the right place. To be in reality means to take a positive decision to arrive at where we really should be. This arriving-in-order-to-be is something active—exemplified, in transcendent terms, in Christ's becoming human flesh; or, more concretely for our purposes, in his making "himself poor though he was rich" (2 Cor. 8:9). This active willingness for an incarnation in the poor of this world, this readiness to allow the poor to impregnate our habits and our attitudes, to direct our cognition and our interests, presupposes a fundamental decision of spirit.

When we grasp poverty from a place and position of incarnation among the poor, we can scarcely doubt that the poor of this world call for a great act of love toward them. This is the only correct, honest response to their reality. And the concrete content of this act of love is dictated by their misery and oppression, which must be overcome, and by their life, which cries out for nurture and fostering. There is no doubt, then, that the only correct way to love the poor will be to struggle for their liberation. This liberation will consist, first and foremost, in their liberation at the most elementary level—that of their simple, physical life, which is what is at stake in their present situation:

> I have witnessed the affliction of my people in Egypt and have heard their cry of complaint against their slave drivers, so I know well what they are suffering. Therefore I have come down to rescue them from the hands of the Egyptians and lead them out of that land into a good and spacious land [Exod. 3:7–8].

God thundered of old, and the divine response to the people's suffering is still the transcendent paradigm of the right and proper response to the reality of the poor. There is no need, then, of insistence on the need for structural justice—the need for efficacious love, with all the socio-political mediations that that love requires—in order to achieve liberation. Our present concern, notwithstanding our theoretical familiarity with the matter, will be to stress the concrete meaning of this liberative love for the concrete human being who makes a decision for liberation. By love, human beings "de-center" themselves. They find their self-fulfillment in devotion to an "other." A liberating love for the poor, by its very nature, demands radical dedication, and thereby calls for a de-centering on the part of the lover.

Very concretely, this means that, in the practice of liberation, men and women are being asked whether it is really the pain of the *other* that they seek to overcome, whether it is the liberation of the *other* that they seek. The poor are "other" in such wise and to such an extent as to demand our absolute ex-centricity. The poor demand, absolutely, that the practice of liberation be genuinely a quest for *their* liberation—and not directly, even if subtly, the meaning of one's own life, although indirectly this meaning is indeed attained in the practice of the liberation of the other. The poor very effectively place us before the alternative of choosing ourself or the other—of accepting, or not accepting, such simple New Testament sayings as, "There is more happiness in giving than in receiving" (Acts 20:35).

The liberation of the poor radicalizes the ex-centricity of love to the point of radical forgetfulness of self. But this self-ignoring must be cultivated, lest in actual practice the "I" be introduced all over again, when it ought to continue to be governed by the liberation of the poor "other." The demand for this self-forgetfulness is very real. The liberation of the poor, by its very nature, is accompanied by dangers and persecutions that threaten the "I" and entail the anything but remote possibility of having to renounce oneself absolutely. A liberative love must keep account of death and martyrdom as concrete realities. Thus if a human being is to be consistent with the practice of liberation, that human being must accept the by no means self-evident fact that the whole human being is constituted or lost in the acceptance or rejection of the evangelical principle that in order to find life one must lose it (Mark 8:35), and that "there is no greater love than this: to lay down one's life for one's friends" (John 15:13). Accordingly, the liberation of the poor calls for love. But it calls for that love with a radicality unattainable from a point of departure in either a mere loving intention or a mere practice as such. The latter provides the setting. But the actualization of love is, once again, a question of spirit.

2.3. *The poor and impoverished of this world bring the human being face to face either with hope, or with despair, resignation, or cynicism.*

On the one hand, the historical liberations that have already occurred, however imperfect or threatened, demonstrate the possibility of liberation (or of a particular type of liberation). Liberation processes celebrate the partial triumph of liberation as such, and develop new forms of a more just and humane societal life. Certain scientific theories predict the inexorable triumph of such revolutions, and the coming of a society that will in truth be "hearth and home for humankind."

On the other hand, not all liberation processes meet with success, nor are those that do succeed thereby exempt from external and internal dangers. At socio-economic levels it cannot be denied that the future of humanity looks somber. Even apart from the specter of imminent nuclear cataclysm, it scarcely seems that the reign of God is at hand.

Then does it make any sense to hope, and what would be the source of the hope? Would it not be preferable to abandon hope as something illusory—humanly necessary, perhaps, but in the end illusory? My belief is that it is the practice of liberation that makes these questions radical, and that it is the poor who keep hope in the condition of true hope—that is, cling to it in what it contains of the positive, the realistic, and the scandalous. "Nor shall the hope of the afflicted forever perish" (Ps. 9.19). This is the truth. The poor—those whose greatest task is survival and whose imminent lot is death—have, and maintain, hope.

This hope of the poor is nurtured by their partial triumphs and their concrete solidarity. But their roots have another sap. It is not that the poor disdain scientific analyses of the triumph of a revolution, when they know them. Only, they do not base their hope on them. The hope of the poor is a primordial act of confidence in reality despite all, a hope explicitated as confidence in a God who is Father. That "the reign of God is at hand"(Mark 1:15), that there will be "new heavens and a new earth"(Rev. 21:1), are, in the mouth of the poor,

expressions of the primordial hope. This is how the poor express their conviction that reality, at its deepest, is textured of justice and goodness—that,
despite all, good is mightier and more basic than evil. Indeed, the poor accept,
at least in fact, and at times in words as well, that true salvation comes only by
way of their own crucifixion: that the one who gives them true hope is the
servant of Yahweh. None of this divests the poor of the spirit of active toil for
liberation. After all, it is the anointed of Yahweh who will bring liberation,
good news, right, and justice. But they accept the scandal that the anointed
must pass by way of the cross, and they integrate that scandal into their hope.

The hope of the poor bears no further analysis. It is just "there." And it
challenges, it interrogates, the radical hope of anyone committed to liberation.
How each one of us will respond, in all seriousness, to this question will vary
from person to person and circumstance to circumstance. But in every case the
poor will have rendered the service of shifting the focus of hope from self to
other.

What it is that sustains our hope in the midst of a practice of liberation can
have no a priori answer. But perhaps we can say this: that, when all is said and
done, hope lives by love. One who has radically, disinterestedly, loved the poor
of this world, has done something absolutely good, something that has been
assimilated by history once and for all. Perhaps, from the midst of hope,
nothing more can be asserted than a negative theology of hope: that it is better
to suffer for love of the poor than not to—that nothing better can be done than
to give the poor some hope. The first Christians thought of it in these terms:
"Who indeed can harm you if you are committed deeply to doing what is
right?" (1 Peter 3:13). But to express hope positively, to express the conviction
of the supremacy of love and justice in a positive form, is not easy.

One thing, of course, remains certain: the fact that conviction always goes
hand in hand with love. Paul says: "God makes all things work together for the
good of those who love him"(Rom. 8:28). Resurrection, the supreme symbol
of Christian hope, speaks to us of nothing else: the supremacy of love and
justice. Those who have totally dedicated themselves to the poor, who have
kept nothing back for themselves—not even their trusted relationship with the
Father—those who have died alone, crucified for love, have performed the
absolute good, and it has been gathered up by God for everlasting remembrance.

Liberation practice, then, brings the human being face to face with hope.
From the poor themselves we learn that, despite all, hope is more judicious
than is hopelessness. Here we confront the ultimate truth of reality. How we
ought to respond cannot be programed. We know only this: if we respond in
hope, we are proclaiming that the ultimate mystery of reality—whether that
mystery be expressed in biblical symbols or formulated in some other way—is a
mystery of goodness and salvation. And to face reality in this posture is, once
again, an act of spirit.

2.4. *The practice of the liberation of the poor is itself a great expression of
love, and therefore of spirit. When no limits are placed on that practice, it*

confronts its agent with realities of supreme importance—ultimately, with love itself, hence also with truth and hope. The practice of the liberation of the poor, then, is the channel that demands, and sets the stage for, a fundamental spirituality in its human agent.

We have seen that the spirituality of liberation is a *basic* spirituality, because it demands of the human being a basic honesty with reality; that it is an *ultimate* spirituality, because the human being has to face up to, and deal with, genuinely ultimate realities—life and death, justice and injustice, giving life to others and giving one's own life—and that it is a *Christian* spirituality, because it forces the human being into direct converse with the ultimacy of others, the poor, with their life and their death, and in so doing brings them into contact with the question of their own ultimacy as well, with the meaning of their own lives. The ultimacy of the spirituality of liberation is an ultimacy that actually and concretely shifts the central concern of the human agent of that liberation from self to other.

Thus the practice of liberation performs an incalculable service to the human being's basic spirituality. Ultimately it sets us in confrontation with ourselves, constraining us to make a free choice regarding our very selfhood—to opt to "become" in one way and not in another. If we are faithful to and consistent with the dynamics of the practice of liberation, we become men and women of truth, men and women of absolute, disinterested love, men and women of hope. Theoretically we could come to this condition from a starting point in other practices than those of liberation. In current history, however, a practice without a core of liberative love will hardly occasion the formation of a person with spirit. Or to express it positively: the practice of liberation has indeed shown us this type of human being.

I call this basic spirituality "theologal," because honesty with the truth, absolute dedication in love, and a hope that never dies are the mediations by way of which women and men join themselves with the ultimate mystery of reality. I make this statement in all confidence even though I have not as yet explicitly formulated the relationship between the human being and God.

3. Necessity of the Practice of Spirituality for Liberation: The Christian Spiritual Mind-Set

I regard it as established that the practice of liberation prepares the ground for a basic spirituality. Now I wish to add that there are other spiritual attitudes and values that, taken jointly, might be styled a "spiritual mind-set": a particular kind of abiding disposition in the agent of liberation that secures, shapes, and invests with its proper dynamism both the basic spirituality and the practice of liberation.

As with the spirituality of liberation, the description that I shall now be making of the "spiritual mind-set" will not be an abstract or general one but, once again, a description of the abiding disposition of the Christian as it functions in relation to the liberation of the poor. It is a spiritual attitude characterized by a determination that the righteous struggle for liberation be good, and continually better, that this struggle be ever more and more open to the reign of God and the specific values of the reign of God. Let us examine this "mind-set," this abiding disposition, in its programmatic presentation by Jesus in the Sermon on the Mount, singling out some of its particular values. It is no accident that the Sermon on the Mount opens with the Beatitude addressed to the poor. It is a practice of liberation in behalf of the poor that, once more, renders this mind-set possible, and calls for the realization of its possibility.

3.1. *The pure of heart are those who see God.*

There is a purity of gaze that maintains human beings in a steadfast openness to truth, even after they have already grasped the basic truth of history. The pure of heart are those who are open to the truth. They have no desire to dominate or manipulate that truth. There is no self-deception, either with regard to oneself or with regard to liberation processes. The pure of heart never succumb to the temptation to equivalate propaganda with truth. More concretely, purity of heart is a persevering attitude of discernment and conversion. These are never guaranteed, however surely a person may have undergone the first great conversion to liberation. Purity of heart is deep chastity of intellect and will: those possessed of it do not seek themselves, do not impose their own ideas, or maintain their own interests in the practice of liberation.

The merciful are those who initiate and carry forward the struggle for liberation, beginning with a profound act of compassion for the suffering of the poor.

To be sure, that pain causes indignation. The prophets, too, and Jesus, were angry with oppressors. But anger is not the prime motivation. The main thing that moved Jesus was his mercy. He pitied the multitudes (Mark 6:34). This mercy, this compassion, should be the heart and soul even of prophetic denunciation. Compassion does not weaken denunciation. We saw that in Archbishop Romero. It becomes a powerful act of love—first for the poor, because it is undertaken in their defense, and then for oppressors, as a call for their conversion (the good news *sub specie contrarii*).

In terms of concrete history, we keep the suffering of the poor before our mind's eye as an evil, hence as something to be eliminated. We must not too quickly regard this suffering merely as the social cost of the triumph of liberation—although of course that cost is to a large extent inevitable. In the strategies and tactics of liberation, in our alliances and our divisions, we must keep a careful account of everything that will have an effect on the suffering of the poor, everything that will either increase or diminish their pain. Mercy is not at all a purely psychological, affective feeling, to which some will naturally be more inclined than others. Structurally, mercy is the way in which we express the fact that the struggle for liberation begins and continues with an immense love for a poor people.

Peacemakers are those who have not transformed the struggle itself into the be-all and end-all of their effort and concern. Rather than placing all their trust in the struggle itself, rather than converting the struggle into a mystique, they continue their efforts to reconcile the tragic need for the struggle with their burning desire for peace.

In historical terms, peacemakers are those who, even in a time of struggle and warfare, seek to humanize conflicts, to conduct armed conflict as humanely as possible, to foster peaceful means for the resolution of conflicts even amid the violence of struggle. In biblical language, peacemakers are those who long to beat their swords into plowshares, indeed, who do all that lies within them to see to it that, even amid the clanging of swords, plowshares ply the earth.

Those who are able to forgive are those who have no desire to close off their adversaries' future absolutely and irrevocably.

Forgiveness is more than an act of the mind, understandably difficult, and yet admirably performed by many of our Christian poor. Forgiveness is the attitude by which we recognize in our adversaries the potential to be humane—and recognize it as a potential that, at least in some small measure, is actualized at this very moment, however blind we tend to be to this fact in the heat of struggle. Historically, forgiveness means welcoming dialogue, and not only out of political calculation, however necessary this may be at times, but, on a deeper level, out of the need to engineer token reconciliations, large and small, even in the midst of conflict—tokens of the fact that without reconciliation, not only will no triumph last, but no society will be humane or human.

Finally, *the poor* are those who believe that in weakness there is strength, poverty is the locus of the spirit.

The material poor (in the Lukan version of the Beatitudes), filled with spirit (Matthew's version), struggle with an unjust and wretched poverty. And yet they see a humanizing element in that poverty. After all, poverty is the very opposite of wealth and power. Wealth and power dehumanize. Poverty points ahead to that society described by Ignacio Ellacuría as the "civilization of poverty," where misery will be a thing of the past, but austerity will enable all to share in everything, and human beings will be rescued from the dehumanization of rampant consumerism.

Historically viewed, again and again in the course of our struggles for liberation, we must return to the poor as our wellspring of spirit. When all is said and done, the struggle of liberation is waged for them and by them.

3.2. *The New Testament shows us another element of the "spiritual mind-set" that impregnates all basic spirituality. The attitudes expressed by Jesus in the Sermon on the Mount fairly resound with it—the element of gratuity.*

The New Testament demands a great deal of Christians. We are asked to put to work all that we have. And yet we are told, and in stern language indeed, that even after we have done all that we should, we may regard ourselves only as "useless servants" (Luke 17:10). To turn it around and put it positively: the entire New Testament is shot through with the concept that the initiative of all good lies in something or someone antecedent to us; indeed, that this something or someone has been given to us not only as a gift, but as the potential for being a gift to others.

Gratuity may be the most difficult reality to conceptualize or verbalize. But we can say something about it and its importance for liberation practice by looking at the "graced" human being. The struggle for liberation calls for great enthusiasm. But gratuity rules out hubris. Gratuity excludes any feeling of ethical superiority. The danger here is not in the fact that some cannot be objectively superior to others. The danger lies in the fact that the hubris of ethical superiority translates into the automatic justification of all that is done by us differently from the way it is done by those to whom we believe ourselves superior. If we fall into this trap, a personality cult springs up with regard to some person or group of persons. Gratuity reminds us that there is limitation and sin in us all, and that—in the words of José Ignacio González Faus—one must wage revolution as one forgiven. The experience of gratuity generates gratitude, and this grateful response invests spirit and practice with a special dynamism. From gratitude springs generous dedication (although the enthusiasm of the "converted" always has its pitfalls), freedom of spirit, and the joy of having found the pearl of great price, the treasure hidden in the earth. Gratuity is creative and fertile.

But once more the question of origin arises—a question all the more difficult in the present case because the reality under consideration—gratuity—is intangible. Theologically, "every worthwhile gift, every genuine benefit comes from above, descending from the Father" (James 1:17). But historically, gratuity has its mediation in the poor. The poor themselves acknowledge that they "have been given something." In formulations of profound biblical inspiration, they recognize that they who before were not, now are; that they who were not a people are now a people, and on the way to becoming God's people. In words of great and tragic depth, a campesino of Aguilares put it this way: "Before, we died, we were killed, and we didn't know why. Now, we may all be going to die—but we're aware that we're dying for a people. And this is completely different."

And these poor, in their totality, as a poor people, with their failings and mistakes, but with values that dwarf their shortcomings, have been transformed into gift and grace for those who seek to walk with them, defend them, and struggle at their side. The experience is universal. Not everything the poor are and do is gospel. But a great deal of it is. At all events, we may quite safely assert that the poor evangelize us (and the assertion is no less true for being so often repeated). And "evangelize" has its original meaning for us: good news that God, out of goodness, has determined to communicate and make present. This good news has been given to us, and inasmuch as it is received as gift, it shapes the deepest reaches of the spirit of those who receive it, so that they not only accept it with gratitude, but put it to work.

3.3. *It might be objected that this spiritual mentality—the attitude of the Beatitudes, and of grace—is sublime, but too idealistic; indeed, that it tends once more to alienation. From the vantage of reality, however, I should like to respond: it is not idealistic—it exists; indeed, its conceptualization has taken shape from a point of departure in reality, and I doubt whether it could have come into being without this reality, even though its "concepts" are scriptural.*

It is an ideal, yes. Accordingly, it is unattainable in its fullness. But this is precisely why I call it a *spiritual mentality*—not because "spiritual" means pure interiority here, as opposed to history, but because it is the fruit and expression of the spirit; and it is the spirit that time and again proposes the ideal, refusing to let us strike a compromise with the factual.

Nor is this spiritual mentality alienating if it accompanies basic spirituality— if spiritual mentality and basic spirituality arise from, take flesh in, and shape the practice of liberation. Furthermore—and we need only open our eyes to observe this—Christians with this mentality have mightily furthered the processes of liberation. Even nonbelievers among revolutionaries acknowledge this. There can be no doubt that Archbishop Romero, that brilliant example of mentality and spirituality, invested the practices of liberation with a unique power as he denounced the failings of liberation and encouraged its successes. Not infrequently, revolutionary groups ask Christians simply to be what they are, to be what I have just described. After all, a revolution has need of spirit, and the deeper the revolution, and the broader the areas of life to which it extends, the greater that need.

4. Spirituality of Liberation as Approach to and Encounter with God

Let me say a word on the relationship between the spirituality just described and the relationship between human beings and God. The spirituality in question is not something arising merely consequent upon faith in and contact with God. True, some manner of faith in and experience of God must be operative in the practice of liberation from the outset. But the spirituality of which I speak is rather the historical actualization of faith as approach to God and as contact with God. I should like to make some brief observations on this problematic from the point of view of spirituality.

4.1. *The spirituality I have described has the two characteristics that, in dialectical unity, shape the human being's approach to God: acquiring a kinship with God and journeying toward God.*

Men and women of truth, love, and hope are caught up in a never-ending process of becoming, in history, persons "akin to God." The God of truth is approached through affinity with God in the recognition of the truth of things, and the refusal to attempt to subjugate that truth by subordinating it to other interests. The God of truth is approached through affinity with God in the forthright denunciation of sin. The God of truth is approached through affinity with God in the maintenance of the purity of heart required to see the changing truth of processes and projects. The God of creation, life, justice, and liberation is approached through a kinship with God in the practice of the bestowal of life and the furthering of justice. God the bountiful and merciful Father, the God of more tenderness than a human mother's, is approached in mercy and compassion. God incarnate, incredibly close to the poor, and oppressed in the scandal of the cross, is approached through a kinship with God in incarnation among the crucified of history—in persecution, in the surrender of our very lives with and for them. The God of hope, of the nearness of the reign, of resurrection, of the new sky and the new earth, is approached by a kinship with God in the stubbornness of hope, in, through, and against history.

Spirituality is kinship with that God. It is walking at God's side. It is being and working in history as God is and works. It is our yes to Jesus' basic demand, which is not just an ethical exigency or a work of supererogation to which the pious may be called, but a paradigm of the very ideal of every woman and man: "You must be made perfect as your heavenly Father is perfect" (Matt. 5:48). "Be compassionate, as your Father is compassionate" (Luke 6:36). Spirituality as kinship with God means imitating in history the holiness of God as God has been revealed in self-revelation—not as distant from the secular and profane world, but as absolute salvific nearness. All of this furthers the liberation of the poor, inasmuch as it furthers real, effective, disinterested love for the poor. This is the prime element of affinity with God as proposed to us in scripture: to know God is to practice right and justice toward the poor and the helpless.

And yet this affinity with God is never possession of God. God is still unfathomable, unmanipulable Mystery. To approach God is to journey toward God and yet let God be God. This is what makes spirituality the true path to God. God's reality as Mystery is an inescapable aspect of God in every element of our existence, and in every starting point for our journey, no matter where we begin. But from a starting point in the liberation of the poor, letting God be God takes specific forms, and these forms make it utterly clear that journeying toward God does not mean possessing God. We come to grasp that there are dialectical elements that strain for reconciliation, and yet achieve it only in partial reconciliations, and only *caminando* ("by walking the way," "moving along"). It is in the experience of never achieving the synthesis, of having to strive for it ceaselessly, that we experience historically the fact that contact with God is necessarily the same thing as moving toward God.

The reason why we must *journey* toward God is that, in liberation, at no moment along the way do struggle and peace, justice and reconciliation, efficacy and gratuity, reach a state of perfect synthesis. We must *journey* because we know neither the day nor the hour of liberation, strong though our hope be. Stated programmatically, we must be ever *in via*—on the way, on the move—because liberation presupposes the reconciliation of a double move-ment: the dogged struggle with the oppression born of poverty, and our own movement in the direction of impoverishment.

Further, we must journey toward God because God draws us. By the power of utopia, God draws us godward. Of course that utopia does not solve all our problems. Nor does it in any way relativize the concrete. But as promise, as salvific future, it moves us. It draws us from the future. It impels history to "give more" of itself. Only *in via*, only in all that the journey contains of limitation and hope, do we experience that God is ever greater, we experience that God is God. Spirituality *in via* consists in reproducing in history the element of mystery in God, reproducing the element of transcendence in God's holiness—transcendence not as distantiation that separates, but as ideal that attracts. Spirituality therefore is directed toward that God, toward the utopia that, time and again, we must seize with our hands in the conviction that we are only seizing what history is holding back. Why? Ultimately, in order that truth, love, and hope may grow ever greater. Ultimately, so that liberation may be ever more profound and more integral.

4.2. *A spirituality that is approach to God makes it possible to encounter God in history as well. It offers the opportunity of a personal relationship with God.*

That God is a personal reality, someone with whom one can and ought to enter into contact, is evident all through scripture. The life and death of Jesus, the believing acceptance of God's son, says to the Christian: God is personal. God's word is to be heard. God's will is to be complied with. God can be trusted. We can find rest in God. We can enter into dialogue with God. We can love God, because God first loved each and every one of us.

From the vantage point of the spirituality I have been describing, we can concretize, to some extent, the personal experience of God. To assert in hope that underlying reality are goodness, justice, mercy, and love is a way of saying that this foundation of the real is personal in its nature. To experience that this foundation of the real issues a call as an individual, a real person, issues a call, that this something has a real, concrete will, that this something calls each of its addressees by name, inviting them all to discern their duty and not simply deduce it from universal principles, is an experience that this foundation of reality is not only some sort of "reality in depth," but reality as personal, reality as "someone"—a someone who calls to us, a someone whose concrete will must be discovered and complied with.

Perhaps the most characteristic element of the spirituality here described, as far as coming to understanding the personal nature of God is concerned, is the experience that the poor are also personal, concrete realities, with their own names; with sufferings and hopes that are generalizable, yes, and that therefore constitute structural reality, but with sufferings and hopes that are noninter-changeable. The world of the poor is made up of the actual poor, one by one. And it is this experience of the concrete human being that intimates the concrete element in God as that human being's correlate. Once we grasp the transcendent correlation between God and the poor (which appears all through scripture) from a point of departure in the concrete, personal, and nontransfer-able nature of each and every one of the poor, then the experience of God has its concrete, personal moment as well.

Surely it should be evident that in engaging in these reflections, I make no pretense of demonstrating the personal nature of God. My concern here is merely to point to, to indicate, God's mediations from the vantage of a spirituality of liberation. The theology of liberation speaks of an "encounter" with God, and agents of liberation assert that they experience this "encounter." It is had in the poor, as we have seen, and it makes a many-faceted demand. It calls for conversion to liberative practice, to the discernment of the signs of the times, to a great love. But it also has the nuance of personal encounter. This is what occurs in the innermost depths of human beings when they make a decision for liberation, when they render that decision explicit in personal and community prayer, when they celebrate that decision in the liturgy and other community gatherings. When all is said and done, what we have here is the synthesis with which we are presented in the exodus, in the prophets, and in Jesus: that God is experienced as initiator of liberation, yes, but that God is also experienced as the one who strikes a covenant with the people, a covenant that penetrates to the human heart. Liberation says affinity with and journey toward God. Covenant says encounter with God.

It is not easy to speak of God. God is ineffable. Human words do not measure up to our expectations. Analogies limp. Concepts serve us inade-quately. What I have attempted to say in these pages is that a spirituality and mind-set springing from and fostered by the practice of liberation permit us (and often enough require us) to speak of God as I have done. Ultimately this God is called Father—a personal reality in which one can place one's trust, and the paradigm of goodness for the practice of liberation. By the same token this Father is called God, and ultimate Mystery—and God's novel and creative word must be hearkened to, and reduced to practice, again and again, as we journey through history toward God, to a meeting with God, but without being able to possess God.

5. Conclusion

There are so many other things that could and should be said about spiritual-ity in relation to liberation. This relationship could also be further clarified from an explicit consideration of christology—although everything I have said is based on Jesus Liberator. Then again, surely the spirituality of liberation ought to be explored in the context of ecclesiology. Here we should have a consideration of the spirituality of the various charisms and functions, and spirituality of the unification of the ecclesial body for the sake of a more effective liberation on the one hand, and on the other a spirituality of the maintenance of the tension between institution and charism in acceptance of intraecclesial conflicts in which that tension sometimes issues. Then there would be a spirituality of solidarity among the various churches and groups (a solidarity so strikingly furthered by the practice of liberation), so that all give and all receive. Then there are certain specific questions that ought to be mentioned in connection with the importance of spirituality for their solution: the problem of Christian membership in non-Christian groups, or in political and revolutionary parties—in view of the key importance of loyalty to the gospel and the church—including the very demanding problem of spirituality and violence. Here, however, I have chosen to approach spirituality "from the roots up," in its deeply human and theo-logal content.

Not only, then, do liberation and spirituality not exclude each other, they require each other, as practice of a spirit and spirit of a practice. The unified duality of spirit and practice expresses the totality of the human being, and corresponds to global reality as seen from the viewpoint of revelation. In revelation, reality always appears as a unified duality, or dual unity: liberation and covenant in the exodus, the reign of God and the God of the reign in Jesus. This has been rediscovered by the Latin American church in the world of today: the struggle for liberation from poverty, and trusting openness to God (Medellín, *Poverty of the Church*, no. 5; Puebla, nos. 1161, 1149). It has worked its way into the religious life, influencing the traditional spiritualities of that life. The unification and inseparability of faith and justice were thematized in the last two general congregations of the Jesuits (in 1974 and 1983)—the proclamation of the good news, and work for justice and peace, in the words of the master general of the Dominicans. At bottom, we have what the prophet Micah asserted in his marvelous synthesis of the human vocation:

> You have been told, O man, what is good,
>   and what the LORD requires of you:
> Only to do right and to love goodness,
>   and to walk humbly with your God
>   [Micah 6:18].

A great many Christians have arrived at the same synthesis. Let me end with some quotations from Archbishop Romero, who was such an outstanding example of the oneness of practice and spirit, of struggle for justice and faith in God. His example also demonstrates that this synthesis can be achieved personally and institutionally. Once made in the furthest depths of a person, it can be expressed in, and charge with dynamism, that person's "professional dimension"—in Archbishop Romero's case, the episcopal ministry.

The need for a practice of justice was absolutely clear to him:

Living as we do in a world in such evident need of social transformation, how shall we not ask Christians to incarnate the justice of Christianity, to live it in their homes and in their lives, to strive to be agents of change, to strive to be new human beings?

And the ultimate foundation of that practice? "There is nothing more important for the church than human life . . . especially the life of the poor and oppressed."

Coolly and calmly he foresaw the historical consequences of this option, and accepted them with courage:

> I rejoice, my brothers and sisters, that our church is persecuted for its efforts of incarnation in the interests of the poor. . . . It would be a sad situation if in a country where such horrible murders are being committed, we had no priests among the victims. They are the witnesses of a church incarnate in the problems of the people.

And he took all of this upon himself personally, as a bishop, a Christian, and a Salvadoran:

> My position as shepherd obliges me to an act of solidarity with everyone who suffers, obliges me to "embody" my every effort in behalf of the dignity of human beings.

He foresaw his martyrdom as his ultimate service to liberation:

> God willing, let my death be a death in behalf of the liberation of my people, and a witness of hope in the future.

None of this withdrew him from God. On the contrary, it drew him immeasurably nearer. In his faith in that God, he saw the importance of spirituality:

> No human being has self-knowledge before having the encounter with God. . . . Brothers and sisters, tell me that my preaching today will bear fruit in the form of the encounter of each and every one of us with God!

And in that practice and that faith, Archbishop Romero was able to keep his people hoping. On other lips his words might have sounded either doctrinaire or propagandistic. But on the lips of Romero they echoed the truth that wells up from the depths of the reality of God and human beings:

> One feels the need of the transcendent, then, something from without! And this shattered Jerusalem will gleam with a new dawn, and that dawn will be God in person. God will take flesh in the bowels of Jerusalem. And we too, brothers and sisters, how full of hope we should be, seeing that our own strength now avails us nothing, seeing our country trapped

in a blind alley, seeing that politics and diplomacy are helpless here now, seeing everything in ruin and disaster! To deny it would be madness! We stand in need of a transcendent salvation! And upon these ruins, the glory of the Lord will blaze forth.

The cry of our people for liberation has reached the ears of the almighty. Nothing can stop it now.

Chapter 3

Spirituality and Theology'

Spirituality has come to be a topic of unusual interest today, and not only in the church or, as so often used to be the case, among those in the church who devoted themselves to the "pursuit of perfection." No, the new interest in spirituality has arisen first and foremost in the world. Current history, with its crises, its doubts and questions, its opportunities and demands for the construction of a human future, challenges human beings, singly and collectively. We can ignore this challenge. We can manipulate it or pervert it. But if we have our ears open, it voices once more the question of what we are and what we ought to be, what we hope for and what we could hope for, what we are doing and what we ought to be doing. From within history itself we hear the call to respond to that history and its truth, to shape it, and not be subjugated by it, or dragged along passively.

The task is endless. But it becomes inescapable, and urgent, in moments of crisis and "unhinging"—when the old, worn-out hinges no longer support the weight of the whole door. The creation of new hinges, so that history may turn again, and turn well—so that it may become a history in which men and women will live as human beings once more—presupposes many things. But the adequate integration of them all is a matter not just of science, or ideology, but of spirit. The "being-human-with-spirit" that will measure up to reality's cargo of crisis and promise, that will unify the various elements of reality in such wise that that reality be, in the event, more promise than crisis, is what I call "spirituality." This description of spirituality may seem rather too vague. But it is important to begin with a correct descriptive definition of spirituality if we hope to be "on the right track" when it comes to speaking of it, and not, consciously or unconsciously, reduce its all-embracing scope, or relegate it to the area of the immaterial or interioristic.

In the church, as well, the question of spirituality has become a factor demanding to be taken into account. After all, like it or not, the church shares current history and its demands. It too has been unhinged, with the unheard-of declarations of Vatican II and Medellín. There is no escaping the new doctrinal, theological, pastoral, and liturgical elements that have taken their place alongside those handed down by tradition. But neither is there any denying that the synthesis of old and new has its difficulties—in theory, and even more in practice—and that the synthesizing is done in different ways. For some of us, the taste for the new is strong, and the challenge of our synthesis consists in somehow integrating the old. In others of us the new is frightening, so that the old is what we long for.

The jigsaw-puzzle mosaic that is the church lies in pieces. It must be reassembled. Confronted with a task this risky, this demanding, we may be sorely tempted to base our reconstruction on doctrinal security and hierarchical authority. Doctrine and discipline remain important, and necessary. But by themselves they will be inadequate to the task of reconstructing the ecclesial edifice. We shall need spirit—great spirit—if we hope to manage a creative synthesis of the heterogeneous construction materials that we shall have to use: transcendence and history, hierarchical ministry and people of God, faith and practice, and the rest. This is why the clearest and most lucid spirits in the church voice not only an interest, but a crying need, for spirituality. This is their way of asserting their driving need to be, and to know themselves to be, believing Christians in the world of today—to be , and to know themselves to be, a sacrament of salvation in the world. The manner in which this goal is to be attained is a question of spirit. Hence the demand for a spirituality capable of effectuating a synthesis between being human and being a believer, saving and being saved, serving God and abandoning oneself to God.

For these reasons, basically, together with other, more specific motivational factors, theology has taken a serious interest in spirituality. The process has been under way for a number of years now. It began with the insight that a purely explicative, deductive, doctrinal theology of the past is no longer equal to the impact of reality on history and the church. We were driven back to the predoctrinal, the globalizing, by the explosive changes in reality. A purely doctrinal theology had become irrelevant. The very truth being proclaimed by that theology in order to maintain the identity of the faith was now seen as merely abstract truth, rather than the concrete truth that any theology based on the premise of God's ongoing activity ought to be developing. Sprinkling theological identity and relevance across dogmatic treatises on the one hand, and moral, pastoral, and spiritual treatises on the other, had failed to resolve the problem—which, after all, lay not in the formal organization of theological content, but in the mentality informing theology as a whole.

In this context, theological renewal has consisted not only in new attention paid to a forgotten content, but in attention paid to a content that of its very nature communicates a particular spirit. To cite one important example: the reign of God as an objective reality, with its subjective correlates of utopian hope and transformative practice, has gradually come into its own as content and "mind-set" of the whole of theology. The basic change here has not consisted in the addition of "reign of God" to other, more familiar theological content, but in the objective demand upon the subject of theology, the agent of theology, to analyze the reign of God with a new spirit, a spirit measuring up to its object, and then to offer that reign—once more, with spirit—to its original addressees. The basic change in a theology that had been purely doctrinal came from the realization that the whole warp and woof of the theological task must be shot through with hope, and thus with a call for Christian practice—and not only when the theological material under consideration happens to be the reign of God, but when theology considers any material at all.

Precisely by adopting a mentality of hope and praxis, theology has become spiritual theology. It only remained to raise its consciousness with respect to its spiritual status. Thus theology continues to treat conventional spiritual topics, but, more importantly, it now recognizes that these considerations must be entertained with spirit, and with the Spirit of God, in order to communicate spirit and the Spirit of God. Let me cite a few statements by well-respected European theologians. As early as 1969, Hans Urs von Balthasar was reinterpreting political theology, then in its infancy, as a rediscovery of "biblical spirituality," and exhorting his readers: "Let us not clip the wings of a generation that has had the sensitivity to discover the unacceptability of a divorce between theology and spirituality, contemplation and action, church and world."[5] Karl Rahner, alluding to the example of St. Thomas, pleaded for a transcendence of "that frightful division, in later theology, between theology and the spiritual life."[6] Political theologian Johannes B. Metz has spoken of a "mystique and policy of discipleship."[7] These citations are merely indicative, of course, but they demonstrate an awareness of the need for an integration of spirituality into theology as one of its essential dimensions.

The same thing has occurred, and is occurring, in the theology of liberation. It should be evident that, from the outset, this theology has professed a utopian and praxic mentality of partiality toward the poor, in virtue of its intended function in the liberation of poor majorities, its very raison d'être. But this has not been an exercise in reductionism, all allegations to the contrary notwithstanding. It has taken place in complementarity with a "spiritual mentality." After all, "from the first steps taken by the theology of liberation, the question of spirituality—precisely the following of Jesus—has constituted a profound concern."[8] It is one thing to say that the theology of liberation did not at first include an explicit consideration of spirituality. This is perfectly true (although it was scarcely without works on spirituality, even in its inception).[9] But it is another matter altogether to deny that the theology of liberation was born with a spiritual mentality. This theology has always been very clear on the insufficiency of purely theoretical categories when it comes to liberation: "We need a vital attitude, all-embracing and synthesizing, informing the totality as well as every detail of our lives; we need a 'spirituality.' "[10] "The encounter with the Lord," and "a living sense of gratuity," were there from the beginning.[11] How could the theology of liberation have done without a spirit and a spirituality? As we have seen, at stake was a new, creative synthesis of the Christian life for the new context of Latin America, where old ideas had become unbearable, and new ones had burst upon the scene with irresistible force.

The implicit spirituality of an infant theology of liberation became more and more explicit in that theology. I shall cite only two examples. In 1979, seven Latin American periodicals simultaneously published a monothematic issue on the "spirituality of liberation."[12] The Presentation speaks of "a phenomenon that has now steeped the life of committed Christians in the renewal of this crucified land," and claims that "only a 'spirituality' is capable of doing justice to the dynamics of Latin American Christianity and its increasing fruitfulness."[13] In 1982, *Espiritualidad y liberación* appeared in Costa Rica—a collection of articles by twelve authors on various aspects of liberation spirituality.[14] An appendix lists seventy-four titles on spirituality from a liberation viewpoint. The Introduction reminds us once more that the theme of spirituality "arises as the consequence of a life committed to a liberative praxis of and among the poor."[15] Conversely, it is among the poor that the "experience of God, and life according to the Spirit, is lived."[16]

Thus the theology of liberation has gradually become a spiritual theology as well. Spirituality is no less a prime dimension of the theology of liberation than is liberation itself. Spirituality and liberation call for one another. This has come to be recognized on a wide scale.[17] It is a pity that the Vatican "Instruction on Certain Aspects of the Theology of Liberation" did not acknowledge it.

I hold that spirituality is not merely a dimension of theology, it is an integral dimension of the whole of theology. Having rediscovered and assimilated the corporeal, societal, praxic, and utopian dimensions of human life, the theology of liberation wishes to integrate all these dimensions into spirituality. This intuition is only a prolongation of the Pauline presentation of the new human being as the spiritual human being. Spirituality here has very little indeed to do with immateriality, or with any subcompartment of the Christian life. It concerns the entirety of that life:

> From the Christian standpoint, spiritual men and women are men and women filled with the spirit of Christ, and filled with it in a living, observable manner. After all, the force and life of that Spirit invades their whole person, and all their activity.[18]

Theology must come to grips with this fact, and plant and water the seeds of a Christian synthesis.

I now propose to (1) present the spirituality of the theology of liberation in terms of Gustavo Gutiérrez's *Beber en su propio pozo**** and (2) mention some reflections of my own on the theology of liberation as a spiritual theology.

---

* This work was published by the Centro de Estudios y Publicaciones, Lima, Peru, in 1971. A revised second edition was published in 1983. The English translation, *We Drink from Our Own Wells* (Orbis Books, Maryknoll, N.Y., and Dove Communications, Melbourne, Australia, 1984), is a translation of the revised edition. In this present chapter, all quotations are (translated) from the 1971 Spanish edition—the edition cited by Sobrino.—ED.

1. Spirituality of Liberation Theology: "Drinking from One's Own Well"

Gutiérrez's work is an important one simply by reason of the identity of its author, who is such a close observer of the development of liberation theology—and more importantly, of liberation processes—together with the life of the church and the relationship of those processes and that life to the theology of liberation. But it is important as well by reason of the light it sheds, however indirectly, on the debate over the inspiring and shaping principle of liberation theology. Finally, it is important by reason of its subject: spirituality. Gutiérrez's book furnishes us with a synthesis of his own spiritual theology, which in turn assimilates the reflections of other authors. Gutiérrez calls his synthesis provisional (p. 139), not only in virtue of any theoretical rough edges it may have, but by the very nature of the subject, for spirituality by definition always stands in relation to real history and its novelty.

Like any synthesis, Gutiérrez's has cost time. He asserts that the explicit treatment contained in his book is "the payment of an old debt" (p. 11). The reason why payment comes so late is not only that the first theoretical efforts of the theology of liberation were devoted to explaining its name—that is, to explaining the nature of liberation and theology—but by the nature of the subject itself. Spirituality is a reality, not just a concept, and realities take more time to be constituted than do concepts. The theology of liberation reflects on the real as it occurs, whereas in the area of doctrine it possesses concepts before their realization. For this twofold reason, the theological treatment of spirituality has taken time. But for the same two reasons, as well, as P. Trigo puts it so well: "It is not a matter of ideology . . . but of theory (that is, of the understanding of a praxis). This is why this book could not have been written earlier."[19] But the delay is offset by the reality of spirituality, and by a theoretical language of the real as well as of the conceptual.

All of this is suggested by the title of Gutiérrez's book (all his titles are rich and suggestive), "Drinking from one's own well." Over and above the beauty of expression, let us note that what we have in this title is an indication of the content, the method, and the basic mind-set of the whole book. The basic image here is that there is a "well" in Latin America that is filled with the water of life, filled with the faith, the hope, the love, the dedication and joy, and often enough the tears and the blood, of Christians who have committed themselves to the liberation of their own poverty-stricken peoples. Thanks to this well of Christian life, there can be a new spirituality. And thanks to the fact that so many drink of this well—first the very poorest, for it is theirs, and then those who have approached these poor persons and devoted themselves to them— there is a new spirituality. Gutiérrez's book, therefore, unlike so many other books on "spirituality," is not a book on the history of spiritualities of the past. It is a book on spirituality as current reality. Therefore, too, its method is basically narrative. Although the book is structured systematically, its nerve center is its narrative theology. It systematizes theoretically what it narrates, but it narrates what exists. Because what exists is a people of faith, hope, and love, the mentality of the book is a joyous one: there are good tidings between its covers. It speaks of spirituality not only in a context of the costly demands of that spirituality, but also as an invitation to make that spirituality real, and thus to come to the deepest identity of being human and being Christian.

Gutiérrez's book presents spirituality as a synthesis of the Christian life, and as standing in essential relationship with liberation. Spirituality does not enter theology by the back door. It enters there with full right. Gutiérrez's book clearly demonstrates the impossibility of a spirituality without liberation. This of course is the original intuition of the theology of liberation. What Gutiérrez makes more explicit, and sets forth in greater detail, is the impossibility of total liberation without spirituality, inasmuch as spirituality endows liberation with a new dimension.

I shall now attempt a systematic presentation of the most important elements of the book: the aspects of spirituality that other Latin American writers have already treated (which shows that spirituality is already part and parcel of the theology of liberation), and especially Gutiérrez's own most novel contributions.[20]

1.1. *Spirituality as Totality of the Christian and Historical Life*

If the theology of liberation insists on anything at all, it insists on spirituality as a totality in the person and group subject, precisely as that subject is referred to in the totality of history. It is not easy, then, to launch a discourse on spirituality. Gutiérrez's book sets forth two unified points of departure, permitting the construction of two unified theoretical frameworks for an understanding of the dimension of totality inherent in spirituality. His twin points of departure are the "irruption" of the Lord, who offers and demands discipleship, and the "irruption" of the poor, who invite and demand liberation. What the reaction between the two experiences and totalities will be, what logical priority one has over the other, is reserved for later analysis. By reason of methodological considerations, these elements will have to be handled separately. But the important thing as we begin is to see them in unity.

1.1.1. *The Following of Christ*

"A Christian is defined as a follower of Jesus, and reflection on the experience of following constitutes the central theme of any solid theology" (*Beber*, p. 11). These are the opening words of the book, as well as its closing words, at the point when the author comes to define spirituality. Discipleship is not something fixed, or an ascetical program, as if Jesus, his attitudes, his practices, and his virtues, were to be the object of imitation by the Christian subject already constituted. The case is just the contrary. The following of Jesus is the *totality* of the Christian life. And precisely in its quality as following, and not pure imitation, it is the *process* of achieving the realization of the Christian life. With these two aspects—totality and process—as his point of departure, Gutiérrez now defines spirituality as "a journey according to the Spirit of Christ" (pp. 59, 73, 85).

In chapter 2 of *Beber* Gutiérrez explicitates his definition in terms of the Holy Trinity: "Encounter with Christ, life in the Spirit, journey to the Father: such, it seems to me, are the dimensions of every spiritual walking in the Spirit according to the Scriptures" (p. 58). Gutiérrez's trinitarian focus on spirituality has important consequences. Formally, spirituality not only is, but can only be, a pilgrimage in history. We have the fundamental normativity of Jesus, and the future of the Father is opened to us, but spanning the norm and the future is a pilgrimage, a journey, a process and a changing, in the Spirit. A number of consequences flow from this. First, spirituality cannot consist of a simple imitation of something already given, some a priori prescription. Spirituality is always and necessarily something to be redone. Secondly, to spirituality belongs, by its essence, novelty, newness—to be judged according to the spirit of Jesus. Thirdly, this novelty stands in relationship with the novelty of history. It must be historical novelty before it can be biographical novelty in the subject, because it is in history that the Spirit of God, manifested in the signs of the times, continues to act. Spirituality is purely and simply a participation in God's own history, history as assumed by God in Christ and the Spirit.

Gutiérrez's trinitarian focus has its consequences as well for the basic *content* of spirituality. Undoubtedly, one must analyze in detail who the trinitarian God is and what the will of God is for history. But we can say a priori—all the more so in view of the situation of Latin America—that the will of this trinitarian God is life. The Father is the origin and fulfillment of life. The Son came that we "might have life and have it to the full" (John 10:10). The Spirit is "Lord and giver of life." The trinitarian God is life, and it is a basic datum of spirituality that God fosters life "trinitarily." In Latin America this translates, as we shall see, into the thesis that the will of God is the promotion of the life of the poor. It will suffice here to recall Archbishop Romero's celebrated paraphrase of St. Irenaeus: *Gloria Dei, vivens pauper*. What Gutiérrez adds—again, as liberation theology has developed the notion from the very beginning—is that this will of God for life is implemented in the presence of death and a will to death. The God of life coexists with the divinities of death. The God of life is locked in mortal combat with them. Thus, right from the start, spirituality finds itself confronted with a fundamental choice. The Christian is at a crossroads. One direction "bears the mark of *death* (sin and law), the other of *life* (grace and freedom)" (p. 109). "Human life unfolds within an option for death or an option for life" (ibid.). "The journey according to the flesh . . . leads to death. . . . The journey according to the Spirit leads to life" (p. 93).

Spirituality, then, is a journey. And it is a journey whose basic direction has already been determined: the promotion of life. But the journey must be walked in the presence of the other choice—the bestowal of death and the fact of dying. It is of crucial importance to approach spirituality in these terms. To approach spirituality, consciously or unconsciously, as something constituted in the area of the incorporeal spiritual, so that the antithesis of spirituality would be materiality, would be to misunderstand spirituality altogether. Spirituality is constituted not in the antithesis of soul and body, spirit and matter, but in that of life and death (p. 111).

Gutiérrez explains that the "journey according to the Spirit" (p. 85) basically means living according to the "principle of dynamism and life" (p. 98), which is love. It means opting, positively, and counter to its contrary, for "life according to the Spirit . . . according to *life*, love, peace, and justice—the great values of the reign of God—and *against death*" (p. 111). It means embracing and assimilating the central paschal event of Christian faith. "Witnessing to life implies the death passage" (p. 73).

This is the overall theological framework of spirituality. Many details will have to be considered within it, but nothing falls outside it. Spirituality is the Christian life in its totality: life in the trinitarian reality of God in a historical manner. The focus here is strictly theologal. At stake is a genuine theology of history, of which spirituality is but the subjective repercussion on the agent of that history.

1.1.2. *Encounter with the Lord in the Poor*

It will be evident from what I have said that spirituality cannot dispense with concrete history. After all, God's own history is concrete. When it comes to Latin America, we begin with the datum that God is passing through history here with novelty and power. But it has ever been thus with the appearance of a great spirituality. "Every great spirituality is bound up with the great historical movements of a given era" (p. 45)—movements that in their inception are not or need not be intraecclesial, being by their essence simply historical (see p. 48).

It is important to stress this, and Gutiérrez makes it emphatically clear. We know from the theological structure of spirituality *that* it ought to be historicized, but we do not know *how* this historicization should occur. Once historicized, the structure of a spirituality can be compared with any other spirituality. But before this happens, something must happen in history. This is why there have been various spiritualities in the history of the church—a variety of syntheses of the pilgrimage in the Spirit. It was inevitable.

It is not, generally speaking, their formal elements—encounter with the Lord, pilgrimage in the Spirit, journey to the Father—that differentiate spiritualities, but rather "the nucleus around which a spiritual pilgrimage is constructed" (p. 135):

A determinate spirituality always entails a rendering of the fundamental axes of the Christian life, beginning with a central intuition. . . . What constitutes the difference between one spirituality and another is not to be found in those axes, which basically are always the same, but in the new order created within them, in how a synthesis takes effect. And this comes from the experience that gives rise to the spiritual journey [p. 135].

In Latin America this experience is the encounter with the Lord in the poor. Gutiérrez emphasizes that the major fact of contemporary Latin American history is the "irruption of the poor" in a part of the world considered to be Christian (p. 12). This appraisal is the original intuition of liberation theology, as we shall see. But let me first examine the essential element of that irruption, and see how it enables the subject to have an experience of totality.

The poor of Latin America are, in the first place and structurally speaking, persons, who live "in a foreign land" (p. 20). This biblical expression is applicable to the poor in every aspect of their existence. The reasons why are, first and generally, because their estrangement extends to their total reality; secondly and specifically, because their poverty arises from their forced estrangement from the land, which belongs to God alone, an estrangement caused by unjust structures (p. 23). These poor are particularized, concrete realities, as well, and Gutiérrez depicts their state in even more graphic language than that of Puebla, referring to the "endless list of the miseries of the poor":

A thousand little things: lacks of every type, abuses and contempt suffered, tortured lives in search of work, incredible ways of making a living or more exactly a crumb of bread, petty quarrels, family separations, illnesses no longer existent at other social levels, malnutrition and infant mortality, substandard payment for their work or merchandise, total disorientation as to what is most necessary for them and their families, delinquency by abandonment or despair, loss of their own cultural values [pp. 171–72].

Here are the real poor, the objects of an active impoverishment. Here, then, are "victims" of impoverishment (p. 23), and victims of an impoverishment that means death (p. 21): physical, real death, first of all, but a more comprehensive death as well—"cultural death, because the dominator seeks the annihilation of all that gives unity and force to the dispossessed, in order to render them easier prey to oppressive machination" (ibid.).

This poverty continues to be the most flagrant phenomenon in Latin America. But it is not the most novel. Suddenly we hear the "song of the poor" (p. 35). What is new is a new awareness, in "a people who begin to perceive the causes of that situation of injustice and seeks to shake it off" (p. 37) with their exploits of solidarity, love, prayer, and so on (pp. 37–44), to become a people with a spirit of its own, a people bearing that ripest and most disconcerting of fruits, joy. The joy of the poor is a theme that Gutiérrez has subjected to an incisive analysis. It is a sign of something very new. "A poor, believing people has never lost its ability to celebrate, despite the harsh living conditions" (p. 173). But now its joy is more conscious, because it has passed the test. Now it is joy in the midst of suffering, poverty, and repression. If joy is maintained now, it is only because of a great hope (p. 172), and hope is mightier than poverty and suffering. "The negation of joy . . . is sorrow, not suffering" (ibid.). Suffering abounds. But sorrow has not carried the day. Therefore can the poor sing, and in their song they show us that they have a spirit of their own.

The irruption of the poor is not simply one more fact or occurrence to be jotted down on the list of socio-economic phenomena in Latin America. It is the complex of all the misery and all the joy of a poor people, as this inescapable reality forces itself on our consciousness. The eruption of the poor discloses the truth of all history from the "underside" of that history, "from beneath," from the lining of history's garment. It shows us the direction of that history, and the correlative obligation to undertake a transforming praxis. In these poor, a concrete universal irrupts upon us with the power to make us see the totality, or at least with more power than that of other concrete universals.

This is why the irruption of the poor can occasion a totalizing spiritual experience. It would be incorrect to regard poverty merely as a material, socio-economic datum—endowed, to be sure, with the power to set in motion a certain analytical, ethical, or praxic potential in its subject. No, the irruption of the poor has the power to set in motion the whole subject. It concerns that subject in its totality. It demands a total response, and it makes that total response possible. And thereby it demands and makes possible a spiritual experience.

Surely it is clear by now that the so-called material element in poverty is something more than material. Life is at stake—the life of my neighbor. And because it is life that is at stake, the life of my neighbor, I can have a spiritual experience of the poor in virtue of the so-called material element in poverty. "It is not *my* body, but the *bodies of the poor*—the feeble, debilitated bodies of the poor—that give us access to the material world from within a spiritual perspective" (p. 154). At the same time, because the poor burst in upon our awareness with a spirit of their own, their irruption constitutes not only a "questioning," a challenge, but an invitation as well. It calls for a liberative response, yes. But it is also gift and grace, the gift of hope and the grace to maintain that hope. It is the grace to proclaim a meaning for history—a history altogether questionable in the eyes of those who view it from the standpoint of the poverty that it generates. That hope is already maintained by those who should seem to have the least reason to hope. Hence we speak of the irruption of the poor as a mediation of the encounter with the Lord.

Whether, then, Latin American reality be regarded from the standpoint of God and the will of God, or from that of the irruption of the poor, it impinges on our awareness as something bearing upon the spirit of the human being as a whole, as demanding a mighty act of human spirit, and as rendering that mighty act possible. Discipleship in our day acquires its concrete characteristics from the irruption of the poor. The following of Jesus today demands that we join the poor on their journey, that we "be for," that we exist for, the poor. In response, the irruption of the poor once more sheds light on the reality of God as God of life, and illuminates our pilgrimage in the Spirit as a fostering of that life.

1.2. *Experience of God*

At the root of all spirituality is a spiritual experience (pp. 14, 16, 59, 61, 83), which Gutiérrez describes as "an encounter with the Lord and his will" (p. 61). In that experience we encounter the will of God, the imperative of building the reign of God, and we encounter the God who wills this reign. And we are interrogated in this encounter. We are asked what we ought to do, we are asked what we are. "God wills the life of those he loves" (p. 49), Gutiérrez reminds us, and he concludes that "to liberate is, definitively, to bestow life. The whole of life" (p. 14). At the same time he emphasizes the genuine presence of God in this experience: "The irruption of the poor into Latin American society and the Latin American church is in the last instance an irruption of God into our lives" (p. 49). Let us follow Gutiérrez's analysis of this experience of an encounter with God.

Spiritual experience is rooted in an encounter with God. Gutiérrez describes this experience, in the most authentic biblical tradition, as something personal, gratuitous, and demanding. "To encounter the Lord is before all else to be encountered by the Lord. . . . In this encounter we discover where the Lord lives and what the mission is with which the Lord entrusts us" (p. 63). To be encountered by the Lord is the experience of the love of God. Indeed it is the experience of the fact that love is the reality that discloses to us, and makes us able to be, what we are. It is God's coming to meet us, simply because God loves us, that renders us capable of defining our very selves as who we are, in order, in our turn, to go forth to meet others. "Gratuity marks our lives in such a way that we are led to love and to seek to be loved gratuitously" (p. 165).

The experience of being met by God cannot be replaced by anything else. It is of a fundamental, foundational nature. It is not only something that occurs in the first beginnings of spirituality. It is something we must return to, as the Apostle John recalled of his encounter with Jesus ("it was about four in the afternoon"—John 1:39) and as the early Christians recalled when speaking of their first assemblies (Acts 2:41–47). St. Ignatius Loyola remembered his experience at Manresa as "his primitive church" (p. 83). To this experience one must return, for it is by this experience that one lives. It is this experience that furnishes the spiritual process with its fundamental direction, and "is the wellspring of a great freedom" (ibid.). The experience of God, then, is absolutely fundamental, and on it depends the depth of the liberation we undertake.

On the foregoing premises, Gutiérrez grounds a powerful thesis: on this experience of God also depends the possibility of a genuine encounter with the poor. Without this experience, we can never hope to allow the poor genuinely to irrupt into our lives. Gutiérrez has spoken of the experience of God and the experience of the poor as a "differentiated unity," such that each pole reinforces the other dialectically. Now he sounds out one of the poles of this dialectic and formulates its absolute necessity. Without a true encounter with God, there can be no true encounter with the poor. And it is important to recall that the need to plunge into the encounter with God proceeds from the reality of the liberation processes themselves—which thus becomes the warranty of their Christian direction besides, for they force us to return to and plumb the depths of our spiritual origins. Gutiérrez writes:

Matthew 25:31-46 makes it very clear that the encounter with the poor, in terms of concrete works, is something mandated by the encounter with Christ. But it also implies, and equally, that a true and full encounter with a neighbor is mediated by the experience of the gratuity of God's love. Liberated from any tendency to impose on others a will alien to them, detached from ourselves, respectful of their personality, needs and aspirations, we reach out to others. If one's neighbor is the path that leads to God, one's relationship to God is what makes possible an encounter, true communion, with that neighbor. . . . The experience of the gratuity of God's love—a basic datum of the Christian faith—not only does not lock itself up in a historical parenthesis, as it were, but gives to the process of human becoming (and from within) its full significance [p. 169].

Historical observation confirms all this. "The practice of these years has demonstrated that the approach to the world of the poor must be effectuated without triumphalism of any sort" (p 189), but rather "calls for a big dose of humility"(ibid.). The Bible calls this attitude "spiritual infancy," which Gutiérrez defines as an "attitude of openness to God, an attitude of the availability of one who looks to the Lord for all things" (ibid.). And he goes on to explain:

Detachment from the goods of this world (an aspect of spiritual poverty) is realized only by inserting oneself into the midst of poverty. This is certainly a valid perception, but there is a deeper one annexed to it: only from an attitude of spiritual infancy is it possible to truly commit oneself to the poor and oppressed in Latin America [p. 90].

Remarkable words. Words that might even seem disconcerting on the lips of a liberation theologian. But they are evangelical words, and they concur with the experience we have in the processes of liberation. Of course, in no way do they deny the decisive importance of the encounter with the poor or the demand for their liberation. On the contrary. Nor do they involve a fall into a dualism of God and the poor, transcendence and history, acceptance of the gift of God and implementation of its demand. Nor, properly speaking, do they set forth a chronology of the spiritual experience, as if first we must secure the experience of God through certain mechanisms absolutely unrelated to the poor, and then, once this has been accomplished, approach the poor. No, what Gutiérrez offers us here is a logical reorganization of the elements of the spiritual experience. In virtue of the very nature of liberation, one must genuinely approach the poor, and genuinely deliver them from their poverty. Precisely on this account, one must make certain that it is the poor that one has met, and their liberation that one strives for. And to this end we are offered the logic of divine revelation. To have genuine love for our sisters and brothers, we must have an experience of the God who first loved us.

What Gutiérrez means here is simply that "it all started with God," and that it is necessary to keep account of this fact in order that everything proceed "according to God." They who really know themselves to be loved by God, will love their brothers and sisters better. They whose vision has been purified by God, will see the world of the poor with more purity. They who have most experienced God's mercy and forgiveness will be most understanding with the poor. Those who have grasped that God is love, and love alone, will seek the liberation of the poor with more disinterestedness and more effectiveness.

The experience of God neither presupposes nor occasions any escape from history on our part. Rather it demands of us, and inspires in us, a greater and better entry into that history—but that entry must be "according to God." The key here is the experience of God, and not any of the conventional practices for achieving it. When does this experience occur? When it will. But once we have encountered God, once we have come to the realization that God has come forth to meet us and has reinserted us into history, then we find that all the elements of our experience are organized in a precise manner:

> The happiness instilled in the human heart by the presence of the love of God engenders thanksgiving and openness to others. In the Magnificat, confidence in and surrender to God are interwoven with readiness for commitment to and proximity with those of God's predilection: the lowly and the hungry [p. 191].

1.3. *Incorporation into the Spirituality of the People*

The foregoing section has been a discussion of the personal dimension of encounter with God, experience of God, and spirituality. But no spirituality of individualism, and no spirituality of elitism, is implied. On the contrary. And so Gutiérrez then presents us with a critque of these two distortions of spirituality. Spirituality must be "popular," the spirituality of a *people*. Granted, with spirituality as with so many other things, there are unique figures who, at a given moment, marvelously express a given spirituality. But the history of spirituality is usually reduced to a study of these figures. In the Old and New Testaments, however, as in Latin American reality, it is peoples and communities who are the primary subjects of spirituality. This is the emphasis of the subtitle of Gutiérrez's book: "In the spiritual journey of a people."

He dwells on the exodus from Egypt and the primitive Christian community as models for spirituality. What gives meaning to God's deed in the exodus, and to Moses' deed as the human protagonist of that exodus, is (1) the liberation of an entire people, and (2) the covenant struck with an entire people. "Leaving Egypt is breaking with death (this is what slavery and want mean) to go forth to meet Yahweh and be transformed into Yahweh's people" (p. 114).

That historical and theological protagonism, or championship, of the people, a priori evident in revelation, is what is being recovered in Latin America. "There is a history that has begun to be forged by the poor and dispossessed, the privileged ones of the reign of God" (p. 20). And it is that history that demands, and is fostering, a new spirituality, whose agent is the people:

> The struggles of the impoverished peoples for liberation represent an affirmation of that people's right to life, granted that the poverty it endures signifies death, a premature and unjust death. In this affirmation of life, the poor of Latin America express their intention to live the faith, to acknowledge the love of God, and to give voice to their hope. Amid their struggles . . . an oppressed people, inspired by faith, becomes more and more the maker of a way being Christian, a spirituality. This people, from being a consumer of spiritualities (valid in themselves no doubt, but corresponding to the experiences and goals of other continents) is now working out its own way of being faithful to the Lord and faithful to the poorest of the poor [p. 48].

This is a new phenomenon. Elitism has gone by the board. "The subject of the experience that opens the road to a spirituality is an entire people, and not an isolated person" (p. 50). Doubtless there are persons who express this spirituality more brilliantly and more clearly than do others. But ultimately their spirituality is not their own creation. Ultimately their spirituality is only the most finished expression and synthesis of a spirituality that has already come into place among their peoples and their communities. Hence Gutiérrez's vigorous conclusion:

> Many Christians in Latin America today have come to the conclusion that for them the following of Jesus will entail an incorporation into the spiritual experience of a poor people. This demands of them a profound conversion: they must make their own the experience that the poor have of God and of God's will for life for every last human being. . . .
>
> This new turn of mind summons them to leave a familiar world, and prompts them to rethink their own spiritual tradition. They must, above all else, make the world of their own the world of the poor, their way of living a relationship with the Lord, and of assuming the historical praxis of Jesus. But they are looking for a path parallel to the path trodden by an oppressed and believing people. They search for ways of establishing contacts with the path of the poor; they take up commitment to the exploited; they enter into friendly relationships with poor persons; they celebrate the eucharist with grassroots communities, and so forth. These

are commendable efforts, no doubt, but they are insufficient: these links with the poor do not eliminate the parallelism mentioned just above. The spiritual experience that a poor people lives is too profound and all-embracing to merit only this type of attention. It merits walking with them on their path [p. 51].

This is an important point. Theoretically it should occasion no surprise. After all, the correlative of God's revelation is first and foremost a people, a people whom God desires to liberate and covenant with: "I shall be your God and you shall be my people." Of the church we say that, before all else, it is the "people of God." Our faith tells us that "the entire body of the faithful . . . cannot err in matters of belief" (*Lumen Gentium,* no. 12). Of liberation we say that the poor must be its primary agents. "The people"—the community in which individuals live, create, and realize their Christian life—is an essential dimension of God's communication to us and of our response to God. This does not abrogate the importance of the "individual, personal" dimension, either with respect to being loved and challenged by God, or with respect to our response to God. After all, each and every human being has an individual face in the sight of God, and no human being can delegate to others his or her acceptance of and response to faith. But all of this transpires with a people, and in such a way that, from the Christian standpoint, an openness to the people, a readiness to give to and receive from that people as a member of it, is essential to the constitution of the believer even qua "individual, personal" believer. Faith has a communitarian facet, essential to its very constitution.

Spirituality, too, at least de jure, has that essential communitarian facet. To be sure, we cannot demand the psychologically or sociologically impossible of persons who are not members of a poor people historically, who must confront crises unknown to the peoples of Latin America (crises deriving from the Enlightenment, for example), and who have specific responsibilities in society and in the church in virtue of the determinate place they occupy. But the spirituality of the people, a people of the poor—the basic element of their faith and their hope, their concrete spiritual values, their generous surrender out of love—must shape the spirituality of everyone else, and give it its concrete direction. Of course, in the realization of this spirituality none of its subjects can prescind from their particular conditions and opportunities, which may be very different from the conditions and opportunities of the people at large.

Paraphrasing the familiar words of Archbishop Romero, Gutiérrez writes: "To this have we been called, to rise with the people in the area of spirituality" (p. 53). This is the fundamental thesis of his "Drinking from one's own well," and this is what the title expresses. "The faith and hope in the God of life that sojourns in the ambit of death and struggle for life—the lived experience of the poor and oppressed in Latin America—this is the well from which we must drink if we would be faithful to Jesus" (p. 54).

1.4. *Concrete Traits of the Spirituality of Liberation*

Thus far the object of my analysis has been the basic structure of spirituality, together with its two principal conditions: that it be theologal, and that it be popular. Now I must explore its concrete content. From this point forward, instead of discussing the nature of spirituality in the abstract, I shall attempt to answer the questions: Who is the concrete spiritual human being, the concrete spiritual people? What does revelation have to say on this point? What does historical reality have to say?

The search for a synthetic formulation of the concrete reality now under consideration is no easy matter. The constitutive elements of spirituality are numerous, and any synthetic formulation is theoretically questionable. Gutiérrez's option is for: "Free to love" (p. 137). After all, "all spirituality is a path available for the better service of God and others: freedom to love" (p. 135). We should take note of the New Testament roots of this formulation from the outset, for in the New Testament spirit and freedom go hand in hand. The freedom of the spiritual human being must be understood in the biblical sense, then, and not in the sense of license. Free human beings are those who are free from themselves, and not for themselves but for others. The "for" between "freedom" and "love" could be misinterpreted, as if one could be free "for" any number of things. No, in the New Testament freedom can only be "for" love of others. Through this love, human beings will "gain themselves" as well. They will also be "for" themselves. But they will not gain this, they will not be this, directly. They will achieve themselves, and be themselves, only by way of the "for others." This is what Gutiérrez expresses so graphically in the pair of New Testament phrases he uses to illustrate this "freedom to love." "Although I am not bound to anyone, I made myself the slave of all" (1 Cor. 9:19). And "No one takes [my life] from me; I lay it down freely" (John 10:18). The freedom of the subject , and the subject's self-bestowal and self-surrender for love, are correlatives. That free subject is the spiritual person.

Gutiérrez sees this synthesis of the spiritual person as a reality now in Latin America—to a greater or lesser degree of perfection and definition, but as a reality nonetheless, and a reality sufficient to warrant designation as a realized spirituality:

> The truth is that daily contact with the experiences of some, reading what is written by many, together with the testimony of others, convince me of the depth of the spiritual experience presently being lived among us [p. 143].

Gutiérrez's concern at this point, then, is to compose a description of these spiritual women and men. To this purpose he selects five concrete traits of spirituality in terms of freedom to love, and analyzes them one by one: "conversion: demand for solidarity" (p. 144); "gratuity: climate of efficacy" (p. 161); "joy: victory over suffering" (p. 171); "spiritual childhood:

precondition of commitment to the poor" (p. 183); and "community: out-growth of solitude" (p. 191). Gutiérrez has selected these headings with great care, in view of the internal dialectic they reflect. He is concerned to render an account of five basic traits of spirituality in such a way that, taken together, they describe its totality. But he is equally concerned to demonstrate the essential need to go beyond the accumulation of these traits and to maintain the difficult dialectic that obtains among them—between each one and all the others, as well as within each one taken separately. "It is important not to isolate the elements, because only in conjunction will each trait demonstrate what it possesses of its own" (p. 143).

What Gutiérrez undertakes here (pp. 137–202) cannot be replaced by a priori analysis. What is being treated here is the reality of the spiritual human being and a spiritual people. I shall limit my own remarks to a few reflections intended to accompany the reading of Gutiérrez's pages.

In the selection and formulation of the traits of the spiritual person, Gutiérrez's emphasis is on the composition of the synthesis and the manner of its attainment. Some of the traits he considers point primarily to the spiritual person as agent of liberation (solidarity, efficacy, suffering, commitment, community). It is not easy to decide to which of the two aspects a given trait belongs. But the basic intent is clear: the historical verification of one's personal liberation is seen in whether he or she produces the fruits of the liberation of others. And these fruits will be deeper and more lasting in the measure that they come forth from a person who has been delivered from self.

Although all, or nearly all, of the traits Gutiérrez examines have been treated elsewhere in the literature of the theology of liberation, there is a relative novelty in his manner of treatment, as well as in his emphasis on the necessity of our own liberation if we are to secure the liberation of our neighbor. The crucial importance not only of a first conversion, but of maintaining a process of self-conversion with the very process of liberation, in a spirit of spiritual infancy, ongoing in joy, solitude in God's presence, and so on, must be kept in explicit account. These elements must be cultivated, not ignored or regarded as derived almost mechanically from liberative activity itself.

The reality and necessity of these traits of a liberated person have been rediscovered within the liberation process. We have rediscovered and reread them in the origins of our faith and in the spiritual tradition of the church. Here is an acknowledgment not only of the formal necessity of a "return to the sources," but of the truth and efficacy of those sources. Here is recognition of the foundational Christian wisdom contained in God's revelation, together with the wisdom accumulated down through the course of history, of which all persons, although of course they live in reference to a concrete history of their own, will have need in order to be liberated from themselves. Here is acknowledgment that the Spirit of God acts not only in the bestowal of life, and in our introduction and insertion into the truth that accompanies history, but also in the deliverance of human beings from themselves, their extraction from themselves. Gutiérrez enables us to recognize our need for purification from ourselves. To this purpose he adduces examples from other ages of history, which retain their importance despite the fact that their praxis of love was different from that of the present age. We should take Gutiérrez's references to St. Francis of Assisi, St. John of the Cross, St. Teresa of Avila, and St. Ignatius Loyola seriously, lest we fail to appreciate the decisive importance he attributes to our deliverance from ourselves in order to be spiritual persons.

When all is said and done, the ideal of the liberated human being is needed in order that that human being be a better liberator—in order that that human being be free to love. This is the original intuition of liberation theology and it not only sustains it, but invests it with new dynamism. The new spirituality springs forth "in the context of the struggle for liberation in view of love and justice" (p. 141), and this context historicizes the timeless traits of liberation from oneself in a new way. In view of one's own sin and that of the world, a death-dealing sin, one must experience a *conversion* (p. 147). In view of this sin we must examine ourselves personally for any connivance with it, whether by commission or by omission, that would leave it intact (pp. 146–47). Even the spiritual experience of conversion, then, is lived in the presence of the misery of the poor and the sin of the world:

> It may be that for a long time this perspective was neglected in the treatment of this theme in the literature of spirituality, but today it cannot be left aside. Encounter with the Lord in one's own depths does not exclude—indeed, it demands—knowing how to make that encounter in the depths of the misery in which the poor peoples of our lands find themselves [p. 149].

Conversion presupposes sin. Sin implies an offense against God and an offense against a poor people. Conversion, then, will be a turning to God and a turning to this people. And the latter element calls for "a conversion more radical in order to enter into another universe, the world of the poor" (ibid.).

Turning to the poor means entering into *solidarity* with them and conceiving a *love* for them. Once again Gutiérrez insists that the love in question is a genuine love for concrete human beings: "Without friendship, without lovingness, without tenderness . . . there is no genuine deed of solidarity" (p. 159). But he insists just as strongly that this love be proportioned and fitted to the oppression from which one wishes to help deliver the poor. It must be a social and effective love, then. For, although the poor are individuals, together they comprise a whole world afflicted by poverty, the majority of the human race, crushed to earth. "To love human beings implies loving them in their social texture" (p. 152). Hence the solidarity and love in question here must analyze the causes of poverty and death, must "discover the social mechanisms that make the worker and campesino marginalized persons" (p. 148), Gutiérrez explains, citing Archbishop Romero. And the only reason for all of this is that love seeks to be efficacious.

At this point Gutiérrez offers us a cogent phenomenology of love, unmasking the dangers and insufficiencies of traditional spiritualities in its regard. A loving intention, without an analysis of the objective results of love, is not enough (p. 161). Nor is it enough to perform acts of love in order to comply with the a priori "duty" to love (p. 162). Love must respond to the objective needs of the poor. We must do our utmost to meet these needs. "Concern for efficacy is a way of expressing love for neighbor" (ibid.). Here we must take into account what has already been said concerning gratuity as characteristic of the spiritual human being. We must live with and in gratuity. It is of the essence of God's communication with human creatures, and our own love for others should be shaped by it. But this climate of gratuity in no way divests love of its urgent demand for efficacy. "The gratuity of the gift of the kingdom does not suppress [efficacy], but actually demands it" (ibid.).

Here Gutiérrez turns to the biblical theme of *interior solitude*. From a positive viewpoint, the desert is necessary as the place where God is experienced. Negatively, and tragically, we have the solitude of Jesus in the garden and on the cross, we have the lamentations of Jeremiah. Interior solitude constitutes a classic theme of mystical spirituality, of existentialism, of theodicy. Gutiérrez does not dissimulate the crucial importance of solitude for the constitution of the liberated spiritual human being. Once more, however, he historicizes it from the vantage of liberation. "This experience of solitude acquires its own traits in our de facto situation," he says (p. 192). "Passing by way of the painful and deep experience of solitude" (p. 191), which is the lot of every human being and every Christian, is first and foremost a "passage through what has been called the 'dark night of injustice' " (p. 192). Injustice inflicts a painful solitude on those who practice liberation. Threats, reprisals on the part of those whose authority or behavior has been called into question, isolation and ostracism because of one's fidelity to a new path of solidarity with the poor, mistrust within the church itself—all this constitutes genuine solitude (p. 193).

But this is not the greatest loneliness. We experience our deepest solitude in our sense of helplessness in the face of "the situation of poverty and exploitation of the poor" (ibid.), the endlessness of their suffering, the obscurity of the tunnel, the extremely high price of the struggle in human terms. This solitude vis-à-vis history and vis-à-vis God is what makes the question posed by theodicy not unreasonable. But this solitude we must accept. When "the only positive experience left to us is the conviction of doing the will of the Father and serving a poor people," we must ever and again raise Jesus' own cry: "My God, my God, why have you forsaken me?" (p. 194).

Solitude here does not mean individuality. Still less does it mean a turning in upon oneself, a flight inward for refuge, a narcissistic preoccupation with self. It is simply an attitude of honesty before and within the history of injustice, and an honest question we put to God. Gutiérrez makes no attempt to conjure away this solitude with facile truisms or false hopes. Rather he calls for its assumption and acceptance, because it is the only path to the constitution of the spiritual person. Then he adds that this solitude, by reason of considerations just adduced, is the locus of prayer, and the precondition for genuine community. "Trust in God and in the church community perdures, even though light still does not appear" (p. 195). Those capable of living this solitude, those whom it has purified, will receive the gift of the community's confidence. Gutiérrez writes:

> The passage through the experience of solitude leads to a deep experience of community. . . . The solitude I am speaking of has nothing in common with individualism. Individualism entails an intentional folding in on oneself, glad to take up residence in the tranquil hermitage of privacy. If someone comes and knocks on the door, the individualist will open the door, as if doing someone a favor. A communitarian dimension is graciously added to a self-sufficiently Christian existence [p. 196].

A new phenomenon in Latin America in our day—a reality most cruel, and yet charged with hope—is *persecution* and *martyrdom*. "Every spirituality has a martyrial dimension" (p. 174) and Latin American spirituality is no exception. But, once more it is our lot not only because of the a priori demand of total self-bestowal in testimony and discipleship with Jesus crucified. It is our lot in virtue of the concrete reality of Latin America. "To defend the poor person's right to life today, in Latin America, readily leads to suffering and even death" (p. 173).

The fact as such is evident. We must be cautious, however, in its interpretation. We dare not glory in the testimony of our martyrs to the point of overlooking the grievous sin it unveils and presupposes. Christian martyrdom in Latin America exposes a much more general death—the structural, gradual, but altogether real, death of entire crucified peoples, together with that of those who defend the rights of the poor. We may not allow ourselves to forget, then, "the cruelty that surrounds this fact, and thereby the rejection of the conditions that give rise to these murders" (p. 175). Some fear that an overemphasis on martyrdom will introduce a morbidity into the practice of the Christian faith here, which would be contrary to the ultimate foundation and goal of that faith: resurrection.

But the fact of martyrdom cannot be denied, any more than the demand in principle that we give our own lives for the life of the poor. When this self-bestowal is expressed in someone's physical death as a martyr, then we see who has been a spiritual human being, who has been a person free to love—for now one more person of this sort has joined the ranks of those who "give their life for their faith in the God of life and God's love for the dispossessed" (p. 174).

Then something else occurs as well—something "unschedulable," and something far more than the desperate compensatory mechanism that "makes a virtue of necessity." Easter joy bursts forth (p. 177). The hope based "on the testimony of those who have known how to surrender their lives" (p. 159) suddenly swells in countless hearts. Nor is this joy some mindless glee, any more than this hope is cheap optimism. Both suddenly abound because the martyrs have created a genuine climate of love. They have exemplified love in themselves, and instilled it in others. And in that climate the profound conviction arises that death does not have the last word. For life to spring forth, death must come first, yes. But death does not have the last word. The scandalous lot of the servant of Yahweh, of Jesus crucified, of the first, persecuted Christian community, recurs ever and again in our day, evoking Easter and the Easter experience, as in days gone by: "the will of life for all, springing from joy after the experience of pain and death" (p. 181).

Stated as simply as possible, spiritual individuals, spiritual communities, spiritual peoples are identifiable by their readiness to celebrate, in their very flesh, Jesus' Passover, in the historical circumstances of their continent and precisely by reason of those circumstances. In their very persons, they relive the theologal experience of Jesus crucified, the experience of his martyrs down through the centuries. They thereby share the experience of all who, in the course of those centuries, from the first Easter down through all the Easters of all the other crucified communities and peoples of history, have met the risen Lord.

All these traits—which synthesize and compose this paschal spirituality—are purely and simply Christian holiness. When all is said and done, spirituality is simply holiness. True, the faith of the people and the theology of liberation have invested the term with a new historical content. Sometimes we even give it a particularizing adjective, as for instance when we speak of "political holiness." We do this lest, bereft of a concretizing modifier, the word "holiness" seems to suggest a reductionism, a verticalism, or lend itself to other misinterpretations. But the holiness I am speaking of is the substance of all Christian life. It is this, in the last analysis, that our communities and their members, the people of the poor, have to offer. This too, when all is said and done, is their mightiest weapon for persuading others and for defending themselves against the assaults of oppressors.

1.5. *Spirituality: A Theoretical Model*

Every great spirituality shows a tendency to be formulated in a synthetic, theoretical model calculated to account for its disparate, complementary moments, the subjective and the objective in the spiritual human being. The spiritual person stands at once in a relationship with the transcendent and with the historical. Such a synthesis is undertaken when there has been enough objective spirituality and enough reflection on it for a synthesis to be expressive—to "say something." To cite some particularly important examples, we have the *ora et labora* of the first monks, we have the *contemplata aliis tradere*, we have the *in actione contemplativus*, all of them theoretical models of spirituality.

Gutiérrez does not subject these models to theoretical analysis. Nor does he settle on any of them as an adequate framework for the conceptual organization of the spirituality he proposes. Nor, finally, does he offer his own synthetic formulation. Doubtless we may ascribe this in part to his modesty, which pervades the whole book. But he also seems to feel that, in order to arrive at the formulation of a new theoretical model, more reflection and time are needed. Doubtless Gutiérrez thinks that, for the moment, rather than coining—and petrifying?—new formulations, the crucial task will be to keep spirituality open to the new opportunities and challenges of history. To be sure, these might then lead to some new formulation.

Gutiérrez neither analyzes existing theoretical syntheses nor proposes one of his own. We may find it useful, however, to examine the conditions he would stipulate for such a synthesis. First, he would give the whole precedence over its parts, in such wise that the historical element (discipleship, pilgrimage, a people on a quest) and the transcendent (the journey with Jesus, in the Spirit, to the Father) would enjoy a mutual reference. Perhaps the totality would be the reign of God, which Gutiérrez mentions so frequently. The various elements in the development of spiritual persons would thus be orientated to the reign of God, the object of their service.

Gutiérrez's second condition would be the transcendence—not the nullification—of the division between the spiritual and the material, to the end that both dimensions may stand in mutual reference in the spiritual person: the tendency to spiritualize the historical, and the tendency to historicize the spiritual. Thus, for example, the historical reality of the poor is something that not only ought to be analyzed and responded to in accordance with its materiality, but ought to be the object of a spiritual experience, a reality that can "implode" into our lives and so become a mediation of the experience of God. On the other hand, the spiritual experience of encountering God, or of being encountered by God, includes, in virtue of its own dynamic, and not only as heterogeneous conclusion of a process of ratiocination, the act of going forth to meet historical poverty and applying a remedy.

The third condition Gutiérrez would require in a legitimate theoretical model of spirituality is an emphasis on the processual aspect of spirituality. Process is the element emphasized in the characterization of spirituality as a "journey" in the Spirit, as in the mystics' spiritual "way" or path. Spirituality must be processual because it takes time for it to form, time for the emergence of such and such concrete emphases in such and such a historical conjuncture, time to gather these emphases together and complement them. Thus the formulation of a theoretical model of spirituality will be an offshoot of that spirituality rather than an initiation of it.

The fourth and last condition is that, unlike the models of spirituality formulated in the grammatical singular, a legitimate model for today ought to include an expression of the collective subject, and especially the people as subject. But this is not to deny that the models of the past envisioned a collective subject in some fashion, for what they inspired and expressed were religious orders, and not simply individuals.

With these four conditions in mind, we are now in a position to make an interpretive statement as to what Gutiérrez's view would be of the models he mentions, and which others have discussed in greater detail.[21] We shall likewise be able to say something about what his own provisional model would be. First, then, the attempt to represent the totality of spirituality by the conjunction of *ora* and *labora* with an *et* will render that theoretical model inadequate. Secondly, the logical priority accorded to contemplation but in the absence of a dialectic of the two poles in *contemplata aliis tradere* will constitute an essential flaw in this model. The first theoretical synthesis fails to underscore the essential unity of spirituality, whereas the second one fails to do justice to the mutual reference of contemplation and action.

Positively, for Gutiérrez spirituality is freedom to love. Love, as the finality of spirituality, would unify the disparate elements in that spirituality. And love presupposes, includes, and fosters contemplation. But love falls per se rather into the category of action. The moment of action is neither separated from, nor subordinate to, nor consequent upon the moment of contemplation. Thus Gutiérrez would seem to be close to the theoretical model of the *in actione contemplativus*, which he cites on page 170. Here contemplation and action enjoy a mutual reference. Contemplation is "the demand for a vivifying element of action in history" (ibid.), but at the same time action is a locus of contemplation. The theoretical model of the *in actione contemplativus* expresses both action upon history with love, and the encounter with God in all things (p. 166).

My concern here is not to identify the spirituality described by Gutiérrez with the spirituality of any of the traditional models. My concern is to unify the dual moments of all spirituality in the manner most adequate to the liberation spirituality of Latin America. In my opinion, Gutiérrez's own model would be found along the lines of what he has formulated in strictly theologal form regarding the relationship between the human being and God: "God is contemplated and practiced."[22] Or again: "The mystery of God is experienced in contemplation and experienced in practice."[23] In the latter proposition we note that the distinction between contemplation and action does not simply disappear, anymore than does the distinction between God and the human being. It is only that the distinct poles of the totality stand in a specific mutual relationship. Contemplation and action are not moments having distinct objects, as if contemplation were directed toward God and action were directed toward the world. It is God who must be contemplated and practiced; and it is in virtue of the unicity of this divine object that both moments find their profound unification. At the same time, the world, too, becomes the object both of action and of contemplation. The contemplation of God is simultaneously a contemplation of the world with God's eyes; and the practice of God is the implementation of God's word according to God's will. Thus the moments of contemplation and action are not "diversified," as if the one were referred to God and the other to the world. God and world alike are the object both of contemplation and of action.

The ultimate, primordial duality that makes spirituality possible cannot be sought in the distinction between contemplation and action. Rather it lies in the irreducible duality implied in the human being's relationship with God. This relationship comprises a moment of initiative and gratuity on the part of God, and another moment, that of response, on the part of the human being. The spiritual person is constituted in the maintenance of both dimensions, gratuity and response, in contemplation as in action. After all, seeing is as gratuitous as is doing. New eyes are as much a gift as are new hands. Allowing myself to be met by God is as much a matter of God's initiative as is allowing myself to be sent forth by God. And then, with reference to the moment of action, my acceptance of God is as much my response to God as is my action upon God's world. The spiritual person is constituted and unified by God's victorious self-manifestation to that person, in the duality of gratuity and response.

It is in this direction, it seems to me, that Gutiérrez's theoretical model of spirituality would doubtless move. The model of "contemplation in action" recognizes the difference between its two constitutive terms, but it subsumes this difference in a more primordial one, that between gratuity and response, which admits of a more complete unity than does the difference between contemplation and action.

Gutiérrez implicitly proposes this strictly theologal model of spirituality in a very simple way at the end of his book: "You must be made perfect as your heavenly Father is perfect" (Matt. 5:48); or, in a Spanish Bible translation, "Be completely good, as your heavenly Father is good" (p. 204). The spiritual human being is the human being divinized historically. Concretely, in Latin America, a spiritual person is someone who sees the poor with God's eyes and deals with them as God does. In thus seeing and relating with the world, the human being enters into a relationship of kinship with God. It all begins with God, Gutiérrez adds. If we allow ourselves to be contemplated by God, and permit God to operate within us, we shall be able to contemplate God and the world in a unified way, and shall be able to love God and the world in a unified way.

This focus does not eliminate the differences with which spirituality must come to grips—the difference between contemplation and action, the difference between relating to God and relating to the world. But it integrates them into another, more comprehensive and basic, difference—the difference between receiving and giving, between gratuity and response. This differentiation and its unification are not attainable by speculation. They express God's mysterious design, which is a matter of fact, and not of any a priori theorization on our part.

God has willed to love human creatures. And God has willed to love them with the radicality with which God is present in Christ. This is why, regarding this existential situation from the point of view of the creature, the most important thing we have to integrate is our condition of being graced and our condition of gracing, and the integration must be effectuated entirely by way of our contemplative and praxic dimensions. At bottom, Gutiérrez is saying only this: a great number of Latin American Christians have been graced by God, and they have been transformed into grace for others.

2. Theology and Spirituality

Gutiérrez's book is a work on spirituality, and it deals with spirituality theologically. Here we see the importance of theology for spirituality. A theological analysis of spirituality can make a useful contribution to the understanding of what spirituality is. But Gutiérrez stresses the converse as well: spirituality is important for theology. Spirituality enters into the constitution of theology and determines its relevancy:

The level of the life of faith sustains the level of the understanding of faith. . . . The firmness and spiritedness of theological reflection are signs of the spiritual experience that supports it. . . . It does not enervate its rigorous and scientific character. It situates it [pp. 60–61].

Referring more concretely to the theology of liberation, Gutiérrez states: "Speaking about God (theo-logy) comes from the silence of prayer and commitment. . . . To put it in a nutshell, our methodology is our spirituality" (pp. 203–4).

That the theology of liberation is a spiritual theology is commonly recognized today both by outsiders and by the liberation theologians themselves. Leonardo Boff claims: "that which sustains liberative practice and theory (theology) is a spiritual experience."[24] Pablo Richard writes: "Our theology is basically a spiritual theology."[25] Such assertions are familiar, but they are demanding as well. They impose serious conditions upon theology and the task of theology. They demand a spiritual experience that will be antecedent to theology: theology is second act here. But then they demand that theology itself be practiced with spirit, and communicate spirit. They require that theology be spiritual from start to finish.

What does it mean to say that theology is spiritual "from start to finish"? It means not only that theology presupposes a spiritual experience, or that it treats of themes conventionally regarded as spiritual, but, as it seems to me, that (1) it is done with spirit, and communicates spirit, in all its dimensions and contents; and (2) in its totality, it enlightens, unifies, and animates the constitution of a spiritual person and a spiritual people.

First, then, for a theology to be spiritual from start to finish means that the very performance of its task, as well as the development of its contents, will be imbued with a spirit, and with a spirit adequate to that task and content. On the formal level, theology, as logos, will explain the truth, will make use of a historical, hermeneutical, and speculative logos, and will avail itself of an instrumentality that is biblical, philosophical, historical, and so on. But this logos is genuinely spiritual when it genuinely enlightens. It is not the same thing merely to treat things scientifically and doctrinally as really to shed light on them. It is not the same thing to speak of many things as to allow things to speak for themselves. In the latter instance theology in its capacity as logos is practiced with an adequate spirit, and communicates light. Its content is not only registered in the cognition of its addressees, it is integrated by them in their spirit as well.

Let me cite a few examples on the level of content. Theology treats of hope, the practice of justice, gratuity, and the like. But it is not the same thing to limit oneself to grouping, ordering, and explaining conceptually the content of the faith as it bears on hope, justice, and gratuity, as to present these contentual elements in such a manner that, from the outset, they generate acts of hope, they move and inspire their addressee to perform acts of justice, they communicate gratuity. When this occurs, theology has been practiced with spirit, and has communicated spirit.

That a theology be spiritual, then, does not mean that it ignores the very demands of theology, much less that it couches the content of theology voluntaristically in spiritualistic or emotional language. Far from it. A theology is "spiritual" when the theological task and content are imbued with the spirit proper to each. Whether a theology meets this requirement or not can ultimately be verified only a posteriori. But it is important to keep the requirement in mind.

There can be little doubt that many contemporary theologies would honestly like to be able to shed light on the content of the faith for the world of today. But only some of these theologies actually succeed in doing so, whereas others, for all their lengthy treatises on that content, fail. Many theologies desire to emphasize hope, the practice of justice and gratuity. But only some of them actually generate those realities, whereas others, for all the length and breadth of their discourse, fail to do so. What is at stake in a spiritual theology, therefore, is the actualization of primordial tautology that theology be a "word that speaks"—that is, a word with a spirit of its own.

Secondly, a theology is spiritual, from beginning to end, when it instills the Christian life with courage, when it gives life (the attribute of the Spirit), while unifying all the dimensions and content of that life, that Christian life. To this purpose, theology must be grounded in an "originating spiritual experience," such as the one described by Gutiérrez, and then maintain that spirit, while keeping it ever open to history. This experience demands, a priori and certainly a posteriori in the world of today, in Latin America as in the First World, that theology, from start to finish, in the development of all its content as in its very task, be a theology that is (1) theologal, (2) popular, and (3) creaturely.

2.1. *A Theologal Theology*

I think it important to dwell on this seeming tautology, especially in view of the world of today. To put it bluntly, theology ought to know what to do with God. It is not enough merely to speak of God. Theology must allow God to speak. Theology must move the human being to speak with God. Theology must relate the human being with God. In a word, God must be a reality for theology, and a reality in action.

In order to achieve this, theology must see to it that its doctrine on God, and its doctrine on whatsoever theological content, genuinely facilitate the experience of God. A theologal theology must be a mystagogy—an introduction into the reality of God as God is: transcendent mystery, utterly resistant to manipulation, and yet our Father, near at hand, good, and saving. The doctrine of God must be such that it both respects God's mystery, and introduces its addressee into that mystery. Theology must know how to speak of God while letting God be God. Theology must integrate into a knowledge of God the ignorance corresponding to that knowledge. Otherwise it will not be genuine knowledge of God. By way of humanistic counterpart to its theological facet, theology ought to know how to dispose its addressees to prayer, to openness to the word of God, to a readiness to discover and accept that word, however novel, in the signs of the times and the call of the heart. But it must also communicate the content of that mystery: God's love. In its theologal aspect, theology must be able to present a God who is a Father, who is near at hand, who is good, and who is our savior—a God who is genuinely good news. This reminder may seem superfluous, but it is absolutely indispensable. In the humanistic counterpart of this aspect, theology must ready its hearers for the gladsome encounter with the God of its discourse, and dispose its hearers to trust and to hope. In presenting God as transcendent, but as a Father who is bounteous and close at hand—and this in transcendence and mystery—theology must help individuals and peoples to an encounter with God, a personal encounter that cannot be replaced by doctrine or culture.

Secondly, for a theology to be theologal it must develop a theology of history. Like spirituality, a theology of history is needed when history enters into a crisis—when its old elements disintegrate and new syntheses are needed. Some theologies of history are explicitly and consciously such. Others are so only implicitly, in the way the Christian community views God and Christ. Consciousness of the presence of Christ in the first Christian communities, the expectation of his imminent Second Coming, and the acknowledgment of the delay of the Parousia are all theologies of history. So is the triumphant sovereignty of Christ in an ecclesial conception of Christianity, or a humble following of Jesus along the road to the absolute future of God. In Latin America there is the germ of a theology of history in the effort to relate God with liberation and captivity. The germ has not yet matured. But the Latin American insistence on a God of life, with a view to endowing history with genuine being, our theology of a God of liberation determined to overcome sin, our focus on a crucified God, and on that God's absolute solidarity with the oppressed of this world, our attention to the God who raises Jesus as the unshakable hope of the poor—all these emphases provide us with the most important elements needed in a theology of history. At all events it cannot be denied that they afford us an outlook on history from God's own vantage, and that they call on us to invest history with its most basic thrust, the thrust toward life. These are the elements that bestow the gift of meaning on those who, from a point of departure in truth about history, put themselves into that history in order to liberate it.

As humanistic counterpart to these theologal elements of content, a theology of history ought to offer human beings an opportunity to do something with this history and demand that they avail themselves of that opportunity. It ought to offer this opportunity and make this demand in such a way that praxis is represented not merely as an ethical demand, but as a theologal demand. We are called on to "make history," and make it "according to God."

Thirdly, a theologal theology must be trinitarian, both in its content and in the execution of its task. God cannot be known only as pure otherness in our respect, even though God is pure otherness, and to an infinite degree. Human beings must encounter God. They must be ushered into the reality of God. This is what God's trinitarian reality both offers and demands. Theology should therefore represent God as approachable in various, of course complementary, ways: in the practice of the following of Jesus, in a pilgrimage according to the Spirit, in an attitude that acknowledges God as absolute, gratuitous origin, in the hope-filled journey toward God as our absolute future. Theology must be careful to present the problem, or the mystery, of God not merely in an intellectualistic correlation between God's truth and human reason, nor merely in an existentialistic correlation between God's meaning and human decision, but in the larger correlation of knowing, hoping, and practicing. If, within this correlation, we become like unto Jesus, and have the spirit of Jesus, we can be very successful in shedding light on the mystery of God.

A conceptual synthesis can be built up by theological demonstrations of certain conceptual interrelationships in the light of God's revelation. A synthesis that "speaks to" the whole human being presupposes the existence of a conceptual synthesis in some form. In the theological task itself—in its intellectual, hope-charged, and praxic content—theology must achieve a conceptual framework of the various elements in its theoretical dynamic. Theology can therefore assist in the unification of knowing, hoping, and acting in a relationship of reciprocity, and thus respond, and correspond, to the God who is Trinity in unity.

As theologal, a theology is spiritual "through and through" when, out of its experience of God and its historical situation, it sets forth that experience and proposes the manner of making history according to God. God is passing through our history today, and it is the task of theology to help us respond and correspond to God. If theology fails to assist the spirit of the believer to do justice to God's passage through history, if it does nothing to help raise the Christian spirit to the level of that passage, it will have done many good deeds perhaps, but it will not have performed the one thing needful today.

2.2. *A Popular Theology*

Theology ought to be practiced among the people of God and in behalf of the people of God. Once more we confront a familiar truth in need of reemphasis. Theology must not only know what to do with God, it must know what to do with God's people as well. To that end it is not enough merely to examine the people of God as a theological concept. Nor will it be enough to recall in some general fashion that the entire people of God is the subject or agent of faith, and that therefore it cannot be deceived with respect to the truth of that faith (see *Lumen Gentium*, no. 12). Theology must emerge from the reality of the people of God, and introduce its addressees into that reality. Theology must lead Christians to the reality of their faith. Theology must enlighten and inspire God's people.

This will not entail a renunciation of a certain legitimate professionalism attaching to the theological task. It only means that we must steep the execution of that task in the popular spirit, and avoid giving the impression that the theologian is somehow above the people—a kind of super-Christian to whom the people of God must have recourse, but who need not have recourse to the people of God. To be sure, theology has certain specific functions of its own, which it can and must perform. Theology must demonstrate the interrelationships of the faith of God's people with revelation, tradition, and the magisterium, and again with the historical situation and its ideologies. Theology must anticipate the dangers of the ideologization of the faith of that people, foresee future problems for that faith, and prepare adequate responses to these dangers and problems. All of this pertains to the specific purview of theology. But none of it exempts theology from its reference, for its very constitution, to God's people and the faith of God's people.

Theology must therefore take seriously into account, and utilize as one of the sources of its knowledge, the faith of the people of God. That faith is the response of a Christian people to God's ongoing manifestation in the present. Hence it will shed light on both what faith is and what God is. Faith and revelation enjoy a circular relationship. Faith sheds light on revelation, and revelation illuminates faith. Testimonials of faith are important for theology, therefore, not only inasmuch as they present a reality that can be capsulized in doctrine, but inasmuch as they present a reality that refers to the reality of God. These testimonials can be offered by individuals, or by a whole people, or by those among the people in whom the faith of the people of God is best expressed. Accordingly, one must of course argue from the testimonials of faith contained in scripture and church tradition, but one must argue as well from the testimonials of faith of the present moment, from what the saints and martyrs of the current age are being and are saying, from what communities— and priests, nuns, and bishops in contact with these communities—are being and are saying. This is what Gutiérrez does in his *Beber en su propio pozo*.

These individuals and groups are the witnesses to the faith who express the genuine theological problems of today. In their own persons, they integrate the essentials of our faith, present in its first beginnings, with the new responses of faith for today. They help us rediscover the radical content, the root content, of our faith, and they point to new syntheses that theology will have to develop.

In Latin America, as in so many other parts of the world, the people of God is a people of the poor. This is why theology must be popular—and not only formally, in virtue of a general reference to the people of God, but, more concretely, in virtue of a reference to the poor, who are the primary addressees and correlates of the revelation of God. It is in virtue of this latter reference that theology becomes genuinely popular, both historically and theologically. In other words, precisely in becoming "partial" in its location and its finality, theology also achieves its genuine universality. And then—as Archbishop Romero pointed out with respect to the evangelizing mission of the church—in its novel concretization of its content, theology rediscovers the content that revelation has always had.

It is impossible to overestimate the value to theology of the people of the poor in the rediscovery of content as central as sin, idolatry, liberation, the gospel as the good news, the Beatitudes and the anathemas, the activity of the prophets of Israel, the denunciation of injustice, the relationship between the practice of justice and knowledge of God, the crucial importance of Matthew 25, and so on. Nor is the value of such content any less in virtue of its concretizing, together with its integration of new elements, of theological content already reinstated outside Latin America, such as the discernment of the signs of the times, the conception of the church as a church of the poor (a seed planted by Vatican II, but which failed to germinate), the following of Jesus the pauper, our nearness to him as our elder brother, the servant of Yahweh as an individual and as an entire crucified people, Jesus' resurrection as the indestructible hope of the oppressed, the God of life as defender and advocate of the poor, the Spirit of God as life-giver with the power to make of humiliated, downtrodden nonpersons, and nonpeoples persons with dignity and people with the awareness of being a people, the reign of God as a transcendent utopia but as a historical reality as well (a reality to be worked on—we must not fall into an equalizing, a "leveling," relativization of all historical expressions in the name of the "eschatological reserve"), and so on.

This people of God, this people of the poor in Latin America and the rest of the Third World, has been transformed into a veritable letter written by God to humankind, to the church, and to theology, in virtue of what this people is, what it suffers, and what it does and creates. To be sure, not all that transpires among the people of God is an automatic manifestation of God and a correct response of faith. The poor are well aware of it. Indeed, one of their most frequent exercises is in the form of self-examination, together with a petition to God for their own conversion.

Obviously theology must keep account of the originating pole constituted by revelation and faith, revelation and scripture. Obviously theology must attend to tradition, and to the pronouncements of the magisterium on new discoveries being made and expressed by God's people. Obviously theology must keep account of intratheological dialogue, and dialogue with the sciences, with philosophies, with ideologies. But if theology does not also, and principally, have recourse to the locus of the realization of the faith of a poor people, it will be a truncated theology. Ever and again it will become abstractivist and elitist, thus depriving itself of an irreplaceable font of theological cognition. Nor may theology permit itself to neglect a serious interest in "the evangelizing potential of the poor" (Puebla, no. 1147). It must drink from their well, for here are waters with the potential to enlighten and purify theology, although of course they can neither create nor replace other theological means of cognition.

This popular theology is spiritual, for it is imbued with the spirit of God's people, with whom it has entered into solidarity and thereby become a theology of reality, "real theology." A theology isolated from the people of God—or even worse, at odds with that people—and feeding only on its own resources, will betray its irreality, however true its propositions. And it will betray its helplessness to extricate itself from this irreality, which can be overcome only when theology is undertaken in genuine solidarity with the people of God, not only in order to be at its service, but in order to receive its own inspiration from that people. Then it will come to pass that theology possesses the spirit of God's people, for in this people God's very Spirit dwells, filling it with life. In order to be "popular," in the best and most authentic sense of the word, it must be to the measure of the reality of the people of God, and of the Spirit living in that people.

2.3. *A Creaturely Theology*

Today, and today especially, a spiritual theology must be a genuinely creaturely theology. It must be open to the world and its problems, open to human beings universally and to the being-human of the believer in particular. It must not, either subtly or crudely, withdraw the believer from the world. It must be willing to make an appeal even to nonbelievers, or at least to those among nonbelievers who have genuine interest in making the world more human and more humane, and who have a sense of their own being-human.

Consequently, theology must avoid communicating the impression that the problem of being human has been solved, at least in principle, and that the task of theology is only to superadd the reality of being-Christian to that of being-human. Doubtless theology has the obligation of reminding us that true being-human has already appeared in Christ. It may not renounce this affirmation at once joyous and scandalous. But it must also emphasize, and efficaciously, that the Christian faith itself refers its believers to their being-human, and to solidarity with real human beings with their real problems and real hopes.

This means that theology must be practiced with humility and without triumphalism, in and with humankind today. It must be practiced with humility because, for all its elaborate doctrine, it knows very little more, in the concrete, than does the majority of humankind. Theology knows of—and believes in—God's love. Theology knows and believes that in Jesus is manifested the way, the truth, and the life. This furnishes it with a basic manner of orientation in history, and basic principles for discerning the direction history ought to take and for which theology must toil. But it is not spared the quest for concrete solutions to be found only along the pathways of the concrete questioning that constitutes the pilgrimage of all human beings. Theology is not exempt from the duty of inquiring into its own nature, any more than it is exempt from the duty of inquiring into the meaning of history, into the reality of the world today where poverty is on the upsurge and where more and more millions of the poor and downtrodden are appearing on the face of the earth. Theology too, part and parcel, must pass by way of the solitude of which Gutiérrez speaks.

And we must practice theology without triumphalism. Theology is not the only source of knowledge of God in the church. For that matter, not even the church is the only locus of God's manifestation. Archbishop Romero put this very clearly:

> The church believes that the action of the Spirit who brings Christ to life in human beings is greater than itself. Far beyond the confines of the church, Christ's redemption is powerfully at work. The strivings of individuals and groups [in behalf of freedom], even if they do not profess to be Christian, derive their impetus from the Spirit of Jesus.[26]

Theology must analyze what is taking place in history, its ideologies and social movements, "in order to purify them, encourage and incorporate them . . . into the overall plan of Christian redemption," he adds.[27] But it must not attempt to accomplish this by erecting itself into a distant, infallible arbiter, hurling condemnations right and left as we sometimes see it do, bereft of the spirit of self-analysis, failing to take into account the fact that at times it is guilty of the very things of which it accuses the world. Theology, too, can be sinful. Indeed it has a sinfulness peculiar to itself: a concupiscence for self-absolutization. And so it too must undergo the conversion process. It must engage in self-examination, and submit to a verification of whether it is being practiced for humankind or for its own sake.

It is this humility on the part of theology that insures its creatureliness. It is this humility that permits it to approach real human beings and enter into solidarity with them. Now it can speak with men and women face to face instead of thundering at them from that presumptuous distance at which so many Christians, in the First World especially, have been led to renounce both theology and faith. In solidarity with men and women of today, a creaturely theology is, first, honest about reality. It receives its agenda from reality as it is, rather than imposing its own agenda on reality. Its contact with reality motivates theology to revise its content, even if the new content alienates it from the old. Honesty with the real is absolutely necessary if theology is to be practiced in solidarity with the women and men of today. But intrinsically as well, in virtue of its ultimate premise, theology must *remain* with the real. For if violence is done to the truth of things, as Paul warns, things will no longer manifest God, and the human heart, which is the light of theology, will brown out.

Next, along with honesty, theology must maintain fidelity to the real and its demands. Theology must walk with reality, and not pretend anachronistically that reality must walk with it. Surely theologians, like the rest of humankind, must discern the loci in which theology gives more of itself. Or, in theological terms, theology must endeavor to discern where history is becoming more and more a history of grace and less and less a history of sin. Theology must avoid giving the impression that history may go along as it will and the truth of theology will nevertheless abide intact. This is true only where "the basics" are concerned. A renunciation of history would mean infidelity to the theological premise of God's passage through that history.

If theology is practiced, in genuine solidarity with the women and men of today, and practiced in the manner indicated, it will at least be able to speak to them and there will be the possibility that they may listen. Theology will be credible when it tells them that genuine being-human is to be a creature of God, when it offers them Jesus' path as the actualization of that being-human, and when it tells them that this path in no way withdraws them from real history but on the contrary inserts them into it, in a greater or lesser degree, according to their faith.

This creaturely theology will now be discharging the role of what has been traditionally called *fundamental theology*. Fundamental theology has been practiced in various ways in various locales down through the centuries, in response to the variety of challenges to faith throughout those centuries and in those locales. Today theology becomes fundamental theology when it becomes invitation and promise. Both the invitation and the promise will stand in need of some *a priori* rationality. But the rationality to be furnished by this creaturely theology will be *a simultaneo*. It will be a rationality emerging in the actualization of the very content of this theology. If theology is practiced with the humility and solidarity sketched above, a certain credibility will attach to it by that very fact. If it helps to actualize hope, if it can present witnesses to that hope, if that hope is itself a testimonial, then this creaturely theology may well be able to issue an invitation acceptable to others to follow in the footsteps of Jesus and thereby enter the ranks of renewed humankind.

In order to present a genuinely adequate analysis of a theology that would be spiritual from start to finish, spiritual through and through, we should have to analyze a good many other things, perhaps more important things. However, it seems to me that this may surely be said: a theology practiced from a radical point of departure in the reality of God, and in the reality of the poor among the people of God, and practiced in the midst of human life, will possess spirit—will be practiced and offered with spirit. Ultimately this is not so much a claim on my part as it is a deduction from the reaction the theology of liberation has aroused. It is not only, or even principally, a particular method, or a novelty of content, that can explain the serious interest shown in this theology. The reaction can be explained only by the fact that the theology of liberation, in "putting its finger into the wound of reality" (Bishop Méndez de Almeida), has touched many a spirit as well. So many persons are sincerely grateful to have rediscovered themselves as believers and as human beings, to have been able to rebuild the scattered mosaic of their faith and their life!

The premise, as well as the content, of a spiritual theology is the passage of the Spirit of the Lord through hearts and history. Many believe that this is what is happening in Latin America today. To recognize this phenomenon for what it is, is in itself a powerful act of the spirit, and Gutiérrez makes this recognition in *Beber en su propio pozo*. He speaks of a "favorable time" (p. 36), and draws this conclusion:

Something new is being born in Latin America, amid numerous and diverse sufferings. It has led to talk of a *kairos*, a favorable time, when the Lord knocks on the doors of the ecclesial community in Latin America, inviting it to a banquet (see Rev. 3:20) [p. 203].

Chapter 4

Political Holiness:
A Profile[28]

1. Holiness and Politics

The expression "political holiness"[29] may seem odd, even nowadays, because it links two realities normally presumed to be separate not just in fact but because they ought to be. It is also an ambiguous expression until its terms are clearly explained. In general, by holiness I mean the outstanding practice of faith, hope, and especially charity and the virtues generated by the following of Jesus. By politics I mean action directed toward structurally transforming society in the direction of the reign of God, by doing justice to the poor and oppressed majorities, so that they obtain life and historical salvation.

Linking these two things means taking two new steps. The first is the presenting of a new environment for holiness as both possible and necessary. Throughout the history of the church, it has been assumed that the proper environment for holiness is personal ascesis, contemplation, the exercise of charity in the form of almsgiving. Now, because they have become aware of the misery and oppression of the majority of the human race and of the processes of liberation set in motion in the Third World (with their analogies in the First World in the form of resistance to dictatorships, efforts at democratization, etc.), many Christians feel that the area of political action is the right place to seek holiness. This of course does not exclude other ways of seeking holiness, but politics is one possible way and because of the signs of the times it has become a historical necessity.

The second, more recent step, which was taken because of Christians' experiences of political involvement, means that now we are not talking about linking faith and politics, Christianity and politics, analyzing their theoretical compatibility, the need for political involvement in the name of faith, but of linking *holiness* and politics. This stage has been reached, I believe, because Christians have realized two things: (1) in order to live a Christian political life it is not enough to be theoretically clear about its possibility and legitimacy; we have to practice and create specifically Christian values in an outstanding manner; (2) by-products inherent in this action and in order to make this action historically effective.

Thus politics today offers a sphere for holiness and holiness makes political action more humanizing for those engaged in it and for the political project in which they are engaged. This is what I want to show in this chapter, and I base my claim on the existence of this type of holiness, not on a merely conceptual analysis.

2. A Holiness That Requires Politics

Religion held with deep conviction leads to political involvement and tends to create conflicts in a country like ours where there is a crying need for social justice.

—Archbishop Romero

2.1. The development of Christian holiness always presupposes that it is in answer to God's will. This may be different for different persons, but it must, essentially, include what is God's clear will in a particular moment of history. At the moment, as Medellín and Puebla remind us, God's primary will is that the poor majority should have life, that they should "build houses and live in them, plant vines and eat their fruits" (Isa. 65:21). Or to put it in negative terms: that the poverty and oppression of millions of human beings should stop, that there should be an end to their constant deprivation of human dignity, the horrible violation of their rights, the massacres, mass expulsions, arrests, tortures, and murders. The response to this primary will of God is a specific type of love for persons, which does not exhaust other forms of love but is not reducible to them either: love for those most deprived of life and working so that they may have life, in the words of Archbishop Romero, "defending the minimum that is God's greatest gift: life." This love, which is both a response to God's will and to the present enormous suffering of humanity, is what I call political love.

This political love has certain specific characteristics that differentiate it from other forms of love. In the first place it requires a *metanoia* to see the truth of the world as it is, in the manifestations of death, which are visible, and its structural causes, which are hidden and take care to be hidden, to see in this generalized death the most important fact and the most serious problem of humanity, the greatest challenge to the meaning of history and humanity, so that we do not imprison the truth of things through injustice (Rom. 1:18). It requires *pity* for the unhealed but not unhealable suffering of the oppressed majority, Jesus' pity for the multitude. It requires an awareness of *responsibility* when asked the question, "What have you done with your brother?" (Gen. 4:10) and co-responsibility for his condition and his destiny. This co-responsibility also allows persons to start recovering their dignity by sharing the suffering of humanity.

Political love tries to be *effective*. This means it must be expressed in a fitting manner to try to eradicate the death and bring about the life of the poor. To understand how this love can be effective we have to think first of those to whom this love wants to offer itself. These are the poor considered as a collectivity, group, or social class, not the poor individual but the *polis*, the world of the poor. They are the poor in the material sense. What needs to be eradicated is not just the inner shame to which they are subjected but their material poverty. Moreover they are poor because of and in opposition to the powerful. They are dialectically poor and in conflict by their very existence.[30]

The political love that seeks to transform the situation of *these* poor must have its specific mechanisms, distinct from those belonging to other forms of love; it must seek structural efficacy. It must denounce oppression and unmask its structural causes, plead for basic human social and political rights, help to bring about "bold and urgent" structural changes, as Paul VI said.

It must also see the poor not only as the *objects* of beneficial political actions but also—especially now in many Third World countries—the enactors of their own destiny as a people fighting for liberation; *they* have the largest share in this struggle and must direct it objectively toward the creation of a new society. For this reason political love must also share—in very different ways—in the struggle of the poor, which takes place on the ideological and social level but also the political level and—in strictly limited cases—the military.[31]

2.2. This political love is the fundamental material of political holiness. But the practice of political love offers a structural causality favorable to specific virtues more difficult to attain by other means. It favors a specific form of ascesis that goes back to fundamental Christian ascesis: *kenosis*, going down into the world of poverty and the poor, a stripping of self; the ascesis necessary in order to denounce and unmask oppression, to have historical patience and solidarity with the poor. It favors the growth of a mature faith and hope in a situation where they will be tried to the utmost. It favors Christian creativity (pastoral, liturgical, theological, spiritual) generated from the underside of history.

It also leads, almost *ex opere operato*, to persecution. This is the inexorable fulfillment of Jesus' preaching. Political love, unlike other forms of love, leads to the specific suffering of persecution by all the powers of this world. Not all Christians, but *political* Christians, are attacked, vilified, threatened, expelled, arrested, tortured, and murdered.

This persecution proves that there has been a love that is fundamental; remaining in it means an outstanding exercise of Christian fortitude and a notable witness to faith. If persecution leads to the sacrifice of our own life, if in this sacrifice there is love for the poor majority, the beginning of the whole process of political love, then the sacrifice of our life becomes martyrdom. This bears witness to the greatest love for the poor and also bears witness objectively to the God of life. Our death is for the cause of justice, but either explicitly or anonymously, for the cause of God's justice. That is why I speak of martyrdom. Of course it is a different matter whether each and every one of those who have fallen or been assassinated for political causes were perfect in all the orders of Christian life. But we cannot deny the great and fundamental love with which they gave their lives. As Archbishop Romero said about murdered priests:

> To my mind they are truly martyrs in the popular sense. They are men who went all the way in their preaching of solidarity with poverty. They are real men who went to the most dangerous limits to say what they wanted to tell someone and they ended up being killed as Christ was killed.[32]

The great numbers of these deaths is what not only enables us to speak a priori of the possibility of political holiness, but what forces us to speak of it a posteriori. If the spilt blood of so many bishops, priests, nuns, catechists, teachers, and also of Christians who are peasants, workers, trade unionists, and combatants, is not a convincing argument that the political is a proper sphere for holiness, and moreover that at the moment holiness normally means involvement with politics, then there is no theological discourse that could be convincing.[33]

Those who are not convinced, even by the clearest examples, are unable to interpret Jesus' death as the death of the Just One. They would be left with the alternative of interpreting his death as that of a blasphemer and subversive, as the powers of his time wanted it to be understood.

2.3. This political holiness is what bears witness structurally today to God's holiness in its incarnate form. God is holy mystery. As mystery, God is always beyond human beings and history: hence the essence of holiness came to be defined as separation and distance from the profane. But since the Jesus-event this has to be corrected.

The God who is holy mystery has come close to us, and has broken the symmetry of being either salvation or condemnation. And this nearness is doubly scandalous: it is a nearness of the mystery of God and a *special* nearness to the poor and oppressed. Because God loves them (Puebla, no. 1142), God has come out on their side, fights against the idols of death, and is clearly revealed as the God of justice who truly wants the life of the poor. And since the Jesus-event, this is the new and scandalous holiness of God: coming close to the poor to save them and sharing their lot on the cross of Jesus.

This is what the *political* saints or holy persons are saying today. They are doing no more than repeating God's action in approaching the poor majorities for the sake of their liberation and assuming the destiny of this nearness. This is the final theological reason why political holiness is a possibility and historically a necessity. There is no other way of telling the world today that God truly loves the poor.

3. A Politics That Requires Holiness

I believe that the saints were the most ambitious persons. And this is my ambition for all of you and for myself: that we may be great, ambitiously great, because we are images of God and we cannot be content with mediocre greatness.

—Archbishop Romero

3.1. The area of politics is necessary for holiness: but it remains a creaturely area. This means it is a limited area, it has its own special temptations and tends to have its own special sins because, especially because, it is about the use of power.

There are historical—not necessarily ethical—limitations for the poor in keeping in proper perspective the simultaneity of revolution and reconciliation, justice and freedom, new stuctures and a new humankind, the messianic ideal and the reality that mitigates it. There also exists *at* the ethical level, the concupiscence active in those who practise political action even with the intentions described above. By its very nature political action may tempt us, to a greater or lesser degree, to exchange the liberation of the poor for the triumph of what we have converted into our own personal or collective cause, the pain of the poor for the passion that politics generates, service for hegemony, truth for propaganda, humility for dominance, gratitude for moral superiority. There is the danger of making absolute the sphere of reality in which the struggle for social, political, or military liberation takes place and thus abandoning other important spheres of reality—including the reality of a poor people—which sooner or later will avenge themselves on this absoluteness. Finally there is the difficulty of keeping up the political love described above to its ultimate consequences, because of the conflicts and risks that go with it.

This limitation and concupiscence of the political sphere in no way invalidates the need for it to be a sphere for holiness. Other spheres too (personal ascesis, prayer, the practice of charity)—and this is too often forgotten—are limited and have their own temptations. But these dangers show the need to engage in politics in the right spirit, so that political love may be and remain *love*. Liberating political projects should always remain open to the kingdom of God.

3.2. We see this necessity today, but not just—although also—because human beings need spirit by the mere fact that they *are* spiritual and need it in every area of their lives, but also because Christians who most fully practice political love need it.

We need the spirit of Jesus in political action too and in those areas that have most to do with politics. We need purity of heart to see the truth of things, to analyze successes and failures in struggles and plans for liberation, to keep as a criterion for action what will most benefit the poor majorities, to overcome the temptation to dogmatism, to which it is so easy to succumb in all political activity. We need to seek peace even in the midst of struggle without turning violence, even when it is just and legitimate, into a kind of mysticism, and without placing all our confidence in it to resolve objective problems and neglecting other more peaceful forms of struggle both before and during armed struggle. We need pity so that we do not relativize disproportionately the people's pain and reduce it to an unavoidable social cost, so that we do not close off the future from the enemy, so that we do not suppress the difficult possibility of forgiveness and reconciliation. We need the humility to know that fundamentally we are "unprofitable servants," sinners, so that in action we remain grateful, in difficulty we ask for help, and we do the work of liberation as forgiven sinners.

3.3. This spirit is the holiness that political action demands if it is to remain and grow in love. Attaining it is personally difficult and structurally utopian. But this does not mean that this holiness is simply idealistic. On the contrary it is historically effective.

This holiness in the political sphere is what today bears witness to the holiness of God in eschatological formality. The God come close is also the God who transcends history not as a pure being beyond but as a utopian principle. As utopian, God's reality is never adequately realizable; but as a principle, God rules over historical realities. This does not mean that the "eschatological reserve" makes all historical realities and all political action relative, but it is the touchstone of history, and political action always has a zenith toward which it should direct itself.

Those with political holiness always keep in view the ideal of the reign of God and the God of that reign, to which they seek to conform history and their own practice. In spite of the difficulties they encounter, they always maintain the primacy of life, justice, obligatory struggle, the revolutions and structural reforms seen to be necessary. But they also maintain the necessity for life to be made full, for truth and freedom, reconciliation and change of heart. They also seek to maintain the even more difficult simultaneity of both types of ideal.

This holiness is repeating in history God's action, which is eschatologically holy. It is necessary for Christians to maintain their specificity in political action, but also to be more effective and succumb less easily to temptations. In the short term this holiness may seem like a hindrance, because it dedicates energies to what is not purely political action. It may appear idealist because of its intrinsic difficulty. But in the long run it is also fruitful historically, as Archbishop Romero demonstrated in an exemplary manner.[34] By his word and example he introduced spirit into the reality and the struggle of the Salvadoran people; by this spirit he made the people more firmly committed to liberation, more politically effective, and more awake to rejecting political action that did not take the good of the poor majority with absolute seriousness.

4. The Necessity and Importance of Political Holiness

Political saints are a reality. Suffering peoples recognize as saints those who incarnate themselves through love in the political and they recognize as saints of today only those who take the risks of this incarnation.

This may be done in different ways and the sacrifice of their lives is their ultimate justification. Some examples are the pastoral work of the four U.S. missionaries, Maura, Ita, Jean, and Kathy, the ministerial work of Archbishop Romero, and the explicitly revolutionary engagement of Gaspar García Laviana. At the moment we also need to speak not only of individual saints but collectives of the poor, whole peoples who share in political holiness when they fight for the liberation of the poor, filling these struggles with Christian spirit, and share in the fate of the servant of Yahweh by their very condition as a crucified people.

There are of course various degrees of this holiness. It does not tend to coincide with what the church still means by holiness in the processes of canonization. In the end only God knows the measure of real love in these new saints. But none of this should lead us to ignore this new, surprising, and massive fact or fail to see its full importance. Political holiness is historically necessary today for the poor to receive the good news and for history to move toward the coming of God's kingdom. It is also important for the church itself, so that it may recover the truth of the gospel and make this the foundation of its mission, and so that externally it may retain its credibility, which it can keep among humankind today only if it offers effective love to the poor. Only thus will it be able to face the challenge to the future of the faith when other struggles for the salvation of the poor are undertaken by those who do not accept the God of Jesus Christ.

It is difficult to maintain political holiness in the two aspects mentioned, and maintain it in both simultaneously. But now it is a necessity and it is not at all falsely spiritual to call it a gift of God. This is how Archbishop Romero saw it. Far better than a long analysis, some of his words explain what is political holiness, how to find it and how to be grateful for it: "I rejoice that our church is persecuted because it has opted for the poor and because it has tried to become incarnate with the poor. . . . [Assassinated priests] are the witness of the church incarnate in the problems of the people."

Translated by Dinah Livingstone

Chapter 5

The Spirituality of Persecution and Martyrdom[35]

Persecuted and Assassinated for the Reign of God in Central America

Name	Nationality	Ministry	Country	Date
Héctor Gallego*	Colombian	Diocesan Priest	Panama	June 9, 1971
Iván Bethancourt	Colombian	Diocesan Priest	Honduras	June 25, 1975
Jerome Cypher	American	Franciscan Priest	Honduras	June 25, 1975
William Woods	American	Maryknoll Priest	Guatemala	Nov. 20, 1976
Rutilio Grande	Salvadoran	Jesuit Priest	El Salvador	Mar. 12, 1977
Alfonso Navarro	Salvadoran	Diocesan Priest	El Salvador	May 11, 1977
Hermógenes López	Guatemalan	Diocesan Priest	Guatemala	June 30, 1978
Francisco Epinoza	Nicaraguan	Diocesan Priest	Nicaragua	Sept. 20, 1978
Ernesto Barrera	Salvadoran	Diocesan Priest	El Salvador	Nov. 28, 1978
Octavio Ortiz	Salvadoran	Diocesan Priest	El Salvador	Jan. 20, 1979
Rafael Palacios	Salvadoran	Diocesan Priest	El Salvador	June 20, 1979
Alirio Macias	Salvadoran	Diocesan Priest	El Salvador	Aug. 4, 1979
Oscar Romero	Salvadoran	Bishop	El Salvador	Mar. 24, 1980
Conrado de la Cruz	Filipino	C.C.M. Priest	Guatemala	May 1, 1980
Walter Woerdeckers	Belgian	C.C.M. Priest	Guatemala	May 12, 1980
José M. Grau Cirera	Spaniard	M.S.C. Priest	Guatemala	June 4, 1980
Cosme Spezzotto	Italian	Franciscan Priest	El Salvador	June 14, 1980
Faustino Villanueva	Spaniard	M.S.C. Priest	Guatemala	July 1, 1980
José Othmaro Cáceres	Salvadoran	Diocesan Seminarian	El Salvador	July 25, 1980
Manuel Reyes	Salvadoran	Diocesan Priest	El Salvador	Oct. 7, 1980
Ernesto Abrego*	Salvadoran	Diocesan Priest	El Salvador	Nov. 23, 1980
Marcial Serrano	Salvadoran	Diocesan Priest	El Salvador	Nov. 28, 1980
Ita Ford	American	Maryknoll Sister	El Salvador	Dec. 2, 1980
Maura Clarke	American	Maryknoll Sister	El Salvador	Dec. 2, 1980
Dorothy Kazel	American	Ursuline Sister	El Salvador	Dec. 2, 1980

Jean Donovan	American	Lay Missionary	El Salvador	Dec. 2, 1980
Silvia Arriola	Salvadoran	Sister	El Salvador	Jan. 17, 1981
Juan Alonso Fernández	Spaniard	M.S.C. Priest	Guatemala	Feb. 15, 1981
Carlos Gálvez Galindo	Guatemalan	Diocesan Priest	Guatemala	May 14, 1981
Marco Tulio Maruzzo	Italian	Franciscan Priest	Guatemala	July 2, 1981
Stanley Rother	American	Diocesan Priest	Guatemala	July 28, 1981
Carlos Pérez Alonso*	Spaniard	Jesuit Priest	Guatemala	Aug. 2, 1981
John David Troyer	American	Diocesan Priest	Guatemala	Sept. 17, 1981
Victoria de la Roca	Guatemalan	Bethlemite Sister	Guatemala	Jan. 6, 1982
Carlos Morales López	Guatemalan	Dominican Priest	Guatemala	Jan. 20, 1982
James Miller	American	Salesian Brother	Guatemala	Feb. 14, 1982

And many other pastoral ministers and lay missionaries,
delegates and ministers of the Word,
catechists and sacristans,
Caritas workers and human rights groups;

many Protestant brothers and sisters,
pastors and ministers,
deacons and preachers;

countless campesinos and Amerindians,
workers and students,
teachers and journalists,
nurses, doctors, and intellectuals;

persecuted and murdered for the reign of God.

1. Spirituality: A Necessity

By the spirituality of persecution and martyrdom I mean the spirit with which they must be confronted in order to prevent their difficulty from constituting an insuperable obstacle to their endurance; as well as to ensure that they be experienced in such a Christian manner as will ensure a burgeoning of new fruits for the Christian life.

Before addressing this theme, let me make a few brief preliminary observations.

1. I propose to focus my attention in this chapter on the spirit of the individual or group subject. That is, I propose to examine the subjective attitudes and virtues that will enable a person or persons to face persecution and martyrdom courageously and with full awareness, and to render them both fruitful in terms of Christian values. I shall not, therefore, be analyzing

---

* = disappeared

the objective reality of persecution and martyrdom, although I shall have occasion to refer to it.[36]

2. By "spirit" I mean, of course, the Christian spirit, which will already be familiar in its general lines to subjects of spirituality before their encounter with persecution and martyrdom, but which will achieve its plenitude as Christian precisely in that encounter. The Christian spirit becomes known in the measure in which it becomes reality.

3. Although spirit is a reality of a subject, it has a relationship with the objective reality of persecution and martyrdom. Thus spirituality is never totally autonomous or intentional, either in its content or with respect to the degree of its intensity. Rather it develops in strict relationship with its real object.

4. I shall be considering persecution and martyrdom as a single, homogeneous reality. I shall treat martyrdom not as an isolated, autonomous occurrence, but as the culmination of the process of persecution. Conversely, I shall treat persecution as the preparation for, and inchoative mode of, martyrdom. From this point forward, therefore, I shall speak of the spirituality of persecution and martyrdom in terms simply of the spirituality of persecution.

5. My direct reference to persecution will be to that occurring in Central America over these last years, although persecution has also been, and continues to be, a reality in many other parts of Latin America and the rest of the Third World as well. Thus I shall be speaking only of one type of persecution, but an important and widespread one, and the one that, in my opinion, most resembles the persecution inflicted on Jesus.

In terms of these preliminary observations, then, the first thing I must assert of the spirituality of persecution is that it is necessary. It is necessary not only because the New Testament insists on its necessity as a matter of principle, but also because persecution actually exists, and this as a result of ongoing historical causes.

1.1. The table appearing at the head of this article speaks for itself.[37] Had we been able to add to the list the priests, sisters, brothers, catechists, delegates of the Word, and simple Christian faithful who have been threatened, slandered, expelled, imprisoned, and tortured; the churches, homes, printing shops, libraries, schools, and chanceries that have been broken into, machine-gunned, dynamited, and ransacked—then we could have shown persecution and martyrdom in their massive, cruel reality. True, persecution and martyrdom are selective, but at the same time, in recent years, they have been generalized.

Further: these facts cannot be adequately explained simply by the perversion or evil nature of persecutors. These facts have *structural* causes, and those structural causes contribute to their inevitability. A church that seeks to be faithful to the impetus of Vatican II and, especially, Medellín, was promptly regarded as a threat to the interests of the powerful. After all, this church has (1) denounced structural injustice and institutionalized violence, exposing prevailing economic, social, and political principles and thus depriving them of religious legitimation; and (2) defended the hopes of the poor for their liberation, defending the poor themselves and encouraging them to organize for the attainment of that liberation. The goal of the powerful was to neutralize that church by various means, or else to convince it of the error of its ways. Pressure was brought to bear with a view to forcing the church to return to a more spiritualistic mission, one that would defend the Western world and its religious values. Alienating religious movements were encouraged, and they have proliferated.

But these strategies failed. The only alternative, then, is to eliminate this church. Persecution is the means to this end, but not a persecution directed upon all Christians equally. It is those Christians who threaten the status quo who must bear the brunt of it. To this same end, once more, persecution has not, by and large, taken the form of legal strictures directed against the church as an institution, in whose good graces the powers that be are most concerned to abide. Persecution has taken the form of acts against individual members of the church—which incidentally is thought to make denial of persecution possible.

The church itself has understood the attacks and murders that victimize its members precisely in categories of persecution and martyrdom for fidelity to its truth. This consciousness on the part of the church further points up the inevitability of persecution of a church that would continue to be the true church of Jesus Christ, and of course the church will never say that it is anything else. Bishops Romero and Rivera have made this declaration in El Salvador, along with many of their fellow bishops. Persecuted Christians themselves, in particular, insist on this. Puebla, too, speaks of "persecutions and deaths" (nos. 92, 668, 1138)—taking them for granted when the church performs its true mission—and adduces, as historical causes, "the testimony of the prophetic mission, the defense of human dignity, concrete commitments to the poor" (ibid.). The ultimate root of persecution, then, is the victims' solidarity with the poor. Persecution first strikes the poor, and with particular savagery. Then the sight of this brutality inspires others to share in their lot. Archbishop Romero puts it this way:

> Real persecution has been directed against the poor, the body of Christ in history today. They, like Jesus, are the crucified, the persecuted servant of Yahweh. They are the ones who make up in their own bodies that which is lacking in the passion of Christ. And for that reason, when the church has organized and united itself around the hopes and the anxieties of the poor, it has incurred the same fate as that of Jesus and of the poor.[38]

1.2. But persecution arises not only by historical necessity. It is not the sheer product of our historical circumstances. It is an a priori theological necessity as well, as we read in the earliest writings of the New Testament. To Christians in the throes of tribulation, Paul writes:

You have been made like the churches of God in Judea which are in Christ Jesus. You suffered the same treatment from your fellow countrymen as they did from [those] who killed the Lord Jesus and the prophets, and persecuted us. . . . You know well enough that such trials are our common lot. When we were still with you, we used to warn you that we would undergo trial; now it has happened, and you know what we meant [1 Thess. 2:14-15, 3:3-4].

The inevitability of persecution was established very early, then, and it was established—radically—in virtue of the very lot of Jesus. The reason why Christians will be persecuted is that "no pupil outranks his teacher" (Matt. 10:24). After all, "they will harry you as they harried me" (John 15:20). In other words, loyalty to Christ necessarily occasions persecution. The conflictuality inherent in the person of Christ endures to our own day. Conflict was not only the historical lot of Jesus personally. Even the risen Christ continues to instigate conflict. Succinctly: the conflictuality of Christ was universalized as "a sign that will be opposed" (Luke 2:34), and Christians were not in the least surprised when they found themselves the victims of persecution. They discovered the theological key to their persecution in the concept of having to suffer "for Christ's sake."

Persecution of Christians will be universal, then, in virtue of the conflict that Christ himself provokes. But we may not allow this to obscure the precise element that occasioned the concrete, historical persecution of Jesus, or ever cease to regard persecution for this cause as *the* Christian persecution, by antonomasia—especially in view of the fact that the persecutions raging around us in our own day have the same origin. Jesus was persecuted for his proclamation of good news to the poor and his service in its implementation. This led him into controversy, denunciation, an unmasking of ugly truths, anathemas hurled against the mighty—and death. Hence the first historical interpretation of the death of Christ—preceding other, more universalizing theologizations—would be constructed from a point of departure in the lot of the prophets (1 Thess. 2:14). The persecution of Christians, then, would be interpreted in the same sense: as the lot of a prophet (Matt. 5:12). Persecution was seen as the upshot of Jesus' practice in behalf of the reign of God, and the necessity of persecution was regarded as emerging from the violence inevitably perpetrated on that reign by the anti-reigns of this world.

1.3. What has been said thus far makes it clear that (1) persecution is a massive fact of our time and place, and (2) its enduring historical roots render it inevitable if the church and its members are to carry out their mission in fidelity to the following of Jesus and in solidarity with the poor. At once, then, we discern in persecution certain elements of spirituality that, although in a sense antecedent to the spirit with which one must confront actual persecution, are nonetheless important.

1. In view of the fact and the roots of persecution, its spirituality is, first of all, necessary. It is not optional. It is demanded in principle by the New Testament itself, as well as, a posteriori, by the historical reality that we have considered. Secondly, it is real, not merely the object of one's intention. Pious souls have practiced its intention and desire, independent of the likelihood of the object of their desire. But the spirituality of actual persecution must respond to an objective reality, whether desired or not.

It is the task of this spirituality to grasp persecution as something important, central, and globalizing. It is not something secondary or "particularizing," therefore, as if it bore upon merely one or a number of the various dimensions of our existence. It bears upon the central element of history and of the faith of Christians, as it shapes the spirituality of other areas of life. It is important because it affects the very kernel of Christian holiness—not that it is sought for the sake of one's own holiness, but because it occurs on account of one's solidarity with the poor and dedication to their welfare.

My purpose in these reflections is only to make this basic statement: that the spirituality of persecution is a demand of reality itself, and that therefore a readiness for persecution will be part and parcel of that spirituality. What is crucial, then, is that the possibility and reality of persecution in some form and in some degree be taken seriously as an essential ingredient of the Christian life. If no persecution were at hand, in any form or any degree, Christians and their churches would at least wonder why, and they would regard the question as a basic one.

2. Persecution does not burst over our heads "out of the blue." Certain things have to happen first. Concretely, what has to happen is: someone chooses to become incarnate in the world of the poor and to live for their defense. In order to be prepared for persecution, one must be ready for this incarnation as a previous step, and have the lucidity to grasp that it will lead to persecution.

The steps that lead to the persecution of an individual or group are invested with a certain ultimacy that is impossible to subject to further analysis. On the other hand, the motivation for these steps can be demonstrated by definitive argumentation. Indeed there are a number of arguments that can be adduced. What happens is that someone simply becomes honest with the reality of the world, the world of the poor as expressing the deepest truth of our world. One comes to grasp that one shares in the truth of humanity in this world of the poor. One comes to grasp that, by defending the poor, one is responding truly and genuinely to the demands of reality.

It is a prerequisite of the spirituality of persecution, then, that we conceive and maintain this honesty with our reality, despite the practical difficulties generated by such honesty—persecution itself—and despite the "theoretical difficulties," such as the injustice, misery, and death with which humanity is plagued in any case and which constitute its most challenging datum. (After all, even if these negative realities could be shown to present no metaphysical problem, the attempt to remedy them would be the most urgent—and consistently urgent—task that could ever face us.) This attitude of honesty with the real may well be accompanied by any of a large number of other attitudes, and psychological motivations—disenchantment with a bourgeois consumer society, naivety, a desire for the limelight, perhaps indeed the need to still within oneself the pain occasioned by the suffering of the poor, compassion for these poor, and so on; but the basic element will be the honesty underlying any of these secondary attitudes. In theological terms, what is at stake is an attitude of honesty with the primary judgment of a God who condemns this world of sin and death, and honesty with God's primary will to deliver that world from misery, injustice, and death.

A spirituality of persecution presupposes an active readiness for persecution by way of a basic honesty with reality. This honesty, in turn, becomes the mediation for an honest grasp of the reality of God and Jesus Christ, and an honest response to their demands.

2. A Theologal Spirituality

Any type of spirituality should be theologal, for any reality that can and ought to be lived with spirit can and ought to refer to God. I speak of the spirituality of persecution, however, as theologal in a more precise sense. Here, in virtue of the very reality of the object of their spirituality, men and women make a quantum leap in the character of their confrontation with God, both (1) in the element of ultimacy attaching to God, and (2) in the element of paradox and scandal in God (although once these are transcended, we come face to face with the positivity of God as well, the goodness and love of God). In other words, the three theologal virtues—faith, hope, and love—are essential to a spirituality of persecution. The theologal virtues are necessary if one is to remain steadfast in persecution. Of course, once persecution is experienced "with spirit," these virtues in turn acquire a new, more dynamic, dimension.

2.1. Of their very nature, persecution and martyrdom bring us face to face with our own life and death, as well as with the death, and hopes for life, of others. Thereby we perceive ourselves to be confronted with things genuinely ultimate. But there is more. In the concrete reality of persecution and martyrdom, we are confronted with the paradox that in order to be able to give life, one must give of one's own life, and even give one's own life. And we are confronted with the scandalous fact that, frequently, giving one's own life does not directly generate life in others—indeed, more radically, that the lot of the just actually worsens.

The so-called question of the ultimate, of God, of the meaning of life and history, imposes itself by its very nature, without needing to be induced, or reduced to the question of God and of the ultimate that human beings themselves are by the simple fact of being creatures. And the question of the right manner of one's relationship with God and with the ultimate likewise imposes itself of its very nature. Furthermore, the very reality of these questions forces us to the conclusion that our responses will be invested with a special radicality.

Let us delve a little deeper into the elements of paradox and scandal in the Christian ultimacy of God. There are certain basic assertions in the New Testament that cannot be omitted in a context of persecution and martyrdom. With regard to the human being, we read in the New Testament that the poor, the weeping, and the persecuted are blessed; that in weakness there is strength; that hope is against hope; that if we would win life, we must be prepared to lose it. In Christ's regard, we read that he was constituted Lord by way of suffering; that he saved the world by suffering the lot of the servant; that on the cross he heard his Father's silence. With regard to God, we read that the Father was on the cross, in the handing over of his Son, and that only at the last—that is, not yet—will God be all in all.

I could go on citing such New Testament assertions. They may not be the only ones that bear on persecution and martyrdom, but they are certainly central, and to fail to recognize them as such would be to deprive the Christian faith of a part of its specific originality. In any event they resound mightily in a situation of persecution and martyrdom, and vain would be our attempt to avoid taking a position in their respect. To be sure, a Christian already in possession of the faith can accept their truth beforehand. And surely a Christian engulfed by persecution will complement them with other New Testament citations—on God's power in the resurrection, and on the meaning of injustice and death as issuing in justice and life. But our paradoxical, scandalous, challenging passages lose none of their incisiveness thereby.

Historically, experience shows that life does not always follow death. Theologically, surely a faith untried by persecution can be true, and integrative, so that it will already include the elements of a correct response to these challenges. But it is a general faith by comparison with the faith that persecution will demand, and in any case it has not yet passed the test of persecution. Faith is concretized, and thus grows (or fails to grow) in its very reality, by way of persecution and martyrdom, in which the Christian responds positively (or negatively) to the ultimate human questions on the meaning of history, life, and God. Faith is also victory, then, for it comes into being by way of a trial. At all events the response that will be forthcoming is theologal, either positively or negatively, and it will be genuinely integrative, because, by the very nature of persecution and martyrdom, the surrender that will be forthcoming if the response is positive is more than a *sacrificium intellectus*. It is a *sacrificium vitae*.

2.2. The ultimacy with which a Christian is confronted in persecution can call forth a variety of responses. The response can be resignation, or despair, or cynicism. It can consist in the optimism of a "scientificism" that thinks to have come upon the infallible dialectic in which death must necessarily issue in life. It can even be a sort of latter-day Epicurean *carpe diem*: "Eat, drink, and be merry, for tomorrow we live!"

But the response with whose analysis we are now concerned is the response of faith. And the first thing to be said of the response of faith is that reasoning about it comes after the response itself. It is in the act of responding that response is constituted precisely response. Thus it is only in the act of responding that the truth of response is asserted. *Acceptance* of persecution and martyrdom as something good comes before its intellectual formulation.

This acceptance is often formulated in the language of negative theology, in the simple statement: "Here I stand. I can do nothing else." This is basically Peter's argumentation when he addresses Christians who are suffering persecution (although in the passage as a whole we also have a positive theology of the Christian response):

> Who indeed can harm you if you are committed deeply to doing what is right? Even if you should have to suffer for justice' sake, happy will you be. "Fear not and do not stand in awe. . . . " Venerate the Lord, that is, Christ, in your hearts. Should anyone ask you the reason for this hope of yours, be ever ready to reply. . . . If it should be God's will that you suffer, it is better to do so for good deeds. . . . [1 Pet. 3:13–17].

In other words, when all is said and done, it is better to give one's life than to keep it. We are more faithful to objective reality and our own subjective conscience when we accept persecution than when we reject it. "We can do nothing else"—and for those who do good and practice justice though they suffer for doing so, and yet maintain hope, no further justification is needed.

But it is not that men and women simply happen to be unable to discover a further justification. The ultimate reason why they can find none is that they have struck bottom where reality is concerned, and they have related it to the reality of God. What they are expressing in their assertion that they "can do nothing else" is the ultimacy of love, hope, and faith. To live persecution and martyrdom with spirit is to accord absolute supremacy to love, which has now been tested in persecution, but which thereby has also been asserted to be something absolutely paramount. It is this love, beyond all desire or calculation, and regardless of the realization or failure of such desires and calculations, that generates hope—the hope that, despite all else and contrary to all else, the future is beatitude. With that love and that hope, women and men make their journey through history learning as they go that it is this love and this hope that opens the road before them, even as they direct their steps toward a place that is not yet theirs. And this is the surrender of faith.

Love, hope, and faith constitute ultimate human realities. Therefore they are demanded when persecution and martyrdom confront one with the ultimate creaturely reality. And yet, precisely in their ultimacy, they are also mediations of the correct relationship between the human being and God. That is, they are theologal. With this love, one corresponds to the ultimate loving and saving reality of God. With this hope, one accepts God's future. With this faith, one respects God's being-God.

It is in the sense of the theologal virtues, then, that the spirituality of persecution is theologal. Persecution and martyrdom, realities in which the ultimate appears in scandalous and paradoxical forms, can be confronted only with an objectively theologal spirituality. And then both poles of the confrontation, persecution and its spirituality, generate and swell the reality of the theologal relationship of the human being with God.

3. A Fruitful Spirituality

Our reflections, first on the importance of being honest with the truth, and then on love, hope, and faith, turn out to be reflections on the foundational presence of spirit in persecution. Now I should like to describe certain more concrete manifestations of that spirit, as these manifestations appear in the dialectical interplay of the challenge and stimulation of persecution. My argumentation will not be a priori, but will consist in a simple narrative of what has occurred in El Salvador when persecution has been lived with spirit. By way of illustration, I shall quote a series of statements by Archbishop Romero, selected from among the many made by him and by other Christians in this same vein. Together with what has been said above, this description will afford us a vision of the spirituality of persecution.

3.1. *Spirit of Fortitude*

It is no hardship to be a good shepherd to this people. Here is a people attracting to its service those of us who have been called to defend its rights and to be its voice. . . .

I wish to assure you—and I ask your prayers that I may be faithful to this promise—that I shall not abandon my people, but shall walk with the people in all the risks that my ministry demands. . . .

I am very grateful for a wonderful letter sent by market women of Cine México. They sent a financial contribution, what they could as poor persons, and said: "Receive our congratulations, and may God ever enlighten you to keep on in your commitment and your love in this struggle for the Salvadoran people."

Obviously persecution calls for fortitude, not only to carry on the hard labors of the gospel, but to accomplish them amid an increasing and menacing brutality that, for the Christian, can be a matter of life and death. The ultimate source of this fortitude, this courage, is precisely the theologal attitude described above—coupled, of course, with the example of Jesus and so many martyrs before us. But the source to which I now refer is the historical font of this fortitude, which is also the source of the persecution we must endure. That font is our Christian presence with the poor.

In drawing close to the poor, and sharing their lot, the Christian experiences a great consolation. This consolation can be described theologically as encounter with God, and historically as the encounter with oneself simply as a human being. Sharing in the lot of the poor enables Christians to rediscover their human dignity, a dignity hitherto concealed or disfigured in the competitive, consumerist creature known as "the modern person." Paradoxically, it is persecution that reveals to Christians what true humanity is and grants them a share in it. It makes them feel themselves to be real citizens of the world of human beings. This discovery, paradoxically a joyful one, is of no small moment: it highlights for us the meaning of our life as a Christian life, and roots us in the place where we have begun to know who we are.

At the same time, as we draw near the poor, the poor behold a sacrament of the nearness of God. Consequently we acquire a Christian and ecclesial responsibility toward them. Perhaps without realizing it at first, and without intending it explicitly as the discharge of an ecclesial duty, Christians feel a most serious responsibility to be here among the poor. We feel that we may not abandon them, cost what it may. If, in these moments, we were to withdraw our presence from them, we should have to hear the terrible biblical judgment: "They served to profane my holy name" (Ezek. 36:20).

Positively, we feel that it is our unwavering presence among the poor that will ultimately bestow credibility on the church, and at a deeper level, on the faith itself, together with other vehicles of sacramentality that are salvific. The Christian intuition is that the choice between nearness to and estrangement from the poor constitutes more than simply one more Christian option. Somehow we grasp that the future of the faith hangs in the balance.

Fortitude in persecution can be translated as the refusal to abandon the poor in their sufferings. And these same poor—by what they give and by what they ask—inspire us with that fortitude, the strength to remain steadfast in persecution.

3.2. *Spirit of Impoverishment*

> My business is scooping up the outrages, the corpses, everything that persecution leaves in its wake. . . .
>
> The day the forces of evil leave us without this marvel [the radio], which they themselves have at their disposition with no curtailment, and the church has to bargain away its last shred, may we know that they have not touched us with evil. . . .

For its victims, persecution is spoliation, and martyrdom the supreme spoliation. But there are repercussions on the rest of the community as well. A massive, prolonged persecution creates a general impoverishment. Eventually the whole Christian community finds itself harassed by grave difficulties. Deprived of so many, and so highly qualified, pastoral ministers, and the use of other apostolic means and platforms for the proclamation of the good news, the community has fallen on hard times indeed. If the persecution is sufficiently prolonged, it may even lose its spectacular aspect and become routine. Now the gleaming cross loses its sheen and lapses into anonymity. To an objective spoliation of the direct victims, then, accrues a general subjective impoverishment, as can be observed in the relative resignation with which we experience persecution today as contrasted with the indignation it aroused in Archbishop Romero's time.

In order to endure this impoverishment—which is even more painful than the suffering of persecution itself—we have need of spirit, especially when our impoverishment seems to lead to silence and futility. The time comes when we must live the fundamental Christian law, "for your sake [Christ] made himself poor though he was rich, so that you might become rich by his poverty" [2 Cor. 8:9], without so much as the opportunity to choose an impoverishment that might seem enriching, and having to accept an impoverishment that seems simply impoverishing. We need spirit then. "May we know that they have not touched us with evil," Archbishop Romero said.

This spirit of impoverishment constitutes no impediment whatever to the struggle with the causes of impoverishment, or the effort to render the impoverishment enriching, as we shall see, or the exercise of the prudence (Matt. 10:16) and shrewdness necessary for the struggle with the children of gloom, the "worldly" (Luke 16:8). But it does forbid us to regard impoverishment as an evil, so that the church would flee the persecution that produced it on the strength of the rationalization that this is the way to strengthen the church and make it more effective. No, we must accept the Christian fact that, in order to win, we must lose, if the losing comes upon us for the sake of the reign of God and God's justice. Indeed, we must lose if we would gain life. We must resist the ever-present personal and ecclesial temptation to attempt to win life directly.

3.3. *Spirit of Creativity*

If they ever take away our radio, suspend our newspaper, stop our mouths, kill all our priests, and the bishop too, and leave you a people without a clergy—then each of you will have to be a messenger and a prophet.

We need creativity if we are to survive persecution. We need to find ways and means of keeping on with the task of the church and the faith in difficult situations, even if that task must now be discharged in total or partial clandestinity. Here Feuerbach's maxim proves a good one: "Suffering comes before thought."

But survival is not the only object of the creativity demanded by the spirituality of persecution. The "survivors" themselves must develop a great deal of creativity in order to live a fuller Christian life. This is what Archbishop Romero indicates in his rhetorical but profound statement about the importance of transforming poverty into plenitude: "If they take away our radio," he said, "we shall then be all the more the 'living microphones of the Lord' to declare his word everywhere."

And persecution has in fact produced magnificent creativity. It produces

Christian and historical clarity of vision. When what befell Jesus, and what befalls the poor of the world, befalls other Christians as well, they grasp the truth of the gospel and of history. Hence the doctrinal creativity of homilies, pastoral letters, reflections of priests and communities, theological studies, and so on. Creativity is demonstrated in the very fact of an investigation into the topic of persecution and martyrdom—matters so important for the faith a priori, but frequently so completely overlooked; or treating new subjects that arise in tandem with persecution or stand in relation to it, such as human rights, the organization of the poor, injustice, violence, and the like; finally, treating the traditional perennial themes, but from a new perspective, an outlook that recovers the viewpoint of the gospel, such as God, the reign of God, Christ, grace and sin, and so on.

Persecution also produces pastoral and liturgical creativity. It gives us sharp eyes, that we may discern the historical realities best calculated to mediate the theological realities to be communicated and celebrated. To cite merely one example, the eucharist can be celebrated in a number of different authentic dimensions—as the presence of Christ, as the celebration of the assembly of those around him, as a celebration of hope and thanksgiving, as a memorial of his sacrifice—because we are in the presence not only of a material crucifix and the relics of the martyrs of bygone times, but of bodies of the martyrs of our own day and place. And also because the persons gathered about the altar are there not just out of obligation, but out of their need to express their hope, and their gratitude to the martyred witnesses of our faith.

Persecution, then, calls for a spirit of creativity merely for the sake of survival. But on a deeper level, persecution leads to great creativity if it is suffered with spirit. And then we experience the truth of Paul's proclamation that in weakness is strength, and that poverty is enriching.

3.4. *Spirit of Solidarity*

I should like to express my solidarity with the priests, religious, and other pastoral ministers whose lives are in danger. . . . Let them not lose heart. Let us offer one another our mutual support. . . .

Service of the gospel and the persecution of the church have brought forth, as a precious fruit, a unity in the archdiocese hitherto unknown. . . . Letters of solidarity and of encouragement to go on living out this testimony have been innumerable. . . . Support has also come from many of our separated brothers and sisters, both inside and outside the country.[39]

At a time of persecution victims will unite, of course, the better to bear the burden by sharing it. And it is equally clear that persecution will divide those who seek to flee from those who hope to remain steadfast. But there is an element in persecution that, of its very nature, impels Christians to strike a relationship of solidarity with one another.

Furthermore, seen from a Christian viewpoint, persecution generates a solidarity of a particularly high order—one that goes beyond mutual consolation to equalize the unequal, and to impel Christians to conceive of the Christian life in terms of a relationship with their neighbor.

Persecution befalls the church first and foremost on account of the solidarity of that church with a poor and suffering people. From the outset, then, a secular barrier is burst. Inequalities of class, culture, and ecclesiastical function notwithstanding, a fundamental unity springs up, at the very least in virtue of a common hope for the end of the persecution and the dawn of the day of liberation. This solidarity generates a oneness within the local church and a solidarity between that church and other churches.

This first, basic unity also leads to a grasp of the fact that it is a unity among persons who are different, and to an appreciation of that fact. These differences do not lend themselves to division, but to complementarity and mutual enrichment. It is a well-known fact that persecution has motivated its victims to place at one another's disposition any contributions made on an individual basis, and not only as regards material goods, but also in terms of pastoral and theological contributions. On a deeper level, persecution has accustomed Christians to recognize their relationship with their neighbor as an element, and an essential one, of the Christian life. Faith itself is not exempt from the Christian law of "share and share alike." To be sure, faith includes a moment of personal responsibility that cannot be delegated to someone else. But it includes as well an essential moment of openness to the other, that that other may receive from my faith and confirm me in my own.

Thus persecution occasions the creation of a oneness, a unity, that is thereupon transformed into genuine solidarity, and it is in virtue of this solidarity that we bear not only one another's burdens, but one another. Individual Christians in small groups, groups throughout an entire local church, the local churches vis-à-vis one another, and even the various Christian confessions, once strengthened, confirm one another.

At bottom, the spirit of solidarity is the attitude and conviction that the Christian does not go to God alone. We are saved as members of a people. Persecution only manifests that spirit of solidarity in all its evidence. Persecution demands solidarity lest Christians falter, and persecution generates solidarity by instilling in Christians at a time of persecution a fixed attitude for all time thereafter: the knowledge that each of us lives our faith in reference to others, bestowing it on them and receiving it from them again.

3.5. *Spirit of Joy*

I rejoice, brothers and sisters, that our church is persecuted precisely for its preferential option for the poor, and for its quest for an incarnation in the interests of the poor. . . .

Sisters and brothers, how lovely the experience of seeking to follow, in some measure, Christ, and to receive in return such insults in the world, a torrent of vilification and calumny, the loss of friendship and the pall of suspicion! . . .

Christians ought always to foster in their hearts the fullness of joy. Try it, brothers and sisters. I have tried it time and again, yes, and in the bitterest hours of the worst circumstances, when calumny and persecution was at its wildest. I have felt the gladness of grafting myself onto Christ, my Friend, and have tasted the sweetness that the joys of this world cannot give. I have felt the joy of feeling myself intimately "God's"—a gladness beyond human comprehension. This is the deepest joy the heart can have.

Persecution is a Beatitude. "Be glad and rejoice" (Matt. 5:12), Jesus encourages the persecuted. "Rejoice and exult," leap for joy on that day (Luke 6:23). Paradoxical words but true. In Matthew and Luke the reason for this joy is the magnificent reward to be received in heaven. But the joy begins today.

The joy of the Beatitude of persecution is, first, the serene gladness of knowing that we resemble Jesus, that we are a member of a genuine church, that we have at long last understood what faith is "all about." It is the serene joy of the awareness that one is a human being and a citizen of this world without having to abdicate this in order to be a Christian. It is the serene joy of having found the meaning of life, inasmuch as, after years of searching, perhaps, the meaning of life has found us. It is the serene pride of being a Christian: at last we have something to offer the world—with humility, not with a superiority complex—at last we have something in which we can cooperate for our salvation.

But secondly, the joy of the Beatitude of persecution is also a joy in oneself, an exultation that of course is not always present, but at certain moments it cannot be repressed. There is joy when we celebrate the eucharist for one of our martyrs, when we sing for joy in the presence of a corpse. There is joy as we watch "these least ones" growing in faith, the hesitant growing in fortitude. There is joy in the experience of oneness and solidarity. There is joy—a humble joy, in which vainglory has no part—in receiving expression of gratitude on the part of other Christians and persons of good will who confess that they have recovered their faith, or the meaning of life, in the presence of the martyrs of their own land.

That joy, experience, received rather than sought, is the "hundredfold" of the gospel. It is the joy of the discovery of the pearl of great price: now the gospel has been presented for what it is, the good news. Here are Christians who, while engulfed in suffering, do not appear sorrowful. Never shall the like of these have to listen to Nietzsche's reproach that Christians do not have the appearance of persons saved. On the contrary, these Christians surprise strangers who had expected to see them sad and distressed but find them serene and joyful. Indeed, had there been no other test of gladness, it would have sufficed to see the pain shown by some of these persecuted Christians when forced to leave their country. Where your treasure is, there is your heart, and the treasure and heart of these is in the land of their persecution and martyrdom.

4. Conclusion

This, in broad strokes, is the spirituality of persecution as manifested in concrete reality. Persecution requires spirit of us if we are to confront it. But it also produces Christian spirit, and the most basic element of that spirit: a correct, theologal relationship with God. Doubtless the description in these pages is an *idealized* one; not all Christians in persecuted lands possess this spirit, nor do all who do possess it, possess it equally. But it is not *idealistic*. My stand is not a priori. Indeed, the traits I have sketched could not have been described in the absence of a real persecution upon which to reflect.

The basic thing persecution has secured for Christians and their church is its "de-centering" of both. No longer is it their own anguish and their own hopes that constitute the focus of their interest. Now it is the anxieties and hopes of others, the poor and oppressed. In El Salvador it is not persecution that saddens the church, but the immense, unabated suffering of the people. It is not for the return of its own peace (and flattery) that the church yearns, but for peace and justice for the suffering people. The spirit of "decentration," of forgetfulness of self, is the right way to correspond to the gospel and to Jesus. It is in the de-centering from self that so many persecuted Christians have discovered the truth of the gospel paradox, and thus find themselves to be "in truth with themselves" and at one with God. Despite the mighty tragedy in their lives, they have the experience of having "been given something." And one who has experienced gratuity has strength for faith, for hope, and for love.

Chapter 6

The Divine Element in the Struggle for Human Rights[40]

The title of this chapter is intended to "bring us up short." What I am suggesting is that the struggle for human rights is not only a categorical ethical demand incumbent on each and every individual, or merely a crucial part of the mission of the church and the praxis of Christians, but a demand and a mission with a divine dimension, an aspect that is theologal. I intend the title seriously. I mean, of course, that God and the struggle for human rights stand in correlation. I mean that with God in mind this struggle can be better understood and better waged. But I also mean that, from within the struggle for human rights, God can be better understood and better "corresponded to."

According to our various historical contexts, the formulation in the title of this chapter will have a different impact. For some of us it will suggest a new apologetics, in the face of the failure of so many others—a new attempt to include God in history when it appears that God has been expelled from nearly all the places in which we have been accustomed to find God. For others it will be the joyful expression of having encountered God, and oneself, in this history. Here it will suggest that there are "places" where, even apart from divine omnipresence, God can be found in a special way—"places" where persons' rights are at stake, places where we could therefore "make history" in a particular way, and where to do so would be to respond to and correspond to God. Surely there are many special "places of God," and many ways of responding to and corresponding to God. I am saying only that these particular places and ways of responding are among them—and I add, for my own part, that these are very special places indeed. Although the title does not say so explicitly, what I am dealing with here is nothing less than the classic, perennial problem of the divine element in history, and the divinization of the human being.[41]

In this chapter I adopt the latter of the two outlooks sketched above. I believe, however, that the second includes the first, not only because it indicates a new type of conceptual apologetics, but because it offers a mystogogy—an introduction into the mystery of God.

I could focus this theme in either of two ways. First—and this would be the easier way today, given the abundance and clarity of the findings of biblical theology in this regard—I could undertake to demonstrate that God's revelation absolutely demands a struggle for human rights. It would be enough to list the passages in scripture showing that God comes to the defense of the rights of the oppressed, widows and orphans, the poor. We could easily show that this pervades the Old and New Testaments. We could indicate how essential the defense of human rights is when it comes to understanding God, how indispensable a hermeneutic principle of everything the Bible says about God. We could establish that such an understanding of God is at the heart of faith in God: "What the Lord requires of you: Only to do right and to love goodness, and to walk humbly with your God" (Micah 6:8). "If you would offer me holocausts, then let justice surge like water, and goodness like an unfailing stream" (Amos 5:23–24). The conclusion would be obvious. For anyone who believes in God, the struggle for human rights is an inescapable imperative. This first focus, however, although correct, would be merely doctrinal, "from above to below"—from what we already think we know about God to what we ought to do about it.

The other way of focusing the problem would be just the opposite of the first. We could examine the struggle for human rights in such a way as to allow it to initiate us into an understanding of the reality of God, the God of Christian revelation. We could come to grasp that this struggle is not only an ethical practice required of us by God, but a practice that introduces us to the reality of God. This is the approach I have chosen. The struggle for human rights is not merely something that should be understood from a teaching about God that we have already accepted, but something that can help us understand that teaching because it actually enters into its constitution. The struggle for human rights is an *in actu* concretization of our faith in God. The God in whom we believe is always better understood in terms of a realized faith.

I might also add that the actualization of our faith—in this case, in the struggle for human rights—restores to God's revelation its primordial character as "word." After all, it is within the actualization of faith that the appeal to scripture has its ultimate meaning. Instead of functioning as a mere thesaurus of citations to be invoked in support of a particular teaching—on human rights or anything else—scripture becomes a demand and a challenge, yes, but then lucidity, inspiration, and beatitude.

1. The Element of the Sacred in the Struggle for Human Rights

I shall begin with a simple question. Is there anything sacred, holy, left in the world? The words "sacred" and "holy" may not mean a great deal in certain milieus, and it seems too close to the religious language of the "divine," as a way to help explain the divine. But it can still have a meaning. "Sacred" is not just a substitute for "ultimate" or "absolute." It also implies salvation for the one who will respond to it and be introduced into it. And so I ask once more: Is there anything that is ultimate and incapable of being manipulated, anything that makes an ultimate demand on human beings in the form of promise and fulfillment? Is there anything that will prevent us from relativizing everything, reducing everything to a lowest common denominator in terms of value, although perhaps without our knowing why we should not make such a reduction? Is there anything that makes a total demand on us—anything to remind us that despite the ideals of a consumer society, despite the growing preoccupation with material security and a life of self-centeredness, as we find for example in many places in the First World, there is after all a "something else," and a "someone else," and not just as a factual datum, but as a "something" and a "someone" in terms of which we either succeed or fail in our own self-fulfillment. Is there anything to stimulate us to reach out beyond our own individual ego or our own group, however worthy, such as family, political party, country, or even church?

All through history, humanity has felt itself to be in the presence of something called the holy, or the sacred. It may have been religious or it may have been secular, and it has varied with time and place, although we could indicate elements of a common substrate. In our own age, there can be little doubt that the defense of human rights represents for many of us something sacred—something that makes ultimate demands on us and holds out the promise of salvation. Certainly this is the case in the countries of the Third World, as well as, in one form or another, in those of the First World. What I shall now attempt to analyze, following a rather phenomenological approach, is why and under what conditions the struggle for human rights is something sacred.

1.1. *Sanctity of the Life of the Poor*

A major characterization of our era is the formulation and doctrine of human rights. And it is of no small merit for our age to have succeeded in conceptualizing and universalizing such rights—to have come to be able to speak of the right to life, to liberty, to dignity, and to so many other blessings accompanying these. But this accomplishment does not yet bring us down to basics. After all, reality is antecedent to doctrine, and to the philosophical or theological founding of doctrine. The concrete is antecedent to the universal. In order to explain what I mean, I could do no better than to return to the historical origin of law and rights:

In a general anthropological approach we could have already supposed as obvious that when in human history the function of judge or of what later came to be called judge was conceived, it was exclusively to help those who because of their weakness could not defend themselves; the others did not need it.[42]

The notion of law, and rights, does not arise in a context of pure human nature. Its origin is in the weakness of that nature, and this not only in the sense of limitation, but in the sense of helplessness in the face of the threats of others. Nor, again, is this helplessness, this defenselessness, experienced in respect to just anything at all. It has to do with the very possibility of life, and with life on its elementary levels:

> When the Bible speaks of Yahweh as judge . . . it is in terms of saving the oppressed from injustice. The concept of right arises when it is realized that in the oppressed life of another person there is a radical this-should-not-be, and there is a radical demand for that person's defense. In the very origin of right, then, there is a partiality for the poor person, because the efficacious rescue of that person is what is at stake. When the utopia of a just king is spoken of, the justice he imparts does not consist primarily in handing down an impartial verdict, but in the protection he offers to the helpless, the weak, and the poor, widows and orphans.[43]

To be sure, things have become a great deal more complex since ancient peoples entertained these reflections. Human rights have been furnished with a much more solid theoretical foundation, and subjected to a much more exhaustive cataloguing. But their source is still in this elementary fact and abiding historical experience: that for very many women and men, to live is a heavy burden, a difficult task, because others interfere with the performance of that task. And here an "ultimate" forces itself on our attention—if only this "ultimate" be spared the universalizing language of human rights. I refer to the ultimacy of historical sin, which threatens life and annihilates it, together with the ultimacy of those who desire to live. The right to life is not a "fringe benefit" added to human nature, however viable such an interpretation may be on the basis of a theoretical conceptualization of the human person. In concrete reality, the right to life is simply a formulation of the concrete ultimacy of life.

The historical reality at the origin of right and law, then, is still very much with us. There are areas of the world in which certain strata of the population possess their lives in sufficient security. But this is scarcely the case with the major portion of humanity. True, the mechanisms threatening the life of the majorities are no longer the same as in the distant past. But the consequences are. It remains important, then, to return to the origin of law and legal rights intended to defend imperiled life. The statistics on hunger, malnutrition, infant mortality, and unemployment in Third World countries are a matter of record. There could be no better definition of our world than "a world of the poor." Even today the poor await the appearance of a "just king" who will protect them from the modern mechanisms of impoverishment and death.

A discourse on human rights must begin with the right to life that is the right precisely of the poor.[44] We have characterized this life as sacred. Freely paraphrasing Rudolph Otto's familiar description of the holy as the *mysterium tremendum et fascinans*, we might wonder whether there is anything more tremendous and terrifying, anything better calculated to fill us with trembling, than the situation of poverty and daily death of humanity's poor. Statistics no longer frighten us. But pictures of the starving children of Biafra, of Haiti, or of India, with thousands sleeping in the streets, ought to. And this entirely apart from the horrors that befall the poor when they struggle to deliver themselves from their poverty: the tortures, the beheadings, the mothers who somehow manage to reach a refuge, but carrying a dead child—a child who could not be nursed in flight and could not be buried after it had died. The catalogue of terrors is endless.

And yet the life of the poor is riveting, fascinating. It attracts and captivates. It lifts one out of oneself and is experienced as something simply good. Apart from all purely sentimental and emotional nuance, all attitude of paternalism, with which the poor are so often regarded, we may well wonder whether there is anything more fascinating than the smile of a child of the poor with a yearning simply to live; or the organization of the poor, on a grand scale or small, simply to live; or the dignity with which the poor begin to carry themselves once they have decided to take their destiny into their own hands; or the pride they show when they have made a commitment, perhaps a commitment of their very lives, to the life of a poor people; or the rejoicing that fills them when they have taken some steps, little or big, in the bettering of that same life.

The experience of the holy is historicized here. But the experience of the holy it surely is. The *tremendum*, the terrifying, is alive and well. It terrifies not only because it is so enormous, and makes us feel so terribly small, but because it shrinks and impoverishes men and women, and puts them to death—and because it puts us to the question: Do we shrink, impoverish, and kill our fellow human beings? But the *fascinans* is here, as well: something that draws us to itself by lying before us as a gift: life and the hope of life. For those who live in this world of the poor, who live in the presence of this world of poverty, the imperiled life of the poor and their hope for life nonetheless, presents itself as ultimate and radical—as an "utterly other," exigent and salvific. Here is an exigency that cannot be relativized in the name of any ideology. But here as well is salvation, in the form of an invitation to introduce ourselves into the actual life of the human race, to share in its truth, in its horror and its hope. And in all of this we intuit salvation, for this is the manner in which one arrives today at being a human being, at simply sharing in life.

The discovery that the life of the poor is a sacred thing is a common experience in the Third World, as well as in the First World. In the human race of today, the life of the poor is ever the prime analogate of the human right. To be sure, this does not mean that there are no other human rights, or that these, as well, are not something sacred. In the First World, it is individual human rights, centering on individual liberty and dignity, that are defended. As for the right to life, the main concern is the very existence of humankind in the face of the threat of a confrontation of the superpowers that will entail the annihilation of us all. Surely this approach to the defense of human rights is necessary, in this age of the mighty, irreversible irruption of the subjectivity of the individual and the dreadful possibility of nuclear catastrophe. But we must insist that the most basic human right of all remains the right of whole peoples, peoples forming the major portion of humanity, to their endangered lives.

This fundamental right ought to be included with the others so legitimately defended by today's champions of "human rights." After all, is this right, too, not sacred? Is its defense, as well, not an experience of the holy?[45] Neglect this most basic right of all, and the defense of other human rights will almost surely degenerate into egocentrism—an understandable egocentrism, to be sure, but an egocentrism all the same—that would annul the sacred element, the experience of the holy, inherent in that defense.

First of all, the poor whose lives are threatened constitute the vast majority of humanity—entire peoples being crucified, slowly or violently. It is these masses of human beings who are ever the major fact, the major truth, of or for all humanity. It is these who are still the great "other" for all men and women, whether in the Third, the Second, or the First World.

Next, the First World must bear a considerable share of the responsibility for this situation of humanity. The poverty of the Third World means, for the First World, not only the prime obligation of defending the life of the poor, but the twofold exigency of restitution and reparation.

Thirdly, a concern for individual liberties ought not to ignore the fact that precisely this right is violated in the Third World more than anywhere else, where the victims are not only individuals, but peoples as such.

Finally, the right to peace (in the present instance, to immunity from the inevitable consequences of a nuclear confrontation between the two superpowers) must not be secured at the expense of regional, vicarious wars between those superpowers in the countries of the Third World. We may well be mindful, and joyful, that there has not yet been any head-on confrontation. But it would be a very serious omission to ignore the wars that have ravaged the Third World.

I have no intention, of course, of soft-pedaling the importance of the threat to life and liberty in the First World. I only wish to add that, if the defense of human rights is to constitute an experience of the holy, the rights to be defended must be seen in a perspective of the right to life of the poor as the major right of our time.

1.2. *The Sanctity of the Struggle for the Life of the Poor*

In the face of the reality just described, there is no room for doubt as to the proper human response: the defense of the life of the poor. And, once more, that defense is a holy thing. There are those who, with Rutilio Grande, can call that defense "humanity's noblest cause." Others will speak of "the sanctity of the revolution." Regardless of the formulation, the intent is the same: in defending the life of the poor, we fulfill ourselves as well.

The life of the poor, then, is an ultimate human concern. It carries us to our deepest roots. These roots are easy to recognize theoretically, but this recognition is easily overwhelmed in practice by self-interest. An honest confrontation with the life of the poor makes it more difficult to conceal these roots, and easier to foster them. In the face of the threat to the life of the poor, we grasp our obligation to respond with mercy and prophecy.

Mercy means genuine com-passion, not merely pity. The greater the passion, the greater the com-passion and mercy. Prophecy means denunciation. Prophecy is truth-telling. It denounces the horrors of death and the causes of death. It does so because this is the truth. The threat to the life of the poor exposes the truth of all humanity—a truth that, because it is sin, takes active measures not to be discovered.

The life of the poor confronts us with our own selves, in those two fundamental dimensions of our reality: co-responsibility with others, and honesty with reality. Both of these elements can be generated in the presence of other historical realities, but the life of the poor demands them with ultimacy, and fosters them with great effectiveness. To stand before the poor with honesty, then, is a first step in the humanization of the human being.

Anyone thus grasping the truth of reality is at once called upon to defend that reality. The imperative issuing from the life of the poor is not merely one more demand among so many demands upon the subject. It is the primary, fundamental demand. Without it, all the others are weakened, evacuated of their meaning. With it, all other exigencies recover their full meaning. Just how that life is to be defended—by what means—remains to be discerned. But as such, the defense of the life of the poor is surely the primary demand of a human being's ethical practice. This is why those who respond positively experience their own humanization.

But the defense of the poor is also, as the title of this chapter warns, a matter of struggle. It is important to have an explicit realization of this fact if we are to have a lucid concept of life and its defense, and a better understanding of the sanctity of that life and that defense. Defending the life of the poor means more than removing the poor from death. It means an active struggle with that death. To defend the life of the poor is to struggle. Why? Because the threat to that life does not proceed from natural causes alone. The threat to the life of the poor results from a death-dealing will, both personal and, especially, structural. The divinities of death really exist, and they must have victims for their sustenance. The defense of life, then, presents itself as one of two irreconcilable alternatives: life and death. Accordingly, the defender of the right to life comes automatically into confrontation with the powers of this world—the forces that strive for the annihilation of life.

This primary fact, so well attested throughout the history of humanity, and so central to divine revelation, comports a crucial corollary: at stake in the defense of the right to life is the very life of those who defend it. At once we have to face the possibility not only of having to give of our own life, but of having to give our very life. And suddenly we are face to face with the question of the holy. Suddenly we must ask ourselves whether or not the defense of the life of the poor is a holy thing. Subjectively, this question takes the form of a choice between coming to be and continuing to be a human being in a movement proceeding from oneself to oneself, or coming to be and continuing to be a human being in a movement from others to others. Objectively, it takes the form of a choice between regarding reality as an absurd, false promise or macabre demand, and as promise of life despite all.

Numerous individuals and groups make the latter option, and take up the struggle for the defense of the life of the poor. They know that their own life is at stake, and are nevertheless ready to give it. And they do so. In this they are affirming *in actu* the truth that there is something of the *tremendum*, the terrifying, here, but something of the *fascinans*, as well, something that attracts and draws us in the direction of self-surrender, in the visceral conviction that here we shall find fulfillment and salvation. These persons and groups know that, in defending the life of the poor, they graft themselves onto very life, and that, even in the giving of their lives, they have attained the plenitude of those lives.

This de-centration of oneself, this transfer of one's ultimate concern from oneself to the life of the poor, redounding as it does to the attainment of one's own life as well, is the subjective experience of the holy. It may be that, at the level of formulation, one cannot go much further. Words may seem insufficient. Theories purporting to demonstrate scientifically that this de-centering is not only necessary, but infallibly efficacious, for the attainment of the life of the majorities, are more voluntaristic than scientific. Perhaps the only thing left to us is the language of negative theo-logy or anthropo-logy: that to lay down one's own life for the life of the poor is better than the contrary: that in failing to do so, one would vitiate one's own life utterly, inasmuch as one had failed to correspond to the demands of life.

Positively, in scripture, and even in secular ideologies, to lay down one's life for the life of the poor has been cast in one concept and term: love. The defense of the life of the poor is love. The defense of that life at the price of our own life is love to the limit, love with ultimacy. And suddenly we are confronted with the intuition that runs like a golden thread throughout the warp and woof of the whole history of humanity: one who lives in love, lives.

2. The Divine Element in the Struggle
for the Life of the Poor

I have laid out a brief phenomenology of the sanctity of the life of the poor and the defense of that life without explicit Christian language. And indeed that sacred quality, that holiness, has its secular expression, as in the formulation, so charged with hope, of Ernst Bloch: "That the world come to be hearth and home for humankind." But this quality of sanctity can and should be formulated in strictly Christian language as well.

The whole of the foregoing is more than evident throughout the Old and

New Testaments, as well as in the life of the church in certain ages of its history—for example, in the defense of the Latin American aborigines by bishops of the sixteenth century—in much of current theology, and in various of the recent documents of the church magisterium. My concern here is to show that the basic justification for denominating the defense of the life of the poor "divine" is not that a particular doctrine of God calls for that defense; or even—although this is of paramount importance—that it responds to the demands of God. The basic justification for calling the defense of the life of the poor "divine" is that, besides all else, that defense bestows upon us a kinship with the very reality of God.

According to Judeo-Christian revelation, the life of the poor is holy because God resides in the poor. Jesus' nearness to the poor makes of them a "place of God." And lest there be any doubt in the matter, scripture tells us explicitly that Jesus is in the hungry and thirsty, the naked, the sick, and strangers (Matt. 25). In most radical terms we hear that God was on Jesus' cross—the cross of the just one slain by sinners. Once more God resides historically in the champion of the hope of the poor, put to death by the mighty. God is present in the poor. God is there, concealed and crucified, but God is there. God is present in other important "places" as well: in the eucharist, in the prayer of the communities, in their priests and ministers, and so on. But these other manners of divine presence do not annul or downgrade that presence in the poor. From the decisive viewpoint of human salvation, we read in our scriptures that our reaction to the presence of God in the poor is fundamental and decisive.

Again according to revelation, God is the defender of the life of the poor. God emerges from divinity and grants self-revelation when God hears the cry of the oppressed and determines to "come down to rescue them" (Exod. 3:8). God defends an oppressed people, who, through the mouth of the prophets, is called God's own people. God draws near, for the sake of the poor, in the reign of God, as Jesus proclaims. This correlation between God and the poor, between the imperiled life of the poor and its divine defense, is one of the essentials of our scriptures.[46] This does not militate against a universalization of the relationship between God and all human beings, or between God and the fullness of life. Only, the concentration is antecedent to the universalization, and not the other way around. This is the self-manifestation God has given, and this is as far as God can possibly go in self-manifestation. To introduce oneself, therefore, into the correlation between God and the poor is a divine mediation.

Puebla's formulation is admirable:

Made in the image and likeness of God (Gen. 1:26–28) to be his children, this image is dimmed, and even defiled. This is why God takes on their defense and loves them (Matt. 5:45; James 2:5).[47]

Archbishop Romero expressed it in pastoral and prophetic terms:

Nothing is more important to the church than human life, the human person—above all, the poor and oppressed person, who, besides being human, is also divine.

In the midst of the barbarities, the supreme poverty, and the death that victimize the poor, Archbishop Romero reaffirmed, in prophetic tones, the correlation between God and the poor: "That blood, that death, touches the very heart of God."

Thus the life of the poor, and the defense of that life, are fundamental both to God's revelation and to human beings' response to that revelation. It is both the most and the least that we can do. It is not everything. But it is the apex, and the foundation, of everything.

First let us recall why it is not everything. Is not the threat to life the supreme peril? And yet it is not everything. It is not everything for the poor themselves: after all, they too are limited, they too are sinners (although their sin is the sin of weakness, and is forgiven in the gospel, where it is mercifully understood and clearly distinguished from the basic sin of oppression). Liberated from one form of their poverty, the poor can become "little oppressors." Besides, God desires their life in plenitude, that they may live by God's word and not by bread alone. There is no question, then, of any a priori idealization of the life of the poor here—although we must add that it is they, too, who, very, very often, for all their lack of material life, are the best examples of Christian spirit, of faith and hope, of dedication and fortitude, of reconciliation and forgiveness.[48]

Nor is it everything, this defense of the life of the poor, for those who defend that life. First, that defense, though supremely necessary, urgent, good, and just, is mounted by human beings, and hubris can enter here. The defense of the life of the poor must be effectuated in the spirit of Jesus, in the spirit of the Beatitudes, with a pervading consciousness of the gratuity of both the gift and the task. Secondly, the defense of life is struggle, and struggle always tends to generate negative by-products. Thirdly, life extends to other levels than of strict survival. Neither, then, do we succumb to an a priori idealization of the defense of the life of the poor—although, again, it is frequently those who engage in that defense who are the best examples of life in its fullness, a life of faith and hope, of prayer and liturgy, which they are accused of seeking to "mutilate."[49] It should be clear, then, that the will of God, as well as the reality of God's own activity, call for the life of the poor in a context of life in plenitude, call for the liberation of the poor in a context culminating in covenant, call for the liberation of a people in the context of the path to becoming a people of God, among whom all men and women will be able to treat one another as sisters and brothers, and God as the Father of them all.

I grant all of this. Nothing could be more evident. But in no way does this truth obscure the evidence of its counterpart. When the life of the poor is under assault, God comes to the rescue. And God's defense of the life of the poor does not become something secondary in virtue of the fact that God is in the process of self-revelation as Father and fulfiller. An "absolute" resides in the death of creation, and God always reacts with ultimacy. Indeed, in scripture, the very revelation of the plenitude of God unfolds from the fundamental fact of God's solidarity with and defense of the poor among human creation. God shows the nature of divine plenitude: far from being independent of that primary solidarity and defense, the fullness of God is a function of God's fidelity to it.

This is why the defense of the life of the poor is necessary for the experience of the Christian God, and of course for the optimum opportunity to develop that experience is plenitude, for that defense is the origin of this plenitude. Therefore the defense of the life of the poor is mystagogy, or initiation into the very mystery of God. Those who defend the life of the poor with mercy, with truth and propheticism, with solidarity and responsibility, with surrender and hope, are re-creating, in historical fashion, the very mercy and tenderness of God, God's own truth and love, God's surrender to the very end on the cross of Jesus. When we proclaim God as the God of life and liberation, we do not do so from somewhere outside God, any more than we proclaim it on the basis of a mere doctrine. We proclaim it from within the history of God.[50]

In acquiring a kinship with God, we find ourselves placed before God and God's mystery. When all is said and done, it is the God crucified in the poor who moves us to conversion—the first great conversion, in which we begin to see and act in a radically new manner, and then the succeeding conversions that the defense of life demands. The God present in the poor comes forth as gift and grace, with the ultimacy of the gift of life itself, and with a bestowal of grace calculated to enable us to defend life and thus come to life ourselves.

We stand before the mystery of this God. We must face the basic questions concerning ourselves, life, and God. We mull over these questions and respond to them in prayer and liturgy, in the solitude of the heart and the objectivity of history. We face the great question of the future, the question of hope. There is nothing naive in our question. "For some time now, I have felt the disappearance of entire peoples to be an absurd mystery of historical wickedness, and my faith is transformed into depression. Lord, why have you abandoned us?" (Pedro Casaldáliga). And still the life of the poor abides in hope. Still we, with them, believe in the God of utopia and resurrection, still we believe in the God whose glory, as Archbishop Romero said, is the poor person who manages to live. In our defense of the life of the poor, we maintain hope in God and the final plenification.

Those who struggle for life encounter God in history, and encounter themselves in history in the sight of God. Thus we can speak of the *divine* element in the struggle for human rights. But this is reality, and reality occurs when it occurs. It will not be enough to invoke a doctrine of human rights coupled with a doctrine of God. It will not be enough even to show the conceptual congruity of both doctrines. The struggle for human rights emerges as divine only in the waging, and only when, on the basis of those rights, the struggle waged is in behalf of the life of the poor of this world.

It should come as no surprise, then, that so many have seen their faith in God increased and christianized when they have dedicated themselves to the defense of that life. Nor should we wonder that this same dedication has aroused in others—in milieus conducive to an acceptance of God—a powerful questioning of faith and of God, a questioning that has even called forth a positive response. And all of this, not because the defense of life furnishes new concepts to the faculty of understanding and thereby renders the concept of God more acceptable, but because, in the actual mounting of a defense of life, that defense reveals more fully the truth of the human being and of God.

Now we see why the struggle for human rights is divine. And this is important—let me note, by way of conclusion—for the church. Obviously the church should be engaged in the struggle for human rights. But this is little. In terms of what we have discovered in the course of our present inquiry, that struggle is an important, indeed essential, mode of expressing the very faith of the church. It is important, and essential, for the very identity of the church, and for its historical relevance. In other words, it is not enough for the church to possess a doctrine of human rights, or even that it preach that doctrine. Indeed, that preaching could actually be transformed into a sterile orthodoxy, a palliative to the conscience in the absence of an actual church praxis of human rights. Nor will it be enough for the church to demand its "own" human rights in society (the right to educate, freedom of expression, and so on) although it certainly has the right to make such a demand. Nor, strictly speaking, will it even suffice that Christians demand their own rights within the church, urgent and necessary though this demand be in terms of the spirit of Vatican II, and necessary though these rights be to the credibility of the church's discourse on the rights of humankind at large.

No, for the human rights struggle to be genuinely ecclesial, it must never lose sight of its theological roots. The most important task on the face of the earth is the struggle for the rights of others, and of those others who are God's privileged persons and peoples, the poor of this world. When this is the struggle that it wages, then the church will really have a contribution to make with its teaching on human rights. Then the church will be able to demand what it regards as its own human rights and have its demand received as an altogether honest one. Then those who struggle for their rights in the church will no longer be doing so directly in their own behalf, but in order the better to serve the world of the poor by demonstrating that human rights can be a reality in the church community itself. Then the struggle for human rights and the defense of the life of the poor will be transformed into a here-and-now, efficacious, sacrament of salvation.

Part Two

DIMENSIONS
of
SPIRITUALITY

Chapter 7

Jesus' Proclamation of the Reign of God: Importance for Today[51]

It is a commonplace today that Jesus of Nazareth preached not himself but the reign of God. This central datum of Jesus' preaching and activity has come to be of increasing and decisive relevance in Christian faith and practice, as well as in theology.

My intent in this chapter is not to set forth once more what the reign of God meant for Jesus, but to reflect on the importance of that reign, as preached by Jesus, for the faith and practice of Christians of the present. Accordingly, I presuppose:

1. That Jesus proclaimed the coming of the reign of God, and that at first he believed it imminent.

2. That he never defines what it is, but speaks of it in parables.

3. That its content is utopian, as already proclaimed in various ways in the prophetic and apocalyptic literature, but that in this utopia is awaited the renewal of persons, of their relationships with one another, and of the relationship of them all with God.

4. That the utopia of the reign of God is proclaimed especially (or only) to the poor.

5. That Jesus not only spoke of that reign, but developed an activity and a practice in its service, and made demands on his hearers.

6. That, on account of his service to the reign, Jesus promptly came into conflict with the powerful, and that this earned him persecution and the cross.

Presupposing these data, then, with respect to what the reign of God meant to Jesus in a bygone time, we now ask: What is the importance today of the fact that the historical Jesus announced that reign, placed his life in its service, and thereby allowed certain important elements of this utopian reign to emerge as salient?

In order to grasp what is at stake here, we might pose the following questions. (They may seem to be rhetorical questions, but in actuality they are not.) Would it make any difference for our faith in Jesus if he were professed as

Son of God but had not proclaimed the reign of God? Would it make any difference for our faith in God if God were, indeed, the Father of Jesus, and the one who raised him from the dead, but not at the same time a God who desires a just life for the poor, and a God who proclaims good news to the poor? Would it make any difference for our Christian life, our life of faith, hope, and love, if their correlate were "God" simply, and not "the reign of God" as well? Or, rephrasing these questions in theoretical, theological terms: Is not the reign of God preached by the historical Jesus, though of course a real datum of his historical life, merely provisional for faith, and at bottom superfluous once Jesus is professed as the Christ, God as the trinitarian God, and the utopia of faith as the resurrection?

The answer to all these questions, to my way of thinking, is a resounding no. Neither would our faith be the same without the reign of God, nor would it be Christian if that reign, along with the historical Jesus, were to become something merely provisional. This problematic cropped up in the infant church itself. The answer given then was in terms of an identification of Christ with Jesus, of the risen one with the one who had been crucified, and gospels were written establishing Jesus and the reign of God at the center of the Christian faith.

On the theoretical level, then, we could say that these questions have been substantially resolved. But special account must be taken of an important fact. Whenever Christians have effectively recovered the centrality of the reign of God—as has happened over the last twenty years in Latin America—suddenly the faith of these Christians is no longer the same. It becomes novel and creative. Further, it becomes more evidently evangelical, more Christian. But in practice it cannot be denied that Christians view themselves as more Christian when they have recovered basic values of their faith—when they have better christianized their traditional faith values. At all events, no observer of the life of the church today can deny that Christians in Latin America today are more like Jesus than they were before.

Undeniably, then, a faith orientation in terms of the reign of God embodies a magnificent potential for the faith and for Christian life, as history itself evinces. But why do I recall this here? In the first place, because it is not easy to maintain one's faith in an orientation to the reign of God. On the level of ecclesial theory and practice, it is not easy to maintain the ultimacy of the reign of God with respect to the church because the reign of God judges and relativizes that church, although it also animates and inspires it, giving its mission proper direction. The reign of God reveals the understandable, but real—and really succumbed to—concupiscence on the part of the church for its own absolutization, as exemplified in the current attempts to invalidate Vatican II, Medellín, and Puebla. Furthermore, the reign of God calls for a practice on the part of the church that will lead to serious conflict and persecution. Not rarely, church officialdom reacts to this threat either with a paralyzing fear, or by giving rein to an instinct for self-preservation.

In the second place, I call attention here to the great potential of the reign of

God for faith and the Christian life because of the need for a clarification of certain questions that, although formulated theoretically, are of great practical consequence. I propose to investigate only three of these questions in this chapter.

1. It is sometimes said that the reign of God is not the monopoly of the biblical, Christian faith, but the legacy of a utopia-minded humanity—and, accordingly, the content of that reign must be analyzed only in its general content.

2. We hear it said that, as a utopia, the reign of God calls for a correspondence in hope—and, accordingly, any demand for faith or a practice of charity would be an open question.

3. We hear it said (more correctly, this time) that Christian spirituality derives from the following of Jesus and the relationship of Jesus with the Father—and, accordingly, what the reign of God requires of, and contributes to, spirituality is a matter for discussion.

1. Reign of God and the Being-Human of a Christian

It has been rightly observed that, as symbolic expression of a utopia to come, the proclamation of a reign of God is not peculiar to the Bible or to Jesus. I admit this. But the important thing here is the conclusion to be drawn for faith today. The quest for, and maintenance of, the specific elements of the Christian faith is a never-ending and important task. But this does not make it the only way to discover the truth of our faith, or exempt that task from the serious dangers of precipitancy in its performance. One of the dangers in question is the possibility that Christians may subtly abandon an incarnation in real history, participation in "the joys and hopes, sorrows and anguishes, of the present age" (*Gaudium et Spes*, no. 1).

Incarnating Christians in the real history of human beings is always the first logical step in Christian existence, which is something to be secured and won over and over again, something that must never be taken for granted, and something that—in practice—is attained with great difficulty. It is precisely because the symbol of the reign of God is so analogous to other utopian symbols of humankind that it performs its first great service—that of directing the Christian, the Christian faith, and the Christian church to real humanity, to the problems and hopes of real women and men. Therefore it is one possible way, and an effective one, whereby the Christian, through faith, can not only "be in" history, but can genuinely share the history of humanity.

But the symbol of the reign of God also contributes a particular concretion to the manner in which human beings experience history and its utopia. There is evil in history. That evil withstands the efforts of men and women to overcome it. And yet these men and women continue to hope that there will be a salvation. In the biblical tradition, and in the mind of Jesus, humanity's utopia is fairly determinate, although of course not absolutely specific.

In the first place, in the Bible, and with Jesus, the evil whose defeat will signal the irruption of the longed-for utopia is not simply a natural evil, nor even merely the death of human beings as their natural fate, but a historical evil. It is the product of the will of human beings. In the second place, this historical evil is basically injustice—the unjust organization of human lives, in the oppression of some persons by others. Thus the reign of God is associated with the triumph of the justice of God, and the practice of that justice. In the third place, the reign of God is presented with "partiality"—presented from the viewpoint of the poor, and presented as a reign in behalf of the poor, although the realized plenitude of God's reign can come to all. From the first origins of the biblical utopia, the awaited king is regarded as just because he will take the side of the poor and helpless.

These simple observations show the importance for today, too, of maintaining Jesus' proclamation of the reign of God at the heart of our faith. Jesus never says exactly what this reign, this utopia, is to be. The gospel narratives interpret it against different backgrounds (the prophetic, with its emphasis on the historical triumph of justice, or the apocalyptic, which postpones to the end time, "eschatologizes," that triumph). Jesus takes up again certain of the wisdom traditions as well. Nevertheless, one key datum emerges again and again as the crucial one: Jesus appears on the scene with a utopia for human beings, and a utopia bestowed directly on the poor majorities. Thus his message is incarnate in humanity, and he himself appears as "true man"— although both truths, that of the reign of God and that of the person of Jesus, will emerge only gradually in their concretion and Christian specificity.

At least two things stand out as important for our present age from the fact that Jesus proclaimed the reign of God. First, we have a positing of the most serious problem of current history. Doubtless the problem could be formulated in other ways as well. But in terms of the reign of God, it becomes the problem of how human beings may have life, or more exactly, come to have life. Accordingly, the problem underlying the prophetical and the apocalyptic backgrounds is a problem of justice. It is the problem of how the great marginalized and oppressed masses of history may cease to be marginalized and oppressed. The problem is not one among many: it is *the* basic problem, and the current situation of humanity keeps making it the basic problem. It is a problem arising out of the very heart of reality, and nothing can make it hold its peace. It acts in the manner of a negative theology, then—as an absolute this-must-not-be. Its solution will not adequately solve the other problems of persons and believers. But without its solution, those other problems will be solved in neither a human nor a Christian way.

A second conclusion to be drawn is that God cannot be understood apart from the reign of God—not only in God's manner of realizing it (whether gratuitously or with human cooperation), but in its content. The utopia of the reign can be expressed in secularized contexts. No reference to God need be made. But if the reign is formulated in religious terms, then not only do we say something about humanity, we also say something about God. To say that God is a God of the reign means that God's reality must become present not only by way of mediators, new human beings who in their holiness reflect something of the holiness and reality of God, but also by way of mediations—historical phenomena shaping the life of persons and embodying fellowship and justice. Hence, very importantly, God is also the God of life—the God of the liberation of those whose life is oppressed, the God of the poor.

Christian faith in God is not reducible to this. Coming to us first of all in Jesus, God comes as one who delivers human beings from their sin, from their concupiscence, from themselves. Again, God is our Father, someone with whom we strike an intimate personal relationship. All this is true. But we would surely fail to do justice to the God of Jesus if we prescinded from the reality of God's reign.

A formulation of history in terms of injustice, and the reality of God in terms of justice, is not adequate and exhaustive for Christian faith. But it is necessary. An appeal to Christian life in its fullness, to the consummation of justice in love, to the eschatological, transcendent plenification, is surely necessary for the expression of Christian faith. But these formulations are "Christian" only if they are not made precipitously and exclusively.

The difficulty of maintaining these elementary truths is demonstrated by current history. It is not easy to maintain the Vatican II option for a church in the service of the world, the Medellín option for liberation, the Puebla option for the poor, or the option for the defense of faith and the promotion of justice of the 1983 general congregation of the Society of Jesus. The reign of God proclaimed by Jesus serves as an ongoing, challenging reminder of these elementary truths, and warns against precipitousness and oversimplification in the formulation of our faith. The reign of God proclaimed by Jesus comes to us with this truth: that at bottom, and before all else, the Christian is a man or a woman immersed in the real history of humanity, which is a history shot through with the enduring, scandalous problem of injustice, and that no one can ignore this problem and hope to attain either human or Christian being; that the locus of the comprehension of the truth of history and of God is the underside of history, where the longing for the utopia of the reign of God has been generated in a secular matrix; that God, religion, faith, and the church must necessarily be seen in a context of the life and death of human beings, that apart from these realities they will neither possess truth nor enjoy credibility. It can seem extremely simple. But what the proclamation of the reign of God has effectuated in our present age is the Christian's reconciliation with human history. Christians now feel genuine membership in the human race. They feel that they can and ought to contribute to humanity from within, not from without. Christians today have the joy of knowing themselves to be genuinely human. They no longer find it in the least necessary to abdicate their human-ness in order to be Christians.

2. Reign of God and Theologal Anthropology: Faith, Hope, and Love

In speaking of the reign of God as utopia, I imply that it has never existed in history. At any rate it has never existed in fullness, and its partial realizations are always tenuous and threatened. Thus the reign of God bespeaks futurity. Let me, then, analyze the meaning of the reign of God for the fundamental posture of believers vis-à-vis the reign of God as utopia.

Like Jesus' own concrete attitude, the utopian concept of the reign of God excludes a view of the future as uncertain or ambiguous. The future is not configured of symmetrical possibilities of salvation and condemnation, life and death. The future is that which is not yet, but which, when it is, will be salvation and fulfillment. Hence in order to correspond to the utopia of God's reign, it is essential that men and women be confidently open to the future.

This trustful openness calls for *hope*, which stands the Christian in a formal relationship with the future. But it also requires an important affirmation of faith, and requires it here and now: that the bottommost stratum of reality is positive, and that therefore history can be salvation. We know all this. Its repetition may seem superfluous. But these propositions are basic for a theologal anthropology. Human beings take various attitudes toward reality. On the one side they may be resigned, skeptical, cynical, or condemning. Or instead, they may view reality with a naive optimism based on rational calculations, blind faith in progress. Betwixt and between, they may place themselves somewhere along the whole epicurean spectrum of those determined only to "get the most out of life while it lasts."

The reign of God certainly excludes this last attitude. It also rejects the first, and calls for hope instead. As for the second posture, the reign of God as proclaimed by Jesus attaches a qualifier: the positive element in history is God. Jesus' formulation is religious. The ultimate element in reality is the goodness of God, indeed the goodness of a God who is our Father, in whom we can place our trust. And yet, God is ever God, beyond manipulation, deduction, and grasp, never a foregone conclusion based on mere calculations and the momentum of history. To respond to the reign of God, then, means to have hope and faith.

But there is more. And this "more" is of the utmost importance for an understanding of the nature of Jesus' utopia and its meaning for today. The reign of God calls for a basic change in persons that I may substantially characterize as the *practice of love*. Hope, understood sheerly conceptually, contains no reference, either by affirmation or negation, to a change to be effected in the one who hopes, other than, of course, a change from not hoping to hoping. And so hope can go hand in hand with passivity, or merely interior activity, without the reference to exteriority that is inherent in the reign of God. But then it will not be the hope that is both demanded and stirred up by the reign of God as proclaimed by Jesus.

We may never allow ourselves to lose sight of this most important datum: that Jesus himself actively toiled for the coming of the reign he proclaimed, and that he demanded radical changes in his hearers in view of its approach. Where Jesus himself is concerned, his prime activity consisted precisely in proclaiming the reign of God—a crucial service to the reign merely in and of itself. This service would have been superfluous, at least logically, unless the coming of the reign was contingent on Jesus' proclamation. But furthermore, Jesus preached the reign not only in words, but in works—works having a relationship to the reign. He performed miracles and exorcisms, he took meals with sinners and social outcasts. His concern was to represent in symbolic form—but also actually to present, at long last—some historical reflex of the reign. In fact his activity was governed, often enough explicitly, by the utopia of the reign: the triumph of justice over injustice.

I am not concerned at this point with the question of whether Jesus had any formal understanding of the stuctural causes of injustice, or of the means whereby that injustice might be overcome. Perhaps he did, and perhaps he did not. The important thing for us here is that his active defense of the poor, in his denunciation and exposé of the mighty, was a social practice that would genuinely tend to the transformation of society in the direction of the utopia of the reign of God. Entirely apart from any reflexive comprehension Jesus may have had of the societal structures of his time and place, irrespective of any subjective intentionality on his part, the conflict into which Jesus entered with the social, political, religious, and economic powers of his time, and his fate on the cross, demonstrate that his activity was objectively a practice that impinged on his society. What guided him in this practice was his ideal of the reign. At least for Jesus himself, the reign of God was not only a utopian symbol of hope, but a utopia for which something—ultimately, everything—had to be done.

It was much the same with his audience. In view of the approaching reign, Jesus always demands something. Conceptually, it may sometimes be unclear whether he demands it precisely because the reign is approaching, or precisely to hasten its coming. But one thing is clear: he requires an interior conversion on the part of all his hearers. Of the poor and oppressed he requires a conversion precisely in the form of hope in God. He calls on the wretched majorities to accept the fact that God is mightier than they, with all their age-old historical experience of misery. This act of hope, although an internal human act, has great potential for external subversion. Jesus also demands certain external fruits of conversion, which, although tiny in comparison with the utopia of the reign, are nevertheless elements that will contribute to its coming.

Together with all this, on the positive side, Jesus requires love—in the form of life according to the ideals of the reign of God, life in a spirit of a communion of sisters and brothers. Often enough Jesus asks for that love in terms of the historical needs of the poor, and always he initiates a process of enlightenment as to the nature of love, lest it continue to be reduced to its conventional notion. Now love is invested with ultimacy. Now love relativizes all other principles of religious fulfillment. Jesus reveals the inadequacy of false notions of the ultimacy of love—for example, in the parables of the last judgment and the good Samaritan. Of some of his hearers Jesus even asks a discipleship that will be explicit service of the reign in the manner of Jesus himself.

The demands of a formally messianic practice, of an activity orientated to the transformation of a society of sin into a society of the reign of God, are not overwhelmingly clear and explicit. But this does not mean that there are no such exigencies. Implicit in the denunciation of oppressors is the demand that the powerful now organize society in a different manner. The subversion of values, and the contrast between rich and poor, in the Beatitudes and anathemas, point to new human relationships. Jesus' call for discipleship in the last moments of his life implies a discipleship laden with not just any cross, but with the cross necessarily accompanying a messianic practice (not just *any* practice).

It is difficult, accordingly, to systematize Jesus' activity and the demands he makes on his hearers. No single category will accommodate them. There is no sharply logical relationship between, on the one hand, the reign of God and, on the other, Jesus' activity and the exigencies he addresses to his hearers. But I believe that these reflections will have been sufficient to justify at least the following conclusion: The "reign of God" is not a merely utopian symbol, to which an adequate response will be sheer hope. It is an ethical symbol as well. It demands a change in attitude and conduct. And ultimately it is a praxic symbol, calling for a determinate activity: in general terms, life in love—the practice of the practical side of charity, the transformation of historical injustice into human relationships of genuine justice.

Jesus' concept of the reign of God signifies, for our time, a particular concretization of the theologal triad, faith-hope-charity—but it signifies that concretization in such a way as to demand as well that "these three" and their mutual relationship become more evident in our day as the basic way of being a Christian, become more capable of unifying the transcendent and historical elements within them, become more relevant, and thereby more credible, in the current situation of humankind. At all events it can be observed that, where the reign of God is proclaimed today, faith, hope, and charity appear in a new, creative, evangelical way, difficult to arrive at from a point of departure in any other Christian reality.

This is especially the case with respect to Christians of the Third World and those who want to be assimilated to them. At first the rediscovery of the reign of God proclaimed by Jesus called forth a recovery of genuine Christian hope, as so much European post-Vatican II theology testifies. Today, especially in the Third World, the reign of God has meant the recovery of the practice of charity in the building of the reign.

The Christian life is hope, which includes a faith view of history, and which is concomitantly—and at bottom preponderantly—the practice of charity.

3. The Spirituality Made Possible and Demanded
by the Reign of God

By spirituality I mean living in history—building and suffering that history according to the Spirit of God in our midst. Spirituality in the concrete is simply the actualization of faith, hope, and charity. But this actualization is an actualization in concrete history, as the Spirit inspires and demands. The Spirit is inexhaustible, and will flow in no preestablished channel (not even in the reign of God as sole channel). But today, as we see, Christians who elect to be governed by the reign of God also explicitly search for a spirituality that will render God present as Father. Hence the renewed emphasis on spiritual themes like prayer, the spirit of the Beatitudes, the holiness of the new human being, and so on.

I do not pretend, then, to deduce the whole of Christian spirituality from the sole premise of the reign of God, or play conceptual games in order to be able to make it appear that the reign of God were indeed the only font of that spirituality. On the other hand, it can scarcely be denied that the proclamation of the reign has generated a powerful spirituality in our day, and that it has done so precisely by way of elements that would be hard to come by without an appeal to that reign. In the light of this observation, then, let me list some of the elements of spirituality that the reign of God logically requires and that the proclamation of the reign has in fact stimulated and inspired.

3.1. *The Stubbornness of Hope*

The reign of God as Jesus has proclaimed it has not come. In terms of a number of outlooks on the human situation, it may even be receding, as poverty and injustice increase in our world. If there is hope despite all this, it must be a steadfast, dialectical hope. Hope has the Pauline nuance now. Now hope means "hoping against hope" (Rom. 4:18), and not only by reason of the obscurity of the future, but also by reason of the misery of the present.

Still there is hope. We see it in Christian hearts. In some of its manifestations, as at times among the poor of the Third World, this hope can seem naive. But it is not. It is a critical, dialectical hope, a hope that knows it runs counter to the misery confronting it. And it is anything but a "hope" maintained by way of raw extrapolation of our desire for change. Enlightened reason might well wonder how our hope is still possible after all these twenty centuries. It could seem more reasonable either to reckon with the hope of human calculations alone, or simply to "face the facts" and give up hoping. And finally, of course, there is a theology that counsels an exclusive apocalypticism: at the last, and only at the last, justice will triumph.

Still, where the approach of the reign of God continues to be proclaimed, where the reign of God is still proclaimed as good news for the poor, ever and again the scandalous miracle of hope is wrought. A sense of the nearness of God is translated into hope for the historical present. Today the proclamation of this reign not only demands this sort of hope, but at the same time makes it possible, and with an efficacy that would be difficult to come by in any other way.

3.2. *Acceptance of Creatureliness*

Being a utopia, the reign of God can never be adequately represented in reality or concept. The moment it is regarded as realized, some human reality must have been absolutized and therefore made the object of idolatry. The moment it is regarded as adequately conceptualizable, some desire to absolutize it must be hiding in the wings. To confront the reign of God, then, requires humility—the humility of the creature, the acceptance of a limited condition and limited knowledge.

At the same time, it cannot be said that there is nothing in the present to reflect the reign of God. Nor does everything simply reflect it and fail to reflect it, indifferently, as a certain interpretation of the "eschatological reserve" would have it. The reign of God is not so easy to discern. Accordingly, the creature's confrontation with the reign of God requires that creature's ability to undertake an active search for, to discern and to construct the particular realities that, at a given moment, appear to be the more likely to hasten or constitute the coming reign.

At the basis of this outlook is a refusal to sunder the tension inherent in creaturely being. An "all or nothing" attitude will have none of this tension. But the creature is neither all, nor nothing. The creature is neither the creator, nor a cipher. The creature is a creature. An internal, visceral acceptance of our creaturely being can constitute an entire spirituality. This spirituality forbids both hubris and self-destruction. It demands both humility and active responsibility. And so it calls for a via media, consisting in a knowing and a doing that fall somewhere between the "all" and the "nothing," and which will translate into an active quest for and discernment of concrete ways to build the reign. More concretely, an authentically creaturely spirituality will seek out and reduce to reality new ways of charity—assistential, promotional, or structural.

This creaturely spirituality, as I style it, can be demanded by other faith realities. But it is surely demanded by the reign of God. That reign calls on us to confront church and society—both of them created realities—in a creaturely fashion. Neither church nor society is the reign of God. And yet we continue to be tempted to make of the church, if no longer in theory, at any rate in practice, a substitute for the reign; and of so-called Western civilization, if not the reign of God proper, at least its natural place. At the same time, the contrary error is just as dangerous: to look upon any configuration of church or society whatever as being equally near or far from the reign. It is not a matter of indifference whether a church comes forward as a genuine servant church, defending the rights of the poor and sharing in their causes, or in effect absolutizes itself, relativizing and ignoring the world of the poor or abandoning the world to its misery. It is not a matter of indifference whether a society sees to, or ignores, the life and fundamental rights of the poor.

To regard things, and oneself, precisely as creaturely—to act upon things, and to act oneself, in a creaturely fashion: such is the challenge of God's reign. This is what is required in order that the reign of God be precisely a utopia—a thing without a place, and yet having a place made for it in history.

3.3. *Perspective of Partiality*

Christian faith makes universal statements about God, Christ, human beings, salvation, and so on. But as we know, that universalization is preceded by a particular, even scandalous, concretion. The Son takes human flesh. But the particular flesh he takes is a flesh of poverty and historical weakness. The Father loves the Son indeed. But the Father delivers him up to be crucified. God raises "the dead." And the first fruits of that resurrection are in a particular individual who has died on a cross. God and human beings are rightly placed by the logic of faith in a correlation that excludes no man or woman. But this universal correlation is preceded by one much more particular. A Christian spirituality must always attend to these preferential, "partial," starting points that issue in a subsequent universalization. Without this "partial particular," the universalization will no longer be precisely Christian. I shall refer to this as the "perspective of partiality."

The reign of God calls for, and most effectively inspires, this perspective of partiality through its correlation with the poor. It is from among the poor, and for the poor, that the utopia of the reign approaches. God is their God, by the mere fact that they are poor. Thus the poor are a theological locus, and their specific contribution is that of furnishing precisely the partiality of the perspective. It is from out of their midst that the truth of things appears, the truth of God, of sin, of grace, of liberation, and the rest. It is from a place among the poor that one is finally able to evaluate the accomplishments of humankind, whether these be designated "reign of God" or something else coming to the same thing. From the underside of history, the truth of history comes to light.

Furthermore, however, the poor have a historical and theological potential in terms of the "other," our "neighbor," that is very important for an experience of gratuity. In virtue of their historical reality, the poor are "other" in a privileged fashion. They mediate the "otherness" of God, and especially the "utter otherness" of God. The astonishment and scandal occasioned by Jesus' activity derived from the fact that his proclamation and service of the reign of God took as its privileged addressees the poor and despised, and placed them in a correlation with God. That this aroused such hostility and incredulity evinces, at least indirectly, the difficulty of accepting the otherness of God.

It is precisely the otherness of the poor that makes it possible to experience the meaning of life itself as emerging from something-other, and thereby to experience that meaning as something gratuitous. And the poor, in their own achievements, as well as in what they make possible for others—demanding it by their very reality—in the way of dedication, service, love, and even martyrdom, are suddenly the place to be and the place to do good. And so their being-other becomes a source of good in others, as well. The sense of being referred to the "other" now goes hand in hand with the experience that something good has been given to us. The formulation may seem very simple. But it is fundamental. There are historical places that are a source of God, and are endowed with the capacity to make us good. But, let us never forget, those places are "partial," preferential, privileged.

3.4. *The Mind-Set of a Person of the Reign*

The reign is a reign for the poor, then, and as such it requires and makes possible a specific mentality or mind-set. This mentality can be promoted in the name of other faith realities, it is true. But it has frequently been either passed over in silence or relegated to the status of a secondary consideration. I am referring to certain basic attitudes, certain ways of reacting to basic human problems. Believers have often ignored those problems. But now, with the proclamation of the reign of God, they have come to light once more—and without being mitigated by a reference to *God*, for this God is precisely the God *of the reign*.

We find the attitude of men and women of the reign described in the Beatitudes, as well as in the Sermon on the Mount. But I shall focus here on certain attitudes that, in a sense, are antecedent to the Beatitudes. The latter are a proclamation of mercy to the great masses that writhe in poverty, oppression, and repression—a proclamation that should fill us with mercy, and inspire us to a practice calculated to overcome these evils. But before all else, here is a mercy that ought to be maintained as something of ultimate value, and not trivialized in the name of eschatology or the plenitude of the Christian life. It is a matter, simply, of recovering, and especially of maintaining, that prioritarian attitude of Jesus, *Misereor super turbas*—"My heart is moved with pity for the crowd" (Matt. 15:32).

Then we shall feel the indignation that the suffering and oppression of the poor arouse in every person of good will, and we shall be led—as Jesus was led—to point the finger of shame at those responsible for this wretched state of affairs: we shall denounce the guilty. Too frequently this indignation has been softened, or even resisted, in the name of other principles of our faith. At the same time, we shall know the gladness of proclaiming a reign that is good news for the poor, as well as the joy produced by the joy of the poor themselves when they hear, understand, and celebrate this good news. We shall know the joy of having found, in this gospel, this good news, the pearl of great price, the treasure hidden in a field, for which we shall want to "sell all we have" and devote ourselves heart and soul to this message.

These basic attitudes—mercy, indignation, joy (to mention only a few)—put a new face on our faith practice. In the first place, they insert our practice into the community of women and men of good will. Suddenly Christians no longer appear, deep down, as alien beings, strangers to the real world, having reactions different from those of other seekers of utopia. And secondly, these attitudes plunge our practice into the deepest heart of the gospel. In their proclamation of the reign and their labors for its realization, Christians have rediscovered this mentality. This proclamation, this toil, far from removing Christians from the rest of humankind, shows them to be messengers of a gospel—the bringers of good tidings for others—and joyful, not downcast messengers, or individuals and groups forever on the defensive.

3.5. *Holiness in Behalf of the Reign*

Christian holiness is nothing more nor less than likeness to Jesus. "Holy" is whatever reproduces, in the best possible manner, the totality of Jesus. The proclamation and practice of the reign are not the totality of Jesus. Consequently, they are not the only road to holiness. But they demand and facilitate a supremely important element of that holiness.

The reign of God is not simply a utopia to be hoped for and striven for. It is a utopia to be anticipated and constructed *in opposition to* historical realities, in opposition to objective sin. This sin is substantially whatever puts persons to death by structural means—by structural injustice, by institutionalized violence—in a word, by repression. The holiness that constructs the reign is altogether conscious of its struggle with this sin. Once more, I am not saying that the sheer struggle with the sin of the world will automatically produce holiness, in the absence of the performance of other tasks of holiness. But neither can holiness come into being apart from this mortal combat with sin. On the contrary, this combat is capable of generating a type of holiness that otherwise would be most difficult of attainment.

Concretely, the struggle with sin in behalf of the reign of God calls for fortitude in the presence of risk, because it stirs up persecution of every kind, including death on the cross—all of which comports a likeness to Jesus on a most fundamental point. If, besides, this struggle is impregnated with a love for the poor, and if the be-all and end-all of this struggle is that the reign of God appear, and that God become more present in our history, then the many deaths of our day are martyrdom. For they are the testimonial of love, the greatest love. And they are the testimonial of faith in a God of the reign.

The readiness to give of one's own life, and actually give one's life, for love, is a central element in Christian spirituality. But in the context of the reign, this readiness cannot be either purely idealistic or merely intentional. It must be real readiness. After all, persecution and death are real possibilities, as current history attests. A totally serious proclamation of God's reign today offers a structural channel for holiness, and for that act that has ever been regarded as the decisive mark of holiness: martyrdom for love.

4. Reign of God and Resurrection

After his resurrection, Jesus is formally professed to be the Christ. Now certain transmutations occur in the reign of God as a symbol of utopia. Now the good news becomes Christ himself, Christ crucified and raised from the dead. The church is now in some sense transformed into the community that expresses the plenitude of the reign of God in history. The resurrection now becomes the symbol of the Christian utopia. This development is in itself legitimate, at least in part. But it holds genuine dangers as well. It may not maintain, within the totality of Christ Jesus, the mutual reference between Christ and Jesus. More specifically: in the tension between "Jesus" and "Christ," "Jesus" and the "reign of God" essential to that "Jesus" could disappear from view. In principle the fact that the gospels, with their "Jesus" content, may well constitute the mightiest bulwark against this threat. In the gospels, as we know, the reign of God is central. In principle, then, it ought to be central today, although of course Jesus' resurrection will contribute new faith elements.

But the reign of God is important not only in principle. It is also important because what this utopian symbol comprises is not purely and simply what the other utopian symbol, the resurrection, comprises. There is always the danger that these two concepts could be regarded as interchangeable. As concepts, they could be interchanged. But this would be to force them. This would be doing them violence, even on the theoretical level. Worse still, it would mean ignoring the fact that, even as formulations of utopia, they generate different, complementary, attitudes and behaviors.

The resurrection of the dead is basic for faith. It points to God's final triumph, and generates a radical hope. It indicates that, even in history, we have an obligation to live in accordance with the plenitude of the resurrection—in accordance with God's guarantee that the new human being is a real possibility. But this basic truth by no manner of means divests the reign of God of its importance. In and of itself, the resurrection is eschatological. The reign of God shows us how to go about constructing the eschatological, how we may journey toward the eschatological.

Let me attempt to capsulize what I mean. In the resurrection we find God's definitive sanction of Jesus as *the* human being. But the truth of Jesus' being-human appears only in his history. In the resurrection we have God's guarantee that the genuine human being appears in Jesus' love and surrender. But the fundamental structure of that love and that surrender appears precisely in Jesus. In the resurrection God declares that there will be a new sky and a new earth, and that the risen Christ constitutes the firstfruits of that new creation. But in Jesus' preaching of the reign of God we see the basic element of this eschatological novelty in our very history, and we hear the demand that we not only look forward to that reign, but actually construct it. In the resurrection we behold how God fulfills history, reconciling the seeming irreconcilables of history. But in the proclamation of the reign we see how to fulfill history gradually, maintaining to the hilt poles so difficult to reconcile historically— justice and mercy, indignation and forgiveness, gratuity and effectiveness, universality and a preference for the poor, structure and person, and so on.

The concept of the reign of God is important today because it teaches us something about Jesus himself. Surely Jesus is none other than Christ Jesus. But whenever, in the course of history, Christians have sought to reinvest Jesus Christ with his totality, they have returned to Jesus of Nazareth. This is what the simple campesinos of Latin America do today. Preaching a Christ Jesus who is Jesus of Nazareth is always a powerful message, and it unleashes Christian history. The same is true of the reign of God. Its proclamation is endowed with a special vigor. It generates a radical hope and a practice in keeping with the discipleship of Jesus.

When all is said and done, all this is true because the reign of God is the utopia of Jesus. This in no way, shape, or form divests of its importance the utopia of the resurrection as the ultimate fulfillment of history. But the reign of

God not only eschatologizes this utopia, it also historicizes it. The reign of God not only tells men and women that there is a utopia, it tells them what to do about it. It not only points to this utopia in all its transcendency, it indicates the road to take to arrive there, and that road is simply the steadfast intent to render that reign a reality in history.

Strangely, the reign of God never leaves anyone in peace. Why? Because it is never realized in all its fullness, and even its partial realizations are provisional, so that Christians must build it again and again. And yet it is precisely in the unending construction of the reign of God that believers encounter the profound meaning of their lives, and true peace in history. Indeed, this historical striving lends all the more conviction to the utopian symbol of the final resurrection in which God will be all in all. This call for the historicization of the utopia that has been the object of my reflections in the pages of this chapter, together with the basic structure of this historicization, bestows permanent value on the reign of God, and brings it about that, where the utopia of the reign of God is proclaimed with the vigor of the gospel, Christians and their churches find renewal.

Chapter 8

Evangelization and Discipleship[52]

1. Following Jesus and Evangelizing

The whole Christian life, and the life of all Christians, ought to consist in evangelization. Here indeed is the identity and raison d'être of the entire church (see *Evangelii Nuntiandi*, no. 15).[53] At the same time, every Christian life consists in being shaped to the image of the Son. Or, in historical terms, the Christian life consists in the *following of Jesus*, which after the first Easter began to be the "absolute expression of Christian existence."[54] Evangelization and discipleship, then, are two dimensions of every Christian life by the mere fact that it is the Christian life. Both, furthermore, are totalizing dimensions of that life. Therefore they must coexist in an interrelated fashion. Mere factual juxtaposition will be insufficient. Generally speaking, we may say: in order to evangelize in Christian fashion, discipleship is required; and discipleship necessarily issues in evangelization.

However, a consideration of this general relationship between evangelization and discipleship will not exhaust a theme as broad as that of the identity of the evangelizer today. By "evangelizer" here I understand not simply the Christian as such, but any Christian endowed with a vocation and charism that demand, and facilitate, the specific task of evangelizing, while shaping the totality of that Christian's personal and professional life. It will not be enough, then, to enunciate the coincidence in every Christian of evangelization and discipleship. We must explain whether and how discipleship is ordered to evangelization. We must explain what it is that enables an evangelizer as such to be a follower of Jesus, and not merely examine the necessity and advantages of discipleship for the evangelizer as a Christian.

In its general formulation, the answer to this question will be obvious. Historically, it is clear that Jesus called certain individuals to follow him, that he might send them to proclaim the good news of the reign of God—that is, to evangelize. Jesus' "Come, follow me" has its raison d'être in the making of "fishers of men" (Matt. 4:19). Discipleship is not self-justifying. The call to discipleship is self-justifying, and by itself alone. Discipleship is justified by the fact of being ordered to evangelization. And conversely, discipleship is the only way of life fully suited to the task of evangelization.

From a systematic viewpoint, it is clear that, after the first Easter, Jesus is recognized as "the very first and the greatest evangelizer" (*Evangelii Nuntiandi*, no. 7), and that his total reality—his deeds and his words, his practice and his prayer, his action and his fate, his death and his resurrection—is seen as evangelizing (ibid., nos. 8–12). *Therefore today's evangelizer must reproduce Jesus' evangelization in Jesus' own fashion.* This "reproduction" of the life of Jesus provides us with the systematic concept of discipleship. It is a notion that goes far beyond the explicit formulas of the gospel texts, but it is necessary for an understanding of the meaning and significance of discipleship for evangelization.

Taking discipleship both in its strict sense, and in its broad sense of the "reproduction" of the life of Jesus, I shall now attempt to set forth some of the traits of discipleship that will illustrate the concept of evangelization, while keeping account of certain particularly current problems, especially those of evangelization in circumstances like those of the Third World. I shall also attempt to relate discipleship to the basic content of evangelization: the proclamation and initiation of the good news—whether formulated from a point of departure in Jesus' preaching the reign of God as drawing near the poor, or from a postpaschal point of departure, including Jesus himself. However, I shall not pause to analyze either the content of the good news or the precise formality of evangelization as the communication of good news.

2. Communicating the Good News as the Truth

The content of the evangelizer's communication is truth: not just any truth, however, but God's truth. The evangelizer proclaims that the reign of God approaches; that in Jesus, God has drawn near; that God is love and that God loves us. This truth, being in the last analysis *God's*, cannot be adequately communicated as pure doctrine—as one among many truths of the deposit of faith, however important the truths of that deposit may be for other concerns. I am dealing with a truth that is and continues to be the basic truth regarding history and human lives.

To allow the good news to be God's truth is the first logical task of evangelizers. If they fail in this task, the good news degenerates into doctrine, and God and God's good news are diminished; the good news degenerates into an ideology, in which personal and church interests are introduced that are not necessarily God's interests; it degenerates into propaganda, and enters into competition with other kinds of good news.

By the same token, the good news, as God's good news, proposes a utopian truth. A utopian truth is never realizable in full and therefore always stands in need of mediations and concretions. The reign of God, love, and justice constitute an ultimate truth. But they can actually exist only as partial truths, whose underlying, ultimate truth must always be the object of a quest if the good news is to be presented historically.

Thus evangelizers find themselves in possession of good news to communicate. But the content of this good news always escapes them. It is greater than their own thoughts, or any doctrine. Furthermore, it is always in danger of manipulation and ideologization. And yet it is always in need of concretion as well. Here, then, is a problem for which theological, pastoral, or catechetical training are not enough. Here, then, is a problem that, in the last analysis, can be confronted only by confronting the very truth of God—by discovering this truth in its ongoing manifestation throughout the course of history, and seeking to concretize it for that history.

Here the evangelizer must deal with the objective character of the following of Jesus as demanding an unending quest for and acceptance of God's truth as it gradually comes to light. We can see that Jesus' own evangelization was not done once and for all, as if he knew the content of the God of the reign and of the reign of God from the outset. Jesus carried out his evangelization gradually, in a spirit of honesty with God in God's ongoing self-manifestation, and in all fidelity to God when God's will called for changes, slight or radical, in the direction in which evangelization was moving. Paradoxically, we also see in Jesus ignorance, doubts, and temptations with respect to evangelization. Is it by power, or by crucifying service, that this evangelizing task is to be performed? What is the day and the hour of the coming of the reign? Jesus hears both the Father's word and the Father's silence. And it is by way of these negative experiences that Jesus demonstrates his immense love for God's truth, which permits him to convey the good news as that truth.

Evangelizers must follow Jesus in Jesus' love for God's truth. Historically, this will entail a process of apprenticeship in and concretion of that truth. Only in this way will evangelizers find gradually concretized the general truths with which evangelization begins—God, the reign of God, Christ. These truths will become real for them. They will be able to communicate them to others genuinely, and not only as doctrine that they have learned and are convinced must be learned and interiorized by others. We might even say that they must learn from Jesus how to be apprentices in the truth of God and the reign of God. In this way they will communicate something that, in the last analysis, is not their possession, but something in fact issuing from God alone. The only way to come to express historically the "provenance" of God's truth is by a sustained, humble apprenticeship in that truth.

3. Communicating the Truth as Good News

The news communicated by evangelizers is good because it is God's own news. Evangelizers not only proclaim God's love for human beings, they initiate it, they make it present. On a theoretical level it might be maintained that, in the division of church labor, evangelizers are responsible only for the proclamation, and may leave its realization, its actualization, to others. In practice, however, this is certainly not the case. Nor could it be. In the first place, we have the example of Jesus. But furthermore, the current situation demands of evangelizers that they demonstrate the content of their word. In many places in the world today the evangelizer's word no longer enjoys an a priori credibility merely in virtue of the fact that it is a religious word, or the word of the church. Besides, an evangelizer's good news finds itself in competition with many other, secular, salvific offers. For today's evangelizer, then, credibility is crucial. And in the last analysis that credibility can be won only by putting the content of the good news into act.

Evangelizers must follow Jesus in putting the good news into act. As we know, it is of the essence of Jesus' evangelization that he performed it in word and deed. We have come to an enormous appreciation of this in our own day and age. Jesus preached, yes, but he also performed miracles and exorcisms. These works were more than simply "good deeds" he did in addition to preaching. Jesus' works were demanded by the content of his preaching. Without them the good news would have been mere promise once more— appealing, surely, to humanity's deepest desires, but without the power to shatter the historical ambiguity inherent in every transcendent promise. Jesus sought to make it altogether clear that God had definitively sundered the symmetry of a God at once saving and damning, a loving Father and implacable judge, a God who is near and yet so far away. To this purpose, the proclamation of God's love simply had to go hand in hand with historical deeds of that love. The proclamation of God's nearness had to go hand in hand with a genuine actualization of God's presence in the midst of humankind.

That Jesus "went about doing good" sums up not only his personal ethical activity, but his evangelizing labor as well. The evangelizer must follow Jesus in *doing* good. The very word of proclamation is already a "doing," but that word must also be consciously ordained to other "doings"—deeds through which women and men may be able to grasp that truly there is good news of God, good news that, because it is God's, is not only communicated, but effective, capable of transforming the misery of personal and historical reality.

4. The Preferential Character of the Good News

Clearly, in the New Testament as in the Old, the good news is "preferential." That is, it is "partial" with respect to certain addressees. Those addressees are the poor. We verify this truth a posteriori in the pages of our scriptures. But it is an a priori truth as well, given the premise that God wishes to manifest love to humankind. It would be rather absurd to God to bestow self-revelation and love on humanity in general and not fix on the majority of humanity—the teeming masses struck down by poverty and accustomed, not to good news, but to horrible reality. To show that God is love and that God has good news, and be believed, God must first address that love and that good news to the poor majorities.

The good news is "partial," or "preferential," today as yesterday. Indeed, it may very well be such today more than ever before, seeing that the poor today constitute an ever-higher percentage of the world population. Corresponding to the partiality of the good news will be a self-abasement, in attitude and in fact, on the part of evangelizers. This, once more, is part and parcel of the following of Jesus.

Jesus humbled himself, lowered himself, in a twofold fashion: in his transcendent incarnation, and in his historical incarnation in the world of the poor. For evangelizers, there is no substitute for this self-humbling if they hope to proclaim the good news to the poor—if they wish to demonstrate something so utterly simple, but so absolutely basic, as the fact that God loves human beings in the lowest abysses of poverty and misery, and that God does so by drawing near them and thus rendering divine love credible.

Evangelizers must recapitulate Jesus' own incarnation, embracing it as a process that generates its own dynamics. Incarnate in the world of the poor, they must share their immense pain, this misery that cries to heaven, the protracted or sudden crucifixion of millions of human beings. Evangelizers must begin as Jesus began—with the *Misereor super turbas*, compassion for the crowds, and without any romanticization or ideologization whatever of the pain of the poor, without making that suffering something ultimately secondary to their evangelizing task, or some purely provisional stepping-stone to a more real existence. As long as the poor are in pain and suffering, evangelizers struggle against that pain with all their might, for they regard it as possessing an ultimacy of its own.

This profound mercy must be transformed into an active defense of the poor. And this will lead evangelizers into controversy, as it did Jesus. Now they will have to denounce those who make the poor poor and keep them poor. Evangelizers will have to tear the masks from their faces. This is the militant dimension of mercy. It has nothing in common with hatred, revenge, or uncontrolled rage. Rather it is the fruit of a love for the poor, and a realistic way of communicating to them that God is really with them.

Thus, active mercy, in virtue of its own dynamic, leads evangelizers into conflict with the mighty of this world. Now evangelizers must face persecution and the cross. Like Jesus, evangelizers spend, pay out their very life in the evangelizing task—and not merely in the sense of the expenditure that any task requires, but in the sense of the expenditure required by the fact that evangelization attracts persecution. The proclamation of the gospel entails its own tribulations. It provokes a hostile reaction. And this reaction can lead to martyrdom—evangelizers' greatest humbling and abasement, and their maximal nearness to the poor. There are countries in the Third World where this happens with considerable regularity.

It is the preference of a loving God for the poor that drives evangelizers to a self-abasement entailing the consequences described above. They are only retracing Jesus' steps. They may not suspect it at first, but this must be their way. They will have their fill of persecution and the cross. Their deepest consolation, amid suffering, will be that there is no other way to present, with credibility, God's love for the poor—the love of a God who took great care to show nearness to these poor, even in the deepest abysses of their poverty, their misery, their repression, and their crucifixion. It falls to evangelizers by way of their own self-humbling and abasement, to generate in the poor the conviction: God *is* with us.

5. Evangelical Mentality of Evangelizers

Evangelizers must maintain an evangelical mentality. They must communicate the good news in the profound conviction that God's approach is truly good news for humankind and its poor. *The evangelical mentality is a habitual attitude of communicating the good news precisely as good news, and therefore communicating it not out of obligation, but with joy.* This does not mean that evangelizers must be endowed with a particular disposition—for example, that they are naturally cheerful and optimistic—or that they must ignore the brute facts of historical reality, or the failures of evangelization and their own failures. It means that evangelizers should transmit joyfully what ought to be joy for human beings; and that for them personally the gospel becomes a burden ever lighter, even though historically it becomes ever heavier.

The evangelical mind-set is expressed in Jesus' relationship with God. Jesus not only listens to God in order to know and accomplish God's will; he also calls him "Father": Abba. In this word Jesus expresses his indestructible conviction that God is good—that God goes ever in search of the lost and the poor, and that God's love is not only justice but tenderness. Those endeavoring to live up to Jesus in this conviction that this is "the way God is," convey in evangelization the unshakable conviction that God is good to human beings, and that women and men can live more fully and more humanly with God than without God. Now evangelization will be more than merely duty—although it surely is a duty, imposed on us by God. It will be an inner need of evangelizers themselves, who will put into words, out of their grateful need and the joy of having found the pearl of great price, what they bear in their heart.

This evangelical mentality may be difficult to come by in certain circumstances today. In a secular milieu, evangelization may degenerate into the mere apologetical attempt to salvage what is left of the faith. Evangelizers may even have personal doubts about God and God's salvific reality. In some circumstances they may suffer a kind of inferiority complex, having to live and work in the shadow of other salvific movements, secular ones, in contrast with which they will have "neither silver nor gold" (Acts 3:6) to offer for the transformation of society; and they will have to listen to the accusation, not always unfounded, that evangelization has functioned as an opium of alienation.

The evangelical mentality is a gift. Precisely how evangelizers acquire it, then, is ultimately a matter between themselves and God. But they will have to be convinced of their need for it if their evangelization is to be effective. They must become convinced that God is not in competition with human nature— that so-called human progress can contribute a great deal to human beings' acquisition of their needed autonomy, but that autonomy does not necessarily guarantee humanity. On the positive side, evangelizers must become convinced that God is good, and humanizing, and the fulfiller and plenifier of human existence, and that for this reason the news of the evangelical message is good news. They must be able to repeat with conviction the words of Archbishop Romero: "Brothers and sisters, tell me that my preaching today will bear fruit in the form of the encounter of each and every one of us with God!" There is no substitute for the salvation bestowed in this encounter.

The specifically evangelical mind-set has, besides, an efficacy of its own today, especially among the poor of the Third World. It enables them to keep hoping. Surely the hope of the poor is encouraged, and rightly, by historical signs of hope—partial liberations, a conscientization on the part of the poor, their progressive organization, and so on. But for the Christian poor, hope has another warranty as well. God is with them. Now they are no longer orphans. In one sense this may seem a small boon. But in another, it is a great one. Their knowledge that they are with God is the mainstay of their historical hope. In order to maintain the poor in this conviction, evangelizers must genuinely communicate a God who is good to the poor.

What I have called an evangelical mind-set is not, then, something that evangelizers can do without. It is a necessity, for evangelizers and evangelization alike.

6. Exigencies of Discipleship and the Good News

I have been recalling some of the traits of Jesus that evangelizers must attempt to re-create, and have thereby attempted to shed some light on the importance of the following of Jesus, in the broad sense, for evangelization. It remains to point up the essential relationship between evangelization and the concrete exigencies of the following of Jesus as evinced in the gospel texts that bear on it. The call to discipleship is for the sake of evangelization. The radical exigencies of the life of discipleship are for the sake of better evangelization. But over and above all this, the very content of those exigencies illuminates, from within, the content of evangelization.

Jesus' injunction to "leave all" for the sake of the reign of God conveys to its addressees the *unconditional character* of the good news. The good news is the pearl of great price par excellence. Once it is found, it relativizes all else absolutely.

The prohibition against "looking back" once one has set one's hand to the plow expresses the *ultimacy* of the good news.

The impossibility of "giving" oneself "to God and money" (Matt. 6:24) manifests the *exclusivity* of the good news. God is a jealous God, and will brook the worship of no other. Thus the prohibition of serving money evinces a *conflictuality* between the good news and any news that attempts to pass off as God something that is not God. The specific conflictuality of the gospel with money inculcates the *preferential nature* of the gospel with respect to the path of poverty. Finally, the call itself—"Come, follow me"—communicates the *gratuity* of the good news. The gospel is from God, and is presented as an invitation—a demanding one, to be sure—and not as the product of human logic.

These attitudes are demanded of evangelizers as followers of Jesus. But when they respond to them, they do more than follow Jesus. In putting them into act, evangelizers shed light on important formalities of the good news: its unconditional character, its ultimacy, its exclusivity, its gratuity, and so on. Evangelizers who follow Jesus' demands to the hilt frame their proclamation in a context that renders it more intelligible for their audience. Their own life of discipleship is not a mere prerequisite for a better evangelization. It is transformed into a concrete elucidation of the proclamation. They become, in a limited way, what Jesus became in an unlimited way: the good news itself. After all, evangelizers manifest God's love precisely as God's love. They breathe a love that can come only from God. Evangelizers follow Jesus, indeed. The ultimate reason for their discipleship is the same as the ultimate reason for the life of Jesus: to render God present and to initiate the reign of God.

7. Spirituality of Evangelizers

Evangelizers are not proprietors, not even in a broad sense, of the good news. Nor may they pride themselves on being its primary addressees, which they are not. They are wholly and entirely its servant. Of course, this does not mean that there is no good news for them as well as for the poor. It is the repeated experience of those who evangelize the poor that they find themselves evangelized in return. In communicating the good news to the poor, they receive it again from them. And suddenly evangelizers find themselves with a broader and deeper knowledge of their own message, and their own existence is filled with new meaning, new vitality.

It is of supreme importance for the human and Christian existence of evangelizers that they be evangelized themselves—that they too, by the indirect route that passes by way of the poor, be addressees of the good news. But this in no way militates against the fact that, formally and directly, evangelizers are only servants of the good news, its vehicle to others—although, in their concrete awareness, both aspects will be intermingled: they will be serving the good news, and served by it.

For the spirituality of evangelizers, then, the crucial aspect is service. The poor are not here to serve evangelizers, although they surely do so. In a profound sense, evangelizers must reproduce a trait of Jesus himself: "The Son of Man has not come to be served but to serve" (Mark 10:45). Amid consolation and desolation, amid jubilation when evangelization is successful and the poor know the mysteries of the reign, and doubt, loneliness, and failure as these are expressed in Jesus' Galilean crisis or in the lamentations of Jeremiah, evangelizers take as their goal one thing alone: To be the servant of the good news in faithfulness and constancy. They take Paul's warning very seriously: "I am ruined if I do not preach [the gospel]!" (1 Cor. 9:16). Any temptation to the contrary they regard as their most dangerous temptation.

The paradox of the personal relationship between evangelizers and their good news is enunciated in another Pauline cry: "I could even wish to be separated from Christ for the sake of my brothers" (Rom. 9:3). Making allowances for some rhetorical exaggeration here, it is a perfect expression of the degree to which evangelization is service to others. Only those who appreciate this, only those who forget themselves and their own interests to the very limit of their capacity, receive the good news for themselves. Total, disinterested service may be astonishing. And well it might. But the astonishing thing is not the evangelization, but evangelization in the following of Jesus. Today's evangelizers accomplish the mission of Jesus in the manner of Jesus himself, and traverse the same historical course as he. But they also evangelize in the way that Jesus made God's reign, and God's salvation, genuinely present in our midst. The difference between Jesus and ourselves is that he was the first to run the race, and that he, and only he, ran it utterly alone. In this sense, Jesus' historical course can never be repeated. No, evangelizers will not be spared the difficulties encountered by Jesus. But they have a hope to live by: the hope that Jesus won for us on the cross. From the moment of the cross onward, service to the gospel has a joy, and an indestructible hope, of its own. It seems to me that the words of Karl Rahner, describing the gospel as a burden the Christian finds at once heavy and light, apply especially to the evangelizer. "Here is a burden," says Rahner, "which, when I take it up, bears down upon me with great weight. But the longer I live, the lighter it becomes." Surely this is the burden taken up by evangelizers the moment they start down the road traversed before them by Jesus himself.

Chapter 9

Conflict in the Church[55]

1. External and Internal Conflict

The basic, quintessential conflict waged by the church is its *external* conflict, its struggle with the world of sin that assaults it when it is faithful to the gospel. Thus it was from the beginning—from the apostolic age onward. Nor was it long before conflict became confrontation and persecution. The New Testament recognized the reality and the inevitability of such conflict and persecution (1 Thess. 3:2-4), and theologized on its inevitability in terms of the fate of Jesus (Matt. 10:24-25; John 15:18-20) and the prophets (Matt. 5:11-12). The theological premise of this conflict is that the good news of the gospel is a two-edged sword (Heb. 4:12), a sign of contradiction (Luke 2:34), a demand for a clear, unambiguous choice between the true God and idols (Matt. 6:24).

In the following pages, however, I propose to examine conflict *within* the church. My standpoint will be that of church unity. Seen from the viewpoint of unity, conflict represents, at first glance, a limitation, even an evil for the church. A deeper look, however, reveals that conflict may be a good thing. It may be the unpleasant, but necessary, historical path to a higher form of church unity, a oneness based on a greater truth and greater holiness. In this perspective the basic premise of internal church conflict is identical with that of its external conflict: the gospel. The two-edged sword divides even the church.

Historically, as is evident, there has always been conflict in the church. Its causes have been manifold. It began in Jesus' own time. Conflict arose between Jesus and his disciples (Mark 8:31-33), as well as among the disciples themselves (Luke 22:24-27). Conflict raged in the primitive church between Hellenistic and Palestinian Jews (Acts 6:1), between Peter and Jewish Christians (Acts 11:1-2), between Paul and the Christians of Corinth (1 Cor., 2 Cor.), and between Peter and Paul (Gal. 2:11), to recall but a few instances.

Throughout history, even since the essential constitution of the norm of church unity, the church has known conflict and confrontation, culminating at times not only in the separation of individuals from the church community (by schism, heresy, and so on) but in disunity within the church itself. Conflict has been generated, or latent conflict has surfaced, in our own day, especially since the time of the Second Vatican Council. We see tensions in the church, confrontations, protests against alleged violations of rights, prophetic denunciations. In Latin America we hear of "parallel magisteriums," a "popular church" distinguished from the official church, and so on. Without pausing to examine the justice of these allegations, let it be noted that tension has always prevailed among the various strata of church membership, but that today— and this is perhaps the most typical characteristic of current church conflict—it cuts across all these strata, dividing bishop from bishop, priest from priest, religious from religious, and lay persons among themselves.

Over and above the concrete issues of a given conflictual situation, the evaluation of conflict becomes another bone of contention. For some, conflict is essentially evil. Ultimately, we hear, conflict is rooted in sin: *Ubi peccatum, ibi multitudo*, where sin abounds, so does division. For others, conflict may be the outgrowth of fidelity to the gospel. Those who take this point of view are fond of reminding us how frequently the saints have led the church into conflict. As a general rule, only later history can show whether a given conflict has been boon or burden for the church and its unity. It can be either, and regardless of whether it originated in sin, sanctity, or a mixture of the two.

2. Diversity within the Church: Prerequisite for Conflict

As with any human society, diversity within the church can be a source of enrichment, or the occasion of conflict and division. Let us analyze the diversity within our church not simply as factual, but as willed and assumed by the church as an integral constituent of church.

1. The decision of the primitive church to reach out to gentiles was predicated on its basic decision to be a *universal* church, and to set no limitations to this universality. Here the church professed *in actu* the universal fatherhood of God and sovereignty of Christ. But it also introduced enormous geographical and historical diversity into the church: diversity of peoples, diversity of cultures, diversity of social classes, and so on. In order to open itself up in this way, the church had to accept the possibility that it would adopt a variety of historical forms. It will be a church of women and men, single and married, poor and rich, a church of the periphery, and a church of the centers of power.

Further, the decision of the church to structure itself *organically and hierarchically* introduced a diversity of functions, and the distinction between the hierarchy and the simple faithful—the distinction between the church *docens* (teaching) and the church *discens* (learning).

But over and above this intentionally generated variety in the church, there obviously is another diversity as well, one demanded by the very nature of God and creature: the *difference between God and the church.* An eternal distinction obtains between the church and the word of God, as the church itself has acknowledged and accepted in recurring moments of truth, as it confesses that it is merely the repository and servant of God's word, never its proprietor and sovereign.

God is greater than the church in its totality, and greater than each of its members or echelons. God's will may become present in the signs of the times, or through prophets, and therefore outside the church or inside it—and inside it, anywhere at all. Hence the possibility arises of a variety of theologal "places."

The courageous acceptance on the part of the church of a genuine universality—cultural, social, and theological—the church's emphatic refusal to degenerate into a closed, elitist sect, is another possible occasion of intramural conflict.

2. There is variety in the church. This variety is sought by the church and required of it. Without it the church would disappear, despite the perennial temptation of uniformism. This variety can be the occasion of enrichment. But it has de facto been the occasion of conflict and disunion as well, due to another fundamental decision on the part of the church—an obvious one, but worth noting—to accept a creaturely membership. Creatures, as we know, are open to the "more," but are structurally limited. They are capable of holiness, but capable of sin as well.

It is not easy for these limited members and echelons of the church to order and arrange their differences into a set of complementary, mutually enhancing elements. As sinners, they have always to face the temptation to absolutize their respective differences—or indeed the even graver temptation to define their respective identities in terms of opposition to the identity of others. As creatures, furthermore, members and strata of the church may well feel the need to maintain their diversity as a matter of responsibility to their consciences and to God. Finally, inasmuch as they seek holiness, members and official functionaries of the church are under an obligation to maintain their diversity in order to see the will of God accomplished and the church grow and develop accordingly.

In view of the variety obtaining among the members and official echelons of the church, it is understandable that conflict visits the church. And given the particular form of variety, which may be sinful or holy, conflict may be the expression of an evil or of a good. To be sure, it may sometimes be difficult to distinguish between the two. And in any event conflict will be painful.

3. Root and Manifestations of Conflict Today

The subjective roots of conflict are always present. They are here today. They must be taken into account, then, in any effort to analyze current conflict. But the basic root of conflict today is the newness willed by God for the church as expressed in Vatican II and Medellín.

1. Vatican II and Medellín represent an epochal newness, novelty, one that, according to Karl Rahner, can only be compared to the decision of the church to evangelize gentiles. Even prescinding from an analysis of its concrete content, the degree of the novelty confronting us bespeaks a historical convul-

sion of unprecedented proportions. A variety of reactions in the face of such an agitation is altogether understandable. There will be crass rejection, subtle rejection, tentative acceptance, and enthusiastic welcome. And of course any readiness for comprehension and implementation, in case of acceptance, will be scattered across a wide spectrum.

Vatican II and Medellín desired church unity. But their manner of addressing the church turns on certain basic elements antecedent to the element of unity. The unity of the church must be built in terms of the structuring of certain prior realities. Understandably, then, the novelty in question has been the occasion of grave conflicts. I deal here with the negative aspects of these conflicts, not with the immense benefits for the church of conflicts that bear, after all, on the very mission of the church and its internal constitution as people of God.

A. The identity of the church must be understood from a point of departure in its mission. But the mission of the church consists in a salvific service to the world, a service to be realized ever more concretely as a preferential service to the poor. We are dealing, then, with nothing less than a Copernican revolution. The church is here to serve, not to be served. It is here to proclaim and initiate the reign of God, not be that reign in its fullness. The church is here to offer God's love, but also to seek it—at times, beyond its own frontiers. This is radical novelty, and difficult to integrate into the totality of the church. Rahner thought it would take us a century. After all, we must be willing not only to wrestle with theoretical difficulties, and to build in the dark (after centuries of "knowing it all"), but to accept a conversion. At bottom, the church is being asked to accept the fact that the only way to gain its life will be to surrender it. Obviously this novelty will be the occasion of grave internal conflicts. Some will be disposed to that conversion, others not, and all in varying degrees.

Furthermore, the implementation of the mission of the church calls for an incarnation of the church in the real world. But the real world is host to enormous conflict and division: poverty and oppression, the life and death of human beings, and all manner of mutually exclusive and irreconcilable realities that cry out for a resolution. Were the church to react with a single stance vis-à-vis that world, there would be no formal problem of church division. Of course it might well wonder whether its stance were the correct one. What is actually taking place, however, is that, in the process of the entry of the church into a divided world, the world introduces itself into the church and divides it. Universal directives offer the church a sufficiently coherent perspective on what is to be done and how one is to accept incarnation in the world. Undeniably, however, the various members of the church—lay persons, priests, and bishops—react in different, even opposing, ways to the sin of the world. Some call for a pluralism that in practice would fall short of the minimal demands of the gravity of the situation and option for the poor. Others reject that world, abandoning it to its misery.

Here, doubtless, is the major source of intrachurch conflicts over the attitude of the church in a divided world. Nor may we expect these conflicts simply to disappear: their root is the option for the poor, and the option for the poor is willed by God. The will of God, as the documents of the church continue to insist, is that the church become incarnate in the world of sin, and in that world make an option.

Finally, when the church serves the world by making a real option for the poor, it enters into conflict with the powers of this world. Then the church suffers persecution and martyrdom. This in turn causes new conflict. On the one side are those who see in persecution and martyrdom a verification of the truth of the church, or in any case something that fidelity to the mission of the church prohibits it from fleeing. On the other side are those who subtly or heavy-handedly advise against the risks of persecution, either because they see persecution as weakening church structures deemed necessary, as they put it, "for a more efficacious church activity in the future," or simply out of an understandable, but unprofessed, fear of persecution and martyrdom. Now suddenly we hear of the dangers of "priests in politics," of mistaking the true nature of martyrdom, of the risk of succumbing to ideologies, and so on. These are all problems, to be sure, calling for theological and ecclesial treatment, but not infrequently they are more expressive of a fear of persecution than of generosity in the service of the church.

As long as this is the conflict of the world, and the world is what the church must serve, there will always be the real possibility of conflict in the church. It is God who assigns the church a mission that it can realize only in the midst of a conflict of irreconcilable alternatives. It must make an option: either service to the God of life and against the idols of death, or the contrary. The ultimate cause of conflict, then, is sin. But the sin in question is more than a mere subjective sinfulness on the part of church members that moves them to defend and impose their own points of view. The sin in question is the much more basic, objective sinfulness of a world of sin that makes its way into the church.

B. The fundamental conceptualization of the church community is that of the "people of God." Thus priority will be assigned to the whole over its parts (prescinding, at this point, from the theologal priority of the poor in the church). This conceptualization has occasioned a theoretical adjustment in our understanding of the relationships among members of the church. In practice, it has occasioned an atmosphere conducive to the recovery of certain elements of an authentic ecclesial mentality: the necessary complementarity of the various charism and functions; a joint quest for the will of God; the faith of a whole people, "from the bishop down to the last of the lay faithful" (*Lumen Gentium*, no. 12); the path of dialogue, communion, and participation as the proper manner of addressing and resolving tensions in a spirit of fellowship; the validity and necessity of public opinion in the church; and so on.

All of this has created a new, and desirable, atmosphere in the church. But it has also created serious difficulties. In this conception of the church the ultimate guarantee of the direction and unity of the church is the Spirit, although the hierarchy retains its functions of direction and unity. It is not easy to accustom oneself to this more pneumatological ecclesial style. It means the loss of a certain security. No longer may we allow ourselves to rely too much for our security on church mechanisms of the past. It means the acceptance of a certain ignorance before the Spirit of God, and the most radical need of faith in the astounding Spirit. It means growing accustomed to the genuine freedom of the Spirit, which forbids authoritarianism and uniformism, as well as the interpretation of liberty as license. It means the honest recognition that the theological superiority historically accorded to some over others in the church (to the hierarchy over the faithful, celibates over married persons, men over women, the churches of the center over those of the periphery, and so on) is the fruit not of the Spirit, but of determinate sociological conditions, not unacquainted with sin.

In this new church atmosphere, the very focus of conflict, along with the manner in which conflict is resolved, causes new internal conflicts. For some, all conflict is perilous and evil, working as it does to the detriment of the prestige and "effectiveness" of the church. For others, conflict is an expression of the sincerity of dialogue, and one of the ways, a historically necessary way, in which the church makes progress, Some, especially after long years of conflict, would invoke strong administrative measures to "clear up the difficulty." Others favor patiently continuing dialogue. Some assume that conflict will be easy to resolve in principle, for the church is a church of one God, one Lord, and one Spirit. Others see all the more difficulty here.

Although a single verbal confession of the faith, and to a lesser degree a single interpretation of the formulas of this confession, may be realized with relative facility, unity in the reality of the faith will be achieved only with great difficulty. Unity in God, in Christ, and in the Spirit is what we must strive for, and achieve in the end. But it will not be a point of departure.

2. Today, it is the stance taken toward Vatican II and Medellín (more concretely, toward the position taken by the church vis-à-vis the new problems of world and church alike)—the decision whether to accept their spirit or not— that continues to be at the real root of church conflict, although the conflict emerges concretely in a plurality of conflicts shot through with human limitation and sinfulness.

Some, although reluctant to assert it explicitly, simply reject Vatican II and Medellín accusing them of fomenting degenerate church practices. Others place too much stress on their novelty, extrapolating from their spirit for their own personal interests, and rightly citing the need for a historicization of faith and the church, but without sufficiently pondering the traditional, transcendent aspects of that faith and that church.

These exaggerations, on both sides of the issue, surely cause conflict. But they are to be ascribed to personal shortcomings. The most acute element of conflictuality is to be found in the difficulty of honestly maintaining the fundamental novelty of Vatican II and Medellín in face of the ever-present danger of involution that would put them both to a thousand kinds of death.

Signs of involution on the level of the relationship of the church with the world. (1) The church would be reduced to judging the sin of the world from without, passing judgment right and left without acknowledging its own historical contribution to the sin in question. (2) The church would cease its incarnation in the real world, appealing either to higher, spiritual missions, or to the alleged dangers of such an incarnation to the church as an institution, as if it feared thereby to be deprived of its ability to render a better and more enduring service to the world. (3) The church would flee an effective option for and partiality toward the poor, and the salvific mission and risks entailed in such an option and such partiality, appealing to the universal salvific will of God, and to an integral, nonreductionistic liberation, which of course is in itself legitimate. (4) The church would decide a priori which situations and which societies are more suitable for its mission and offer a more connatural place for the church, opting, for example, for Western society. (5) In sum, the church would cease to be, of its very essence, the servant of the world, and seek to return to the past.

Signs of involution on the level of the internal reality of the church. (1) Regression to a pyramidal conception of church that would assign priority to the legitimate hierarchical structure of the church while ignoring, in effect, the even more fundamental reality of the church as people of God, entailing the risk of hierarchical absolutism. (2) Neglect or relativization of the specificity of ecclesial groups and local churches—their contributions, not only cultural, but in the area of faith, hope, and charity as well, and on the level of pastoral, liturgical, and theological creativity. (3) Abandonment of the principle of ecclesial solidarity, the spirit of bearing one another's burdens, of giving and receiving, of mutual teaching and learning, among the various churches and the diverse strata of church structure. (4) Abandonment of dialogue or failure to appreciate its value for the common quest for truth, its value for explaining ambiguities of situation and interpretation constituting a bone of contention. (5) Creation of a climate of diffidence in which the mere honest posing of problems in the church would bring on suspicion or persecution.

Of course it is difficult to determine with all precision just when one is abiding by the spirit of Vatican II and Medellín. Hence the need for discernment, periodic evaluation, even casuistry. But it is not difficult to distinguish whether broad lines of activity are engaged in a spirit of fidelity or of involution. In this tension, I think, is the tenderest, most exposed root, structurally speaking, of conflict in the church.

4. Spirituality of Conflict

By spirituality of conflict I understand the particular Christian spirit in which conflict should be dealt with. More concretely, spirituality of conflict consists in certain attitudes that, although demanded by faith generally, are more evidently necessary in situations of concrete conflict.

1. Conflict is a reality in the church. Therefore the prime Christian exigency will be incarnation in that reality. This will require the basic honesty to recognize conflict as such and not attempt to gloss over it. One must have the honesty to recognize and recall that the church is a church at once holy and

sinful, the "chaste prostitute," and at the same time the courage to accept incarnation in what that situation holds of the disagreeable, the painful, and at times the unjust.

In the concrete, this incarnation may generate—and in any case it demands—certain key Christian attitudes. It demands a love for truth, which may entail having to "obey God rather than men" (see Acts 5:29). It demands faith in God alone, whose Spirit is the ultimate norm and guide of the church. Without the Spirit, we may never hope to achieve a satisfactory analysis and resolution of our conflicts. The utopian hope of church unity, though a hope never fully attainable in history, moves us to toil for the increase of unity.

2. Conflict is inevitable. And yet it must be resolved. This presupposes a spirituality that will seek first of all a correct grasp of the roots of a conflict, that will seek the truth rather than the defense of its own truth. For this the unity of the church must be founded more on truth than on administrative measures. As for the determination of the best way to confront conflict and resolve it, a spirituality of honest dialogue will be required—an openness to the argumentation of others, and a conviction that there can be truth in that argumentation. A spirituality of conflict, then, will stand opposed to the use of sheer force as the ultimate means of resolution of conflict, whether this be the force of social pressure, or even the strength of reason alone (when reason is invoked in the form of pressure rather than in the hope of bringing one's adversary to one's own view). Finally, a spirituality of conflict will call for holiness, as the ultimate, definitive means by which truth will triumph in the church—although, as the history of so many saints demonstrates, this resolution may be years in coming.

Besides attempting to resolve conflict, we ought to try to see that it bear fruit. This will call for a spirituality of creativity, and of endless striving for the complementarity of the seemingly opposed. This will call for an unflagging effort to render fruitful the structural tensions, especially between institution and charism, at the heart of the church. We ought to do all that lies within our power to achieve a blend of efficacy and truth, so that the former may be based more and more on the latter, and the latter may acquire more and more institutional substance and thus be more efficacious.

3. Of its very nature, conflict inclines us to see the limitation and sin in others. A spirituality of conflict, however, requires me to examine myself for my own limitation and sin. Thus the conflict becomes the occasion of my own conversion. To boot, in my self-examination I shall have a guarantee that I do not seek conflict in defense of my own truth, but in quest of the truth. And I may hope that the example of this humility on my part may give further stimulus to the process of conversion in my adversary.

Part of this genuine humility consists in a willingness to let history be the judge of which side has had the greater truth. I must be disposed, then, to submit to verification by the facts, and to change my opinion if need be. In any case I may not simply continue dogmatically to maintain an opinion that I have believed at one time to be the truth, regardless of the degree of good will with which I am convinced I have believed this.

In the last analysis, the ultimate criteria of verification are furnished by the Spirit of God in our own day. And these criteria can be set forth in terms of the gospel: the proclamation of the good news to the poor, the espousal of the defense of the poor, and the acceptance of their lot. In this way the church gradually appears more like unto Jesus in his life and in his death, enjoys more and more credibility with the poor, God's favorites, and little by little grows in holiness, whose ultimate verification is persecution and martyrdom for love.

4. Finally, like any created reality, the question of conflict is reducible to a question of love. Redundant as it may appear to speak of a "spirituality of love," it will be useful to speak of a spirituality of love-in-conflict. Within and without conflict, a member of the church should have great love for God and Jesus, for the poor, and for the reign of God. In virtue of this evangelical love, the Christian ought to be ready for conflict, and may not renounce love simply because it generates conflict.

Of its very nature, however, conflict poses the question of my love for my adversary, even for my enemy. That love does not mean that I do not face up to my adversary or enemy. It does, however, preclude the absolutization of my neighbor as my enemy. I may not close off from my adversary all prospect of a future. Ultimately I am forced back on the question of my love for the church. After all, the church is at the root of sins and scandals that cause conflict. A love-in-conflict for the church is far from anything like romanticism or triumphalism. But such a love ought to be there, however great the tensions. Out of love for the church, I shall have to denounce the shortcomings of that church when they are grave and scandalous. Moments may arrive when I shall have to say of the church, with William of Auvergne, bishop of Paris: "Who will not call this horrible specter Babylon and the desert, rather than the City of God?"

But out of love, too, and with joy, I rejoice when the gospel of Jesus has become present, in great and famous saints, or in numberless, unknown persons and groups, at special, heroic moments, or in the everyday practice of charity. At all events it is in the church that the gospel of Jesus continues to be proclaimed. This is where we have received it ourselves. It is likewise in the church that, amid and despite such great shortcomings and sins, each of us lives our own faith in reliance on the faith of others. We ought therefore to feel a fundamental gratitude to the church, and this gratitude (although love does not ask for reasons) can be the basic reason for loving the church. It is anything but superfluous, then, to state that conflicts in the church can emerge precisely from love for the church, and that these conflicts can be, and ought to be, waged with love.

Part Three

SOURCES
of
SPIRITUALITY

Chapter 10

Martyrdom of Maura, Ita,
Dorothy, and Jean[56]

I have stood by the bodies of Maura Clarke, Ita Ford, Dorothy Kazel, and Jean Donovan. Once more I felt what I have felt so often since the murder of Rutilio Grande, in 1977. Then, the martyrs had been a Jesuit priest—my friend and comrade—and two Aguilares campesinos. This time the martyrs were four American women missionaries: two Maryknoll sisters, an Ursuline sister, and a social worker from the diocese of Cleveland, Ohio. Between those two dates— March 12, 1977, and December 2, 1980—there has been martyrdom upon martyrdom—an endless procession of priests, seminarians, students, campesinos, teachers, workers, professionals, and intellectuals murdered for the faith in El Salvador.

Death has come to be the inseparable, dismal companion of our people. And yet, each time we gather to bid our martyrs farewell, the same feelings well up inside, surge to the surface again. First we are filled with indignation and grief, and we cry with the psalmist: "How long, O Lord? How long?" Then comes that feeling of determination and high resolve, and we pray with the psalmist: "Rejoice, Jerusalem. Your deliverance is at hand!"

This time, however, things are different. No one can conceal the new sensation we have. Not since the murder of Archbishop Romero (March 24, 1980) has there been a commotion like the one occasioned by this latest martyrdom. Neither within the country nor abroad has there been such a universal repudiation, such a feeling that God's patience must be exhausted and that this martyrdom is telling us that liberation is in the offing.

There were three hundred of us priests and sisters gathered in the chancery to hear Archbishop Rivera. His voice had a new and different ring, as he denounced the Security Forces of the Christian Democratic Junta. He tore the masks from their faces. He pointed the finger of shame and guilt. Once again the truth was crystal clear. And with the truth came courage, and the Christian resolve to keep on, shoulder to shoulder with a massacred people, even if it meant that the church must march once more to the cross.

It was the first Christian Easter all over again. The horror, the abandonment, the solitude of Jesus' cross had driven the disciples to their refuge in the
upper room. But Jesus' spirit was mightier than death, and it flung the doors
wide apart. The disciples emerged stronger than before, determined to preach
resurrection and life, determined to proclaim the good news of the reign of the
poor. The archbishop's residence had been transformed into a latter-day upper
room. The God of life was there. And that God was stronger than death,
stronger than oppression and repression, stronger than ourselves and our fears
and terrors. There, in the presence of four corpses, the Christian paradox came
to life. Yes, where sin and crime had abounded, life and grace abounded even
more.

This past Easter was a special celebration indeed. With this last murder the
reservoirs of iniquity have overspilled their limits. The dams of evil have burst.
We have seen everything in El Salvador. No barbarity would surprise us, we
thought. But this time we were overwhelmed. Once more we witnessed the
murder of the just, the innocent. But this time the murdered Christ was present
in the person of four women, four missionaries, four Americans. This time the
thick clouds of crime were pierced by a brand-new light.

The murdered Christ is here in the person of four *women*. In the drama of
the world, and the drama of the church, all the actors are human beings. We are
all of us equal, as well as different, in God's eyes. And yet, the two together—
equality and difference—are hard to come by in our history. Then suddenly,
with these four dead bodies, we see something of it. Men and women are
oppressed and repressed in El Salvador. Men and women have raised their
lamentation to God and begged God to hear the cries wrung from them by their
exploiters. Men and women have thrown in their lot with the struggle for
liberation. And men and women have fallen in that struggle. Here is the most
profound equality of all: equality in suffering and in hope.

By making themselves one with the archetypical Salvadoran woman, these
four sisters made themselves one with the whole Salvadoran people. Woman is
the procreator of humankind. But she is the creator of humanity—of human-
ness and humaneness—as well, in a specific manner all her own: in the delicacy
of her service, her limitless self-donation, her affective and effective contact
with the people, and that compassion of hers that simply will not rationalize the
suffering of the poor. Woman is the creator of a courage that will never
abandon the suffering, as these four sisters did not abandon their people when
they saw the danger. Woman is more defenseless physically. This fact points up
the singular barbarity of their murder. It shows that barbarity for what it is.
And it demonstrates the simplicity and gratuity of these women's self-sacrifice.

The murdered Christ is present here in the person of four *religious*. We hear a
great deal about the renewal of the religious life today, in El Salvador as
elsewhere. We hear a great deal about charisms and vows. And now these four
dead bodies show us what a life of consecration to God today is all about. They
make no fuss. They hold no grandiloquent harangues. They show us, simply,
the basic element of all religious charism: service. Religious women today have

been moving out more and more, reaching the most abandoned places, places where others cannot or will not go. They have drawn close to the poor, in genuineness and in truth, the poor of the slums, the poor of the working-class neighborhoods, and especially the poor campesinos. Consecration to God today means service and dedication to the poor.

Just as quietly, women religious have exercised their prophetic charism, which is part and parcel of the religious life. By their presence, by their activity, they have denounced the petrification of other echelons of the church. They have denounced the alienation of the hierarchy from Christian peoples. Above all, they have denounced the death-dealing sin that decimates the Salvadoran population. Therefore they have suffered the fate of the prophets, and shared the people's own lot: martyrdom. And so religious women, too, have their representatives among the martyrs of all social classes. They too have made an option for the poor, and therefore they too had to die.

The dead Christ is present among us in the person of four *Americans*. The United States is everywhere in El Salvador. We have U.S. businessmen and military experts. We have a U.S. embassy here to decide the fate of Salvadorans without consulting them. We have U.S. arms, we have U.S. helicopters to pursue and bombard the civilian population. But we have something else from the United States, too. We have American Christians, priests, and nuns. These have given us the best the United States has to offer: faith in Jesus instead of faith in the almighty dollar; love for persons instead of love for an imperialist plan; a thirst for justice instead of a lust for exploitation. With these four Americans, Christ, although he came from a far-off land, was no stranger in El Salvador. He was a Salvadoran, through and through.

In these four religious women, the churches of El Salvador and of the United States have become sister churches. After all, Christian action is helping others for their own sake, not blackmailing them with economic aid or babying them with paternalism. El Salvador gave these four sisters new eyes, and they beheld the crucified body of Christ in our people. El Salvador gave these four sisters new hands, and they healed Christ's wounds in the people of our land. The United States of America gave us four women who left their native land to give. And they gave all, in utter simplicity. They gave their very lives.

What has brought these two churches together? What has enabled the churches of El Salvador and the United States to contribute so much to the upbuilding of the world church? The poor. Service to the poor. How moved I was to hear from Peggy Healy, the Maryknoll sister who was a friend of the murdered sisters, that the high-ranking officials sent here by President Carter were to investigate not only the death of four American citizens, but the genocide of ten thousand Salvadorans.

Today as yesterday, there is no other Christian formula for building the church or unifying the various churches throughout the world: we must emerge from ourselves, we must devote ourselves to others—to the very poorest, to the oppressed, to the tortured, to the "disappeared," to the murdered. If this is the attitude with which Christians of the church of the United States come to their fellow Christians of the church of El Salvador, then the church of El Salvador can only say: "Welcome." And if that attitude leads Christians of the church of the United States down the path of martyrdom, we can only say: "Thank you, from the bottom of our hearts."

Christ lies dead here among us. He is Maura, Ita, Dorothy, and Jean. But he is risen, too, in these same four women, and he keeps the hope of liberation alive. The world is moved, and indignant, and so are we Christians. But to us Christians, this murder tells us something about God as well. We believe that salvation comes to us from Jesus. And perhaps this is the moment to take seriously something that theology has been telling us in its too spiritualistic and too academic way: salvation comes by way of a woman—Mary, the virgin of the cross and of the Magnificat. Salvation comes to us through all women and men who love truth more than lies, who are more eager to give than to receive, and whose love is that supreme love that gives life rather than keeping it for oneself. God is here today. Yes, their dead bodies fill us with sorrow and indignation. And yet, our last word must be: Thank you. In Maura, Ita, Dorothy, and Jean, God has visited El Salvador.

Chapter 11

The Hope of the Poor
in Latin America[57]

I propose to speak of the hope of the poor in Latin America in terms of the
hope cherished by the poor in countries like El Salvador and Guatemala. I do
this for the evident reason that these are the countries I know best. It seems to
me that direct knowledge is necessary if we are to speak of poverty, and
especially of hope, from a Christian viewpoint.

This methodological restriction will have its disadvantages in terms of the
outlook of those who are studying the theme of the hope of the poor in other
parts of the world. The poverty and the hope of which I speak are different
from poverty, and the hope of the poor, in Spain and in the rest of the First
World. Indeed, even in Latin America the Guatemalan and Salvadoran situations constitute new, extreme cases. But there will be advantages as well. True, I
shall be treating limited, particular situations. But these situations will be more
representative of those of the greater part of current humanity, the two-thirds
of the world population found in the Third World.

I propose to speak of the hope of the poor in Latin America from a
theological viewpoint, and I shall take my point of departure in the *fact* of this
poverty and this hope. I shall not, therefore, commence with philosophical,
biblical, or theological *concepts*, even though such concepts are surely necessary when we wish to present reality in a reflective way—and in the case of
theological reflection, necessary for arriving at some criterion of what poverty
and hope are in a Christian perspective. I shall begin with the reality, then,
which, if important in the case of poverty, lest the tragic reality of poverty be
obscured by the concept, is even more important in the case of hope, where we
are confronted with a genuine miracle, whose existence and content can by no
manner of means be argued a priori, but can be studied only a posteriori, in a
spirit of wonder and thanksgiving.

Accordingly, I should like to engage in some reflective "narrative theology."
Concrete reality, reality as it actually occurs, is the prerequisite for narrative
theology. But on a deeper level, concrete reality must also be a prerequisite for
theology as such. If we are really serious when we say that God continues self-

manifestation in ongoing, current reality, in reality as it occurs, then we must admit the essential dependence of theology on historical reality. I take it as understood, then, that, although words may have a relative importance, their importance cannot be decisive. What is decisive is that the reality of the poor—their hope and their poverty—and, in this hope and this poverty, the word of God, come to expression.

By way of one last introductory caution: I cannot pretend to present the hope of the poor in the form of sheer information—something you can "hear about," as if I were offering one more unit of cognition for the store of knowledge that we possess. Still less shall I be attempting to present that hope with a view to the verification of this or that philosophical or theological thesis, as if the poor and their hope were here to illustrate the theories of Bloch or Moltmann or the theology of liberation. The poor are not here to expand or confirm our knowledge. They are here as a reality, a reality struggling to make itself heard, a reality clamoring to be allowed to speak, a great cry to which justice is simply not done by a mere readiness to record it. The cry of the poor is a cry that calls for a "correspondence."

It seems very important to me that we grasp the reality of the poor as the struggle of a reality to make itself known. This is the profound meaning of what has occurred at this congress and others. Here persons from El Salvador, Guatemala, Nicaragua, Bolivia, and Peru ask, beg, at times on bended knee, to be given a little time to speak of the reality of their countries. You must not interpret this phenomenon, now become so commonplace, from a point of departure in the psychology of your visitors. Your analysis should begin with the reality of their countries. A grasp of the reality of urgency, by the compelling need to speak of what is transpiring there.

One can "correspond" to this crying reality, it seems to me, only by grasping it both as a challenge and as good news. Even in and of itself, this reality is the mediation of God's elementary act of calling human creatures to account. "Where is your brother . . . ? What have you done!" (Gen. 4:9,10). God never fails to demand a reckoning of the perpetrator of oppression, repression, and murder. But this same clamorous reality is also, paradoxically, good news—a message that can give us, all of us, a hope that we so often seek in vain in the illusion of a *total* human being, when we should be looking for it in the utopia of a *new* human being, the human being converted and gripped by poverty, but a human being of dignity, dedication, and hope as well. This may be the most difficult thing to grasp in Latin American reality: that the terrible reality of the Latin American poor is also precisely a matter of good news. After all, although the First World of course earnestly "wants things to get better," there can be grounds here for a basic skepticism that could close us off from the hope of "glad tidings" with respect to any truth at all, let alone the truth of God.

Here I shall offer a theological description of the hope of the poor, both as call or challenge, and as good news. Then I shall reflect on its theological and ecclesial roots.

1. Reality of the Poor in Latin America

Some years ago now—it was at the first of these congresses—Ignacio Ellacuría formulated an in-depth description of the poor in Latin America as a historical, socio-economic and dialectical, theological, and political reality. I need not repeat his exposition here. But I do feel that it would be in order to call attention to certain fundamental points, in order to reinforce the subsequent, incredible assertion that the poor in Latin America have hope.

1.1. *Defending the Bare Minimum: The Poor and Their Endangered Lives*

This congress has been dealing with poverty in Spain. From the first day onward, you have spoken of socio-economic poverty. This seems to me to be altogether "on target." Socio-economic poverty explains a good many of the phenomena that go with poverty. At the same time, however, we should bear in mind that socio-economic poverty, in its historical reality, is an analogous concept, one verging at times on the equivocal. Poverty in Latin America is a socio-economic reality. But it is such poverty, and causes such extreme misery, that what we have heard here about "pockets of poverty," or plant shutdowns and the like, provides precious little in the way of an introduction to the topic of the poor in Latin America.

To put it in systematic terms poverty in the First World is understood in terms of a relative distance from certain standards of human well-being that have been realized in the past but that are now seen less and less frequently. The frame of reference continues to be positive—a degree of well-being attained once upon a time and still attainable. In Latin America, however, the most obvious and spontaneous frame of reference for the concept of poverty is not something positive, but something negative in the extreme: death. In our countries, concrete poverty is misery verging on death. The poor are those whose greatest task is to try to survive. The poor are those whose concrete lives are threatened by socio-economic structures.

In theological and theologal terms, poverty in Latin America amounts to a real, concrete assault on God's creation. Among us, creation, the primary element in God's plan for the human race and each member of that race, not only is not being realized in its totality, or realized only with certain limitations, but is being out-and-out perverted. It is the raw status of creaturely being, the very existence of the vast majority of the human race, that is at stake.

Let me use a comparison to try to explain what I mean. In the First World today, there is a new anxiety, an honest, perfectly understandable one: the threat of nuclear holocaust. This is a fear with a new face. Old anxieties pale by comparison. Anxiety in the First World now is not about some particular area of life, but the very existence of the world. In theological terms, it is no longer merely some level of well-being or progress about which there is anxiety, but created being itself.

Now perhaps we have the wherewithal to understand poverty in the Third World. Poverty in the Third World is a threat analogous to the First World fear of nuclear annihilation. It constitutes the threat of annihilation, of nonexistence. In the Third World, the threat to creation has not been felt in terms of nuclear threat, nor is that threat imagined in terms of apocalyptic destruction. But the daily misery that puts thousands, millions of human beings to death, slowly and effectively, is just as real a holocaust, just as radical a vitiation of God's creation. This is why, in the Third World, we call poverty an expression and product of sin, constituting as it does the absolute negation of God's absolutely basic will for creatures: existence. And we call this sin "mortal" in a new, radically etymological, sense of the word: in our lands, the cancellation of the will of God is represented in *mors*, death, and this objective, literal death manifests sin in its most profound essence.

This is what we understand by poverty in Latin America. I do not have time here to analyze the structural causes of this poverty. From a theological point of view, these structures constitute idols—absolutized capitalism, the national security doctrine, and so on. Nor can I pause to contemplate the real, concrete faces of the poor, the victims these idols require for their sustenance. But perhaps I can say something that will help in an understanding of the supreme urgency that Christians and their churches take poverty absolutely seriously, and then really do something about it. In the sober, profound words of Archbishop Romero: "We must defend the minimum: God's maximal gift, life."

1.2. *Crucified for Being Poor*

"Crucified for being poor." This description of poverty, bitter in the extreme, has a bittersweet taste, as well, in El Salvador and Guatemala today. The poverty under consideration here is not a natural phenomenon of simple want or lack. It is a historical phenomenon of impoverishment. Poverty is dialectical, then: there is poverty because there is wealth, and there is wealth because there is poverty. This structural dialectic becomes highly conflictual when the poor become actively aware of their situation, and organize socially and politically to struggle against unjust structures. When this occurs, the structures of the gods of death turn against the poor once more, and repression is the rule. For the poor who wish to cease to be poor, the slow death that constitutes their historical lot turns violent. Poverty acquires a new relationship with death. Now the poor are murdered—for being poor.

It is important to underscore this elementary truth. The poor are currently the victims of repression because they are seen as dangerous. But the ultimate root of their threat is precisely that they are poor. Accordingly, the poor are either repressed for struggling, or repressed as a precaution, so that they will not struggle. My point is that repression inflicts new forms of death on the poor because they are poor.

The poor, then, are no longer merely those close to death—landless campesinos, babies who die of malnutrition because their mothers cannot nurse them, and so on. Now the poor are, besides and ultimately, the thirty-five thousand Salvadorans murdered mostly by the army and the security forces, the forty thousand Nicaraguans who died during the Sandinista revolution, and the thousands upon thousands of Guatemalans murdered since 1954. The poor are the peasants massacred at the Sumpul River, at El Mozote, at Panzós, the poor are the tortured, those who have been skinned alive, who have had acid poured over their faces, who have been lined up and decapitated one by one, those whose corpses turn up in clandestine cemeteries betrayed by circling buzzards, those found in their death agony in garbage wagons. These are the consummately poor. These are they whose slow death is consummated in violent murder.

If the first poverty—mere want—was a vitiation of creation, this second, violent, ultimate poverty is "the empire of hell," as Archbishop Romero called it, explaining that the slow oppression of unjust structures has "transformed a people into a dungeon and torture chamber." As we know, he was obliged to reinterpret his episcopal ministry in light of the stark fact of death: "My business is scooping up the outrages, the corpses, everything that persecution leaves in its wake." Pope John Paul II, in his letter of August 6, 1982, to the bishops of El Salvador, felt constrained to excoriate the "brutal repression" being perpetrated there in the name of the national security doctrine.

The analogy of poverty broadens tragically. In theological language, the poor become the suffering servant of Yahweh (2 Isaiah). As that suffering servant, the poor have sought to implant right and justice among the nations; and surely enough, their lot is death. Today's poor finish their "lives" faceless and dehumanized. We turn our eyes away; the very sight of them is too much to stomach. They are impoverished, annihilated, by the mighty—weighed down with this sin. How often they go to the slaughter, in massacre after massacre, like sheep without a voice raised in protest! And yes, they are accounted malefactors, subversives—godless individuals who ought to die stripped of any dignity, in one last, utter perversion of their reality, and they are thrown into ditches instead of being buried. The poor today are peoples crucified.

2. Reality of the Hope of the Poor in Latin America

Because the poverty described above is real, it is scandalously tragic. It calls us to account. It unsettles us. And yet these poor have hope. This is scandalous too, and we are simply taken aback. Despite all these years of oppression and repression, and despite the fact that a macrostructural view only threatens the Third World with greater poverty still, the poor of Latin America today are peoples filled with hope. Indeed, hope is one of the essential characteristics of their poverty, so that there is no understanding them apart from it.

Medellín affirmed the material identification of poverty and hope, and then went further, elevating both to the category of "signs of the times"—clear, unambiguous manifestations of the will of God in the present. Ignore these signs, and your search for the will of God elsewhere will be fruitless. Medellín declared this enormous misery to be the product of an injustice that cries to heaven, and called attention to the sigh of the victims for "total emancipation, liberation from all servitude, personal maturation, and collective integration"(Medellín, Intro., no. 4). It qualifies the sigh of longing torn from the breast of these victims as "an evident sign of the Spirit," and "the marrow of the image of God in human nature" (ibid.).

Puebla described poverty in similar terms, calling it the most devastating and humiliating scourge in Latin America, and adding—although with perhaps somewhat less vigor than Medellín—an allusion to the burning aspirations of the Latin American poor. The reference to them was indirect, but dramatic, in Puebla's celebrated text on the "cry of the poor." At Medellín, said Puebla, that cry may have seemed muted, but now it was "clear, growing, impetuous, and on occasions, threatening"(Puebla, no. 89).

These texts, to which so many Old and New Testament passages could be added, show that poverty, as well as hope, constitutes an absolute for our faith and our church. But they also show that, for a Christian, there is a correlation between poverty and hope—of such a nature that one might wonder whether the title of this address, "The Hope of the Poor," at least from the Christian viewpoint, might constitute a tautology. Could there be a Christian hope that were not the "hope of the poor"? Is Christian hope some manner of antecedent, self-constituted reality in which poor and rich, however differently, both share? Is the "hope of the poor" not precisely the prime analogate of Christian hope—something, therefore, in which others may share to the extent that they share the poverty of the poor? Conversely, can there be Christian poor who, precisely as Christian poor, do not have a determinate hope? Is hope not one of the crucial manifestations of the spirit with which the poor are called upon to live their poverty in a Christan manner, and thus realize the evangelical synthesis of a "spiritual poverty" that is neither ahistorical nor spiritualistic?

This is the perspective from which I propose to construct a brief outline of the hope of the poor: as a spirit arising out of a determinate locus—the poverty already described—and constituting the wherewithal to act and react to this poverty in a Christian manner. I shall attempt to describe this hope both in terms of its formal relationship with the future, and in terms of its effectiveness for the present where the poor are concerned.

2.1. *Sober, Moderate Hope: To Live!*

The hope of the poor focuses on a future grasped simultaneously as gift and promise, and as call to action. In formal terms, this hope consists in the coming-to-be-possible of something that for so long seemed impossible. In terms of its content, this hope consists in life. It is difficult to state in abstract terms what this "hope of life" means in its concrete context. Perhaps we may find some help in the words in which Third Isaiah describes God's utopia:

They shall live in the houses they build,
  and eat the fruit of the vineyards they plant;
They shall not build houses for others to live in,
  or plant for others to eat [Isa. 65:21–22].

This is the concrete hope of the poor. It does not consist in the desire to possess more material goods. But neither is it the purely subjective desire to be recognized in one's dignity as a person. Rather, it seems to me, the hope of the poor is a fundamental, foundational hope, antecedent to the familiar distinction between being and having—a distinction that can well be made by those whose "having" is already sufficient. The hope of the poor is demanded by sheer being, merely in order to be that being: hope for housing, hope for employment, a hope in which "having" is not yet oriented to consumerism and the tendency to oppression, but oriented simply to the constitution of "being with dignity." The hope of the poor is the novel conviction that it is possible to succeed in becoming a person—a genuine creature of God, and no longer the perennial victim of idols. The hope of the poor is the curious persuasion that it is possible to live in a society not composed exclusively of wolves and sheep. It is in this change in perspective, seemingly so simple, that the hope of the poor is expressed. For these poor, history is no longer sheer fatalism. History becomes promise, and the possibility of the realization of the promise.

This grasp of history as promise has led the poor to react. It has even led them to take spontaneous action. The discovery of history's potential has coincided with the discovery of their own potential, along with the need to set their hand to a task. The hope of the poor is active, then, issuing in the organization of the poor on the social, political, ecclesial, and, in extreme cases, even military level. The hope of the poor is a dialectical, conflictual hope. After all, the hope of the poor is a "hope against hope" (cf. Rom. 4:18)—hope against the present and hope against the past.

The hope of the First World is a hope for the recovery of a paradise just recently lost. The hope of the poor is a hope that struggles to tear out poverty and death by their very roots, against everything the guardians of the status quo can do to prevent it. It is a sober, moderate hope, despite euphoric moments. It is a persistent hope: it learns not to confuse the potential of history with an imminent Parousia. It is a hope in the liberation of the poor, a hope to be realized substantially by the poor themselves. It is all summed up, even if in a somewhat dramatic and manipulable way, in the ideal of "revolution," in the sense of putting hope of the poor into action.

2.2. *A New Spirit: "Hoping by Being"*

This new hope is already producing fruit—modestly at times, and ambiguous, limited fruit, surely, but fruit. "We were asleep. Then we woke up. We were dying. And we still are. But now we know why. And that's quite a bit

different," said a campesino. The "were" and the "now" imply a change, a
metanoia, in the poor—not necessarily in their situation of poverty, but surely
in the spirit in which they live it.

In the first place, the poor have recovered an awareness of their own dignity
and value here and now. They have made the grand discovery of the encounter
with themselves and one another as persons, as subjects of their history, and no
longer as things and objects constituting the heritage of others. To paraphrase
the Letter to the Romans, we might say that God has called the poor to
existence, and that those who formerly were not, now are (cf. Rom: 9:25, 26;
cf. Hos. 2:25). Therefore indeed the hope of the poor is a "hope by *acting*," as
we have heard in this congress. But it is also—yes, there is really something new
under the sun—it is also a hope by *being*. This really-to-be, in and by way of
being poor, is the pearl of great price, which, once discovered, transforms the
present.

In the second place, the poor now point to a new society, one with two basic
characteristics. The first, of course, is the transcendence of selfishness as the
principle of activity—the transcendence of nonsolidarity, nonfellowship, and
injustice as the shape and form of society. The second characteristic, more
paradoxical at first blush but no less important and needful, is the configuration of a society based on "living poorly" (although not miserably)—a society
that genuinely takes account of the scarcity of the resources at hand for the
benefit of all, but sees to their distribution itself rather than throwing them to
the winds of acquisition and consumerism. The realization of these ideals is
necessarily modest, but they are being realized, in refugee camps, grassroots
communities, and other groups where the sharing of goods is actually planned
out.

The poor live the paradox of the Sermon on the Mount: a life of beatitude in
difficult material conditions. The resolution of the paradox is a matter of living
the difficult material conditions in a particular spirit. Despite the mighty
sorrow, despite the weeping and the lamentation, rarely do the poor give
themselves over to sterile complaint. In fact, in the midst of the sorrow of the
poor, we frequently find a serene joy. There is even time for gaiety, for a
celebration of the triumphs of the people or of the everyday toils of life. There
is gaiety in liturgical celebrations, where occasions as disparate as the memorial
of the fallen and the celebration of a marriage or birth may coincide. There is
solidarity among the poor—a mutual giving and receiving of what one possesses, very frequently the very little that one possesses. There is time to pray
for the living and the dead, time to ask God in song that the day of liberation
may come. There is time to thank God for the solidarity of others, for the visits
and help of those who draw near the poor. There is even time to forgive the
murderers of one's family members.

My description is an idealized one, to be sure. But it is not idealistic. It is
based on reality. The important thing is the fact that the poor, filled with hope,
actually render their hope fruitful in the here and now. Without falling victim
either to the "hope" offered by false messianisms, or to the hopelessness of

resignation, the poor live with a new spirit today. And if there were no other evidence for this spirit and this hope, we should need only to recall the cruel, massive repression mounted to exterminate it. Resigned, hopeless poor are not murdered. Resigned, hopeless poor pose no threat. Our poor, however, are murdered—year after year, and by the thousands. They must be dangerous, then—year after year, and by the thousands. In fact, the reason why they are murdered by torture is that they must be terrorized. Doing away with their lives would not "do the job." It is their spirit that must be done away with. Poor who have spirit, poor who have joy, poor who can sing while they weep, poor who know how to bury their dead but also celebrate them as martyrs, represent an enormous danger for their oppressors. They are dangerous because, in the midst of their poverty, they keep their spirit alive.

2.3. *Trust in the God of the Poor*

It may seem strange that I have as yet made no mention of the transcendent hope of the poor. I have not situated the foregoing analysis in the familiar schema of historical hope versus transcendent hope. Why? To my understanding, the dichotomy is not particularly useful for a grasp of the novelty of the hope of the poor.

The great majority of the Latin American poor are Christians. Transcendent hope? They are filled with it. And they manifest it in all the eucharists they celebrate for their dead and their murdered. Transcendent hope is secure, then, at the level of religious ideology. The novelty, I believe, consists in the fact that this transcendent hope is now subsumed into a more primordial, more elementary hope—a "meta-hope," if you will—in which historical and transcendent hope constitute two distinct but complementary moments. For these poor, historical hope is genuine novelty, miracle, and scandal—the scandal of the Beatitudes. As such it is the mediation of transcendent hope as well, with its transcendent novelty and prodigiousness, and scandalous proclamation of the Beatitudes. Conversely, eschatological hope, as the radical formulation of hope, bestows radicality on this historical hope, emerging and materializing in the joy and freedom with which a life can be lived in conditions of such painful historical slavery.

What I have styled "meta-hope" has, I believe, become reality in virtue of the discovery by the poor of the true God as God of the poor. In this God they place their absolute trust. Such trust cannot exist without hope. And when that trust is placed genuinely in God, it has no intrinsic limits, and thus becomes, altogether naturally, a hope at once historical and transcendent.

3. Theologal Roots of the Hope of the Poor

The roots of the hope of the poor are complex and varied. Latin America has now seen the appearance of the subjective conditions necessary for the poor to be able to reflect seriously on their liberation. The objective conditions as well, for setting their hands to the task, have also partly materialized. Various ideologies, doubtless, have made their contributions to this state of affairs, with their scientific analyses and with the at least implicit faith that animates them. Accordingly, a thoroughgoing analysis of the hope of the poor will necessarily take into account not only the social, economic, and political reality of the poor, but their collective awareness as well. Nevertheless, I shall limit my present considerations to an examination of the religious roots of this hope—a hope that has been latent, or that has manifested itself more in the form of resignation, for centuries now, but that suddenly flashes forth with all its force for having been rendered more explicitly evangelical and Christian. At bottom, the hope of the poor is animated by a new relationship with and correspondence to God. Hence my characterization of that hope as theologal. Hence too the place of this hope as a moment in the threefold theologal relationship of faith, hope, and charity.

3.1. *Discovery of the Nearness of God: Incarnation*

The poor of Latin America have faith in God. And they have faith in God precisely as God of the poor. Nor is this faith one faith among many "faiths" or beliefs. Rather it is a faith signing the archetypal relationship between God and humankind: a relationship by way of the poor. In this faith, God's constitutive partiality toward the poor, toward all who are small, contemned, oppressed, and repressed—the divine partiality as abundantly evidenced in the exodus, in the prophets, and in Jesus—all comes to expression. As Puebla has expressed it so admirably, in virtue of the sheer fact that they are poor, before any other consideration, "God defends and loves them."

The poor know that they stand in this primordial correlation with God, and they grasp the primary element in the correlation. God has good news for them. God has made them a promise, a promise that will bring them to the full realization of their being. To be sure, they also grasp God's demands on them. But the first thing they seize is God's manner of relating to them by communicating to them a hope. That hope is the first thing aroused by God's revelation to them: God's passionate, reeling interest in them. The exodus tells them that God is bent on their deliverance. Jesus inaugurates his ministry with the proclamation of good tidings for the poor—the reign of God. Jesus' resurrection declares that there is justice, and therefore hope, for the crucified.

Faith and hope, therefore, are separable only in the order of its logic. Hope expresses the absolutely basic faith in God that is the faith of the poor. This faith-and-hope has become reality in the poor not only because, in their traditional piety, they have always believed in God, in an ultimate reality, but also because God has become credible for them—in the last analysis, because they have seen that this God is close to them. A vague, undifferentiated faith in God is not enough to generate hope. Not even the admission that God is mighty, or that God has made promises, will do this. Something else besides the generic or abstract attributes of the divinity is necessary in order to generate hope. This distinct element—which, furthermore, is the fundamental characteristic of the Christian God—is something the poor have discovered viscerally, and in reality itself: the nearness of God. God instills hope because God is credible, and God is credible because God is close to the poor.

This is where the figure of Jesus takes on a crucial importance. Jesus is God's Son, yes. But he is our brother, as well, and he is close to us. Of course Jesus is the power of God. The poor understand that. Of course Jesus is someone who makes serious demands of his followers in the hour of their venturing upon his discipleship. The poor understand all this. But, with a kind of anterior logic, they understand Jesus first of all as God's approach to the world of the poor. Hence the unique value of the incarnation. By a kind of connaturality, the poor grasp the core of the New Testament message: Jesus has taken flesh not just in any world, but in the world of the poor. And he has taken not just any flesh, but weak, fragile flesh. He has defended not just any cause, but the cause of the poor. And he has met with not just any fate, but with the fate of the poor. The poor grasp the message of the Letter to the Hebrews: Jesus did not shrink from calling the poor his sisters and brothers. And the reason they are able to comprehend this, at least at first, is that, in virtue of their own historical condition, they have no reason to be ashamed to call Jesus their brother.

The nearness of God that is Jesus, the genuine sharing of the reality and lot of the poor that is Jesus, is what makes God and God's promises credible. The greater the degree of God's nearness, the greater God's credibility, and the greater the hope of the poor. Therefore when the poor hear and understand that God delivers up the Son, and that God is crucified—something that to the mind of the nonpoor will always be either a scandal or a pure anthropomorphism—then, paradoxically, their hope becomes real.

The poor have no problems with God. The classic question of theodicy—the "problem of God," the atheism of protest—so reasonably posed by the nonpoor, is no problem at all for the poor (who in good logic ought of course to be the ones to pose it). The poor have no magician-type God, no *Lückenbüsser* (stopgap) God, and no killjoy God like the one Bonhoeffer was so rightly concerned to dissipate. The God the poor believe in is a God dwelling in their midst with good news. Their faith in God is not naive, although the external expressions of that faith may make it look as if it were. The faith of the poor is deeply dialectical: the poor believe in a liberator God, crucified. It is in virtue of the equilibrium they maintain between these two poles that the poor maintain the stubbornness of their faith.

3.2. *Love for God in a Martyrial Love for One's Brothers and Sisters*

By faith, the poor have come to an understanding that God is "for" them. By that same faith they have grasped as well that they are not "for" themselves. With hope, which is their response to God's good tidings for them, charity goes hand in hand, and charity is correspondence with God's very reality. The practice of charity on the part of the poor takes various forms—some more structural, as the various ways in which they struggle for liberation, and others more immediate, as for example attending to the manifold needs of the poor themselves.

The most important thing is that the practice of the poor includes a focus on the "other"—that great "other" constituted by the poor majorities and by the totality of the society for whose construction the struggle is waged. It is this reference to the other that renders their toil, their struggles, formally love. There is no denying that the concrete realization of this love is beset with errors and sins, and that when it is expressed in certain stages of the revolutionary struggle, many negative, historically inevitable, by-products appear. But it would be a serious mistake to fail to recognize that what has brought so many of the poor to the task and the struggle is love for their brothers and sisters. The hope that God has aroused in them has been transformed into active love for others.

Among the manifestations of this love—one that cannot be silenced—is the unbounded generosity in self-giving that has led, so very many times, to the surrender of the life of the lover. Surely this surrender calls for an interpretation in the light of social psychology as well. There must be a certain element of "desperation" here that would help to motivate someone to leap into the jaws of death. But the love manifested in the massive fact of thousands of martyrs cannot be overlooked. The theological explanation of these deaths is simple. Many of the poor are giving their lives that others may live. They are reproducing what Jesus did, and their lives become theologal. They are "corresponding" to the loving reality of God.

Martyrdom is the expression and product of love. Therefore it generates hope. Again we confront the great paradox: the cross generates hope. It does so not in virtue of its negative element, but in virtue of the fact that it is the maximal expression of love. So many are the martyrs of our lands today, such a "cloud of witnesses" (cf. Heb. 12:1) surrounds the poor, that it is no wonder their faith does not falter. But the martyrs also make it possible for the poor to maintain their hope. It is a "hope against hope," surely. But it is a genuine hope, arising, in the last analysis, from the unshakable conviction that nothing is more real, nothing more fruitful, than love.

When all is said and done, the hope of the poor arises from and is maintained in virtue of the holiness of the lives of the poor themselves. It arises out of their practice of love, a practice so abundantly attested to and verified by martyrdom. The hope of the poor, then, is not an autonomous dimension of the life of the poor, as if the poor could somehow lift themselves by their own bootstraps. True, the material conditions of their lives confront them with hope or despair as the only reasonable alternatives. But concretely, their hope springs from a faith in a God of the poor, and a practice of charity in behalf of these same poor.

Chapter 12

Christ Discovered in Latin America: Toward a New Spirituality [58]

I have been asked to speak about the Christ being discovered in Latin America today, and to relate this discovery to a new spirituality. Both points seem to me to be important. The first presupposes that something new has been discovered in Latin America about Christ, and that this new discovery, scandalous as it is, is good news for those who believe in Christ. Christ, after all, who makes such towering demands and raises such important questions, also provides the strength to meet the demands and willingness to face the questions. The second point calls for a connection between a cognition of Christ and spirituality—between a knowledge of Christ and the personal appropriation of this knowledge that constitutes the life of faith. And the request for an explanation of the relationship between the two points indicates, at least to me, that the need is felt to have theology—in this case, christology—at the service of a spirituality, and conversely, to have a spirituality that will constitute an integral part of the christology in question.

I shall attempt to respond to these two questions. My response will be brief, but will attempt to go to the heart of the matter. An understanding of my response will doubtless require an understanding of the situation of Latin America and its churches, for this reality has become a key hermeneutic principle of christology for us. At the same time, in view of the terms in which I have been asked to speak, I want my response to contain something of importance for the European churches. Accordingly, I shall focus on those particular aspects of this topic that, by reason of their potential for challenge and inspiration, are likely to make a contribution to the churches of Europe.

1. The Figure of Christ in Latin America

A reference to a "discovery of Christ" in Latin America or anywhere else obviously suggests that Christ has been hiding, or better, that we believers have hidden him. And indeed this is the case. Have we perhaps gradually identified him with our own traditions, immobilizing him and depriving him of his eternal novelty? Or have we the intuition that the genuine Christ is always a challenge, and in this sense also a threat, to concupiscent human beings? This is always the root problem. We human beings are ever engaged in the attempt to manufacture our own "christs." It is not easy for us to turn an honest ear to the truth of a Christ who not only goes beyond our expectations and interest, but often enough moves in just the opposite direction.

Very simply, the discovery of Christ in Latin America is the rediscovery of the Christ of the Gospels—the Christ who is none other than Jesus of Nazareth as the Gospels present him to us. To be sure, this rediscovery has its technical difficulties. Jesus as he is handed down to us is the Jesus of the gospel accounts, and these records are faith accounts. The historical Jesus of Nazareth will not always be easy to find. But what is at issue is precisely a return to Jesus of Nazareth, and it is precisely this that so many Latin American Christians have accomplished.

When this Jesus has been rediscovered, we shall do well to ask ourselves how this rediscovery has been possible. The answer, once more, will be of paramount importance. In Latin America the rediscovery of Jesus of Nazareth is to be credited not primarily to theological investigation, but to the fact that the gospel has been restored to its rightful place—to the place where it ought to be read, to the place where it becomes transparent for us all. And where is this place? The world of the poor. "Poor" and "gospel" are correlative terms. They have a mutual reference. In separation, the gospel tends to become pure text, easily transformed into mere doctrine, and gospel passages will be studied that support a "doctrine" of Christ. But when poor and gospel are joined, what the Gospels say of Christ points authentically to the Christ element present in Jesus, and the genuine Jesus appears both as the bearer of good news to the poor and that good news itself. The poor give us new eyes to read the Gospels and to understand the Jesus of the Gospels. Standing "where the poor live," we have the opportunity to overcome a certain evangelical illiteracy, an inability to read the gospel. The rediscovery of Christ has resulted from the rediscovery of the relationship between Jesus and the poor of our time, a relationship mediated by Jesus' message of good news for the poor of his time.

A great deal has been written about the Jesus of the Gospels. It will not be necessary for me to go over in detail all that Jesus was, said, did, and suffered. What I intend to do is present some formal characteristics of the manner in which Jesus is grasped in Latin America. I shall select and stress elements that have not been stressed elsewhere. It seems to me that these characteristics are of very special importance, inasmuch as they afford an insight into certain elements of the gospel content that, although discoverable in many other places, find in Latin America a distinct interpretation, one comporting an immense potential for the transformation of human lives.

1.1. The first characteristic of Christ as discovered in Latin America is that he is grasped as *a Jesus who is close at hand*. The nearness of God and Christ is of course a theological and christological category of the first magnitude. Indeed, the dogma of the incarnation is nothing more than a sanction of the absolute nearness of God to human beings, in Christ. But it is one thing to accept this dogma of the faith as a dogma, and something else to accept the proximity proposed in the doctrine as central to one's lived faith.

In Latin America Jesus is believed in as someone close to us because, first of all, he is seen as someone closely involved with his own real circumstances. I mean that Jesus is seen as someone "right up close" to the reality of his time, and to the major fact of that reality—the poor, oppressed majority, the masses shorn of dignity. Indeed Jesus is seen as one who erected that nearness into the criterion of all his activity. We can see that this closeness of his to the oppressive reality of his time is the fulcrum for his judgments upon that reality, the wellspring of the need he experienced to express that tragic phenomenon in words, denouncing and exposing both the reality itself and those responsible for it.

Jesus' nearness to reality is what caused him to wrench at the sight of his suffering compatriots. It is what caused him to step forward and take an active part in their defense. It is what caused him to enter into their conflicts. It is what occasioned his persecution and cruxifixion. "Nearness," then, is not an abstract category here. It is a historical (in-history) category. "Nearness" here is Jesus' abiding incarnation in his own world of oppression—his honest view of that world, and his reaction to it in the form of compassion for its oppressed members.

It is in virtue of this proximity of Jesus to his own world that he is felt by the poor of Latin America today to be someone who is close to themselves. The "problem" of hermeneutic distance is no problem at all for the poor of Latin America. To their mentality, very simply, a Christ who is essentially near his own world will be automatically understood, accepted, and loved by the poor of the world of today. And thereupon Jesus' nearness becomes the premise of certain conclusions bearing upon the reality of Christ.

First, the poor of today regard the process of Jesus' approach to the poor of his time as his becoming the brother of the poor—his way of genuinely sharing the reality of a humanity composed, in its vast majority, of the poor. And so the poor of today can call Jesus their brother. They will say further that he is their "elder" brother. But by far the main thing is that he is their brother, someone like themselves. They understand very well the assertion of the Letter to the Hebrews that Jesus was not ashamed to call human beings his brothers and sisters.

In the second place, the nearness of the Christ who is Jesus bestows on that Christ an intrinsic credibility. Be the problems of the "truth" of Christ what they may, his credibility is assured as far as the poor are concerned, for he maintained his nearness to them to the end. In this sense the cross of Jesus is seen as the paramount symbol of Jesus' approach to the poor, and hence the guarantee of his indisputable credibility.

Thirdly, Jesus and the gospel now become Latin American. In other words, no longer do the Latin American poor have the impression that the gospel has reached Latin America, and is maintained there, somehow "from without." Not that the poor of Latin America do not accept the universality of the church, or the fact that the church has ecclesial or theological centers at a geographical distance from Latin America. But now the gospel speaks to Latin Americans directly. It is not necessary for the gospel to come filtered through and interpreted by some other culture (although this also continues to happen and it has some positive values to it). In virtue of the experience of a "Jesus near," the poor of Latin America feel this Jesus to be one of them, and they feel they can and should read the gospel. And suddenly something of supreme importance materializes: the possibility and actuality of an authentically Latin American believer. Latin Americans need no longer "borrow" their evangelical identity. It is theirs as Latin Americans, today and tomorrow.

1.2. The second characteristic of Christ as he is grasped in Latin America is that he is *Jesus Liberator*. This is not a fad—something introduced by the theology of liberation, which repeats it "in season and out of season," *oportune et importune*. No, it is an essential of the rediscovery of the Jesus of the Gospels. Liberation—as redemption and salvation—is, once more, a fundamental theological category. What has happened in Latin America is that liberation has been historicized and biblicized—understood as a phenomenon of history and grasped from a starting point in its biblical rootage, and thus spontaneously grasped as good, just, and necessary for the poor of Latin America. If any biblical passage has had an impact on the heart of the poor, and penetrated that heart to its depths, it is the celebrated text of Luke 4:

> The Spirit of the Lord is upon me;
>   therefore, he has anointed me.
> He has sent me to bring glad tidings to the poor,
>   to proclaim liberty to captives,
> Recovery of sight to the blind
>   and release to prisoners,
> To announce a year of favor from the Lord
>   [vv. 18–19].

It is from this fundamental passage that the poor of Latin America draw their understanding of so many key biblical passages guaranteeing the hope that the reign of God is finally drawing near, that the poor are fortunate and blessed because that reign is theirs. The longing of the poor for liberation, recognized by Medellín to be both a sign of the presence of the Spirit and a "sign of the times," becomes an essential element for the understanding of Jesus. The poor see Jesus as the herald and agent of liberation—the one who puts the content of their hope into words and then devotes his life to the service of its realization.

It is not easy to systematize the vision of Jesus Liberator in the eyes of the poor. However, we can say this much: they see him as the one who liberates them to the very depths of their being. He delivers them from their anguish, their resignation, their individualism, their desperation. In Jesus they see the one who conveys to them an interior strength that transforms them, personally and collectively, from terrified human beings into men and women who are free—free to hope, to unite, to struggle. They are aware of Jesus' miracles of healing in the gospel repeated today as well. Touch Jesus and you are no longer sick. And Jesus tells them the reason why: *your* faith has saved you.

In Jesus the poor see the one who carries on a practice calculated to transform an oppressive society into a communion of sisters and brothers, a society of justice in conformity with the ideal of the reign of God. In Jesus the mediations of this practice were constituted first and foremost by his word. But his word was not only doctrine or proclamation. It was practice as well. Jesus' proscriptive and expository word is understood by the poor as social critique, both of a theocratic society organized around the temple, and of a society straightened by coercion issuing from Rome, the Pax Romana. Jesus' death on the cross, his execution as an alleged blasphemer and subversive, is seen in Latin America, where Latin Americans too are slaughtered as blasphemers and subversives, as the most authentic demonstration of Jesus' quest for the transformation of his society—of his love not only for the individual, poor or rich, but for the masses of the poor—as the demonstration, therefore, of a political, liberative love as well.

Finally, Jesus is seen as the agent of a profound liberation as to the very notion of God. The poor in Latin America—by virtue of their traditional religious culture, yes, but also by virtue of the clarification offered by their faith—pose the problem of God not in terms of the simple dilemma of God's existence or nonexistence, but in terms of the choice between the true God and idols. That is, they see God in Jesus. Jesus has shown them what the true God really is, and has unmasked the idols. The idols are genuine deities. They are real, and when they oppress the poor and put them to death, they justify it in the name of their divinity. For Jesus, the true God is the living God who wills the life of human beings, a life in abundance, eventually, but a life that begins with bread, a roof, health, and education. God is truly the God of the exodus, come down from heaven to deliver the people. God is really and truly the God of the prophets, and takes sides with those whom God calls "my people" against their oppressors. These are dynamic concepts, and they have been grasped by the poor of Latin America in their rediscovery of Jesus.

This is the Jesus understood and sought by the poor today: Jesus the liberator. Day by day he generates a dignity in the poor, and this dignity enables them to actualize their potential, and to organize themselves—organize themselves as a people, and as God's people. Day by day Jesus instills in the poor a spirit of commitment, generosity, struggle, and unbounded dedication to the cause of the people's liberation. Day by day Jesus generates in them the hope that liberation and the reign of God will come—despite the enormous obstacles in its way, and despite the fact that it comes neither when one desires it to come, nor with the desired utopian plenitude.

1.3. The third characteristic of Christ as discovered and grasped in Latin America is that he is *a Jesus present in current history*. The currency of Jesus' presence is, once more, a fundamental theological category, although it has been more a matter of spirituality and piety than of christology properly so called. In other words the current presence of Christ has not had a great deal of influence on our knowledge of Christ, and we have had to live with the risk of a reduction of the fonts of that knowledge to texts written in the past. We have felt that in order to know Christ one must basically return to the past. Surely it is important to know Christ from the past (in order not to entertain delusions about him, among other things). But a one-sided attention to the past fails to do full justice to the Jesus of the Gospels—of whom we read again and again in New Testament writings that he is still present among us.

In Latin America, the current presence of Christ is of paramount importance, both for Christians and for their theology. It is not of course a matter of inventing Christ in the present. But we do enter into contact with Christ in the present—a contact that bears scrutiny. Without delving into that scrutiny, I am saying as a minimum, that genuine knowledge of Christ is not to be had from the past alone, but from the present as well. The spirit of Christ, and the signs of the times in which Christ becomes present today, are of the greatest importance if we are to come to know him. To be sure, it is not a matter of just any spirit, but of Jesus' spirit. Our history must be the history of Jesus, in capsule.

Concretely, I regard the presence of Christ in Latin America today as the synthesis of a dialectic between finding him present and working to make him present. We find an essential part of his presence in what Archbishop Romero saw as the poor "filling up in their own flesh what is lacking in the sufferings of Christ" (cf. Col. 1:24)—and not simply in the fashion in which all Christians must do so, but in the suffering of an immense passion. The sufferings of the poor of this world are obviously beyond all bounds, and one of the ways in which the poor genuinely come to a knowledge of Christ is in their visceral grasp of the fact that in their own sufferings, they complement those of Christ. At the same time, they are co-responsible with Christ for his sovereignty in the present, and they know this too. They are the sowers, in ongoing history, of the signs of Christ risen: undying hope, disinterested service, freedom, and joy. This is how Latin American believers regard their identity as the body of Christ in today's history, and this is how they come to an ever more adequate knowledge of the head of that body.

It is in the spirit of this share of theirs in Christ's reality that they celebrate his presence in the eucharist, in the liturgy of the word, and in solidarity—the great solidarity of the Latin American Christian poor with an entire suffering people, and the "little solidarities" of their daily life in community. They accept the sacramental presence of Christ, and they assimilate it: it becomes utterly meaningful to them, in fidelity to Christ's injunction at the Last Supper, "Do this as a remembrance of me" (Luke 22:19). Here again they integrate a discovery of Christ's presence with their obligation to render him present in history. They integrate their fidelity in sharing this bread and drinking from the same cup with their calling to act in such a way that Christ may come to rule over current history.

Finally, Christ's presence in current history is taken seriously in terms of the parable of the last judgment in Matthew 25:40, where the king says: "As often as you did it for one of my least brothers, you did it for me." Christ continues his presence today in a unique manner in the poor. Not that the whole Christ is in the poor, or that Christ is found only in the poor; but Christ is in the poor, and in a unique way, and it is absolutely necessary that this be kept in mind. Christ is present today, hidden and faceless, in the pain of the poor. And he is present there salvifically, for everyone who draws near the poor in order to set them free.

These brief reflections on the current presence of Christ and the ways in which we may contact him, do not, of course, pretend to supplant the historical Jesus of Nazareth. My intent is to indicate that knowledge of Christ develops dialectically from our knowledge of him in the past and our grasp of him in the present. At least this is what is taking place in Latin America. Past and present constitute mutually clarifying poles, and the upshot of their dialectical interplay is an ever-increasing appreciation of who Jesus was and is.

1.4. A last characteristic of Christ in Latin America—a summary, in a way, of the first three—is that he is grasped as *a Jesus who is good news.* By this I mean that, although the Christ we discover is the Christ of the gospels, the discovery we make is no longer purely historical, in virtue of the fact that the gospels are sources of a knowledge of the history of Jesus, but systematic as well, inasmuch as "gospel" and "good news" are synonymous. This discovery ought to be the most obvious of all. But it has not been the most frequent. For manifold reasons, the gospel has been converted into material for the demonstration of a determinate theology or dogma. This is legitimate and necessary. But this is not the original purpose of the gospel. The original purpose of the gospel is to be good news. In certain circumstances the only use made of the gospel may be to defend it from those who impugn truth—that is, the only approach to the gospel may be apologetical. Apologetics is a necessary pastoral task when imposed by, for example, a secularized milieu. But it places the gospel "on the defensive," and deprives it of its original force as glad tidings.

What the poor in Latin America have rediscovered—if I may be permitted the redundancy—is the gospel's "evangelical outlook." Jesus is the bringer of a gospel, of good tidings. These good tidings are constituted by his words and deeds. Who is Jesus? Jesus is the one who says, "The reign of God is at hand" (Matt. 3:2), and "Blest are you poor, the reign of God is yours" (Luke 6:20). Jesus is the one who, when he teaches us to pray, begins with another marvelous piece of news: that we have a God who is a Father, and the Father of us all— "This is how you are to pray: Our Father. . . . " (Matt. 6:9). Jesus is the one who tells the aggrieved human being, "Do not be afraid!" (Matt. 14:27; Mark 6:50); "Go in peace"(Mark 5:34; Luke 7:50; 8:48). Jesus is the one who tells the anguished sinner that God's greatest joy is for sinners to approach God in confidence as a Father.

The poor of Latin America look on this Jesus, this herald of glad tidings, as good news in person—good news himself for the poor of today. Jesus is God's magnificent gift to this world. Now the poor can cry out, with all their hearts, in the words of Paul: "The grace of God has appeared" (Titus 2:11); or in those of John: "Of his fullness we have all had a share" (John 1:16). Or they can develop their own formulations: "Jesus is liberator." The important thing in all these affirmations is that Jesus is himself regarded as good news, glad tidings.

When you have a Christ like that, you have joy. No other outcome is possible. Latin American Christians, if anyone, know how much Jesus can ask. Thousands of their fellow campesinos, workers, students, men and women religious, have shed their blood for this gospel and this Christ on our continent. But Latin American Christians also know the joy and gratitude of the encounter with Jesus. The gospel is a burden, then, a burden both heavy and light. But it is the pearl of great price too, the treasure hidden in a field, and finders are willing to sell all that they possess in order to buy that field.

2. Toward a New Spirituality

The Christ discovered in Latin America is also a "lived" Christ: a Christ of living experience, a Christ known in the personal experience of the following of Jesus. This can of course be regarded as the basic element of any spirituality, which, at bottom, is simply and solely the exercise of the spirit required for, and then acquired in, the following of Jesus. The effort to reproduce such and such a trait of Jesus, such and such an attitude, is not a fractionated, "sideline" spirituality. It is a basic spirituality, for any Christian spirituality must enable us to confront our current history as Jesus confronted his. It is a theologal spirituality, for it sets us in confrontation with the ultimacy of history and therefore with the ultimate that is God. Now we can confront life and death, now we can struggle for the one and against the other, now we are ready to give of our own life, and even give our own life, for the lives of others. It is a christocentric spirituality, for it does all things in the spirit of Jesus, with the mind-set and in the manner of Jesus. Spirituality, then, is the exercise of the spirit that makes its subjects "share the image of [God's] Son," as Paul says (Rom. 8:29).

2.1. What are the concrete traits of this spirituality? We may deduce them, to a large extent, from what has already been said about Jesus. In its origin, this spirituality is the act of the spirit in coming into confrontation with the truth of this world—in discovering, stating, and denouncing it as monstrous sin, and in doing all this from a position among the poor. As it develops, this spirituality engenders a mighty sentiment of mercy toward the poor of this world, a mercy emerging in an efficacious option for, defense of, and struggle in company with these poor for their liberation, so that we ourselves are converted into good news for them—and then fidelity and steadfastness in that original option of ours when the consequences are hard and costly. We enter into the conflicts that that option inevitably generates, and then we refuse to withdraw. We are ready to suffer every manner of persecution that the powers of this world can unleash against the poor and against those who enter into solidarity with them. And we remain faithful to the end, even when the option for the poor demands renunciation not only of oneself, but of one's very life.

Thus the kernel of this spirituality consists in an orientation of one's own life not toward oneself and in behalf of oneself, one's group, or one's church, but toward the poor of this world, just as they themselves genuinely shift from a concentration upon their personal or group ego. This is the spirituality necessary for consistent service to the reign of God, the object of our service. It is a most effective mediation of the demand of Christian love to serve and not be served. It is the option of living one's life in order that the poor of this world may be done justice, in order that life may come into being, and in order that the human order of things, overwhelmingly the producer of death, slow or violent, may produce life instead.

At these levels, spirituality manifests very little sophistication. It does not appear to have led us, thus far, to what has traditionally been regarded as the finality of spirituality: holiness. But it is the absolutely necessary first step for a genuinely human life, Christian life, and holy life. It is this basic spirituality that bestows on us a kinship with the God of life, liberation, and justice who wills the life of the people. It consists in a recognition of the fact that in the life of the poor of this world there is an element of the Ultimate and the Holy, in whose service we ourselves attain, in ever-increasing measure, that which is ultimate for ourselves as well—that apart from which we shall seek in vain the ultimacy of our own life, and our own hope.

2.2. This fundamental alignment with the life of the poor must go hand in hand with a particular spirit: a spirit like the spirit of Jesus. The option for the poor can be exercised in various ways. But a Christian must reproduce the values, the attitudes—the virtues, if you will—that are realized and demanded by Jesus. Accordingly, this spirituality will consist in a reproduction of Jesus' basic attitude in the service and realization of the reign of God: his interior approach to his service of the reign. We see this in programmatic form in so many of Jesus' demands. We see it in the Sermon on the Mount, and especially in the Beatitudes. Here we are told what kind of a person a follower of Jesus, a person who struggles for justice, should be. Spirituality calls for impoverishment, willingness to empty oneself, renunciation. Spirituality calls for acceptance of the fact that there is in weakness a kind of strength that is acquired in no other way, and that this impoverishment is the only antidote for the concupiscence inherent in the exercise of power.

Spirituality calls for a pure heart, and the profound chastity to recognize things for what they really are, rather than manipulating them for one's own benefit—rather than yielding to an inevitably dehumanizing dogmatism bent on forcing reality into the mold of one's own ideas and interests. It calls for a quest for peace in the midst of conflict, even armed conflict, lest violence, so tragically necessary and legitimate on occasion, be transformed into an end in itself (indeed, into a salvific mystique). It calls for a quest for reconciliation and forgiveness—not only in the form of purely psychological attitudes, at times so difficult to come by (although we have moving examples of their attainment), but in the form of a refusal to close off the future from our adversary forever, and a recognition that even in this adversary there may be something positive. It calls for an appreciation of gratuity—an attitude so difficult to conceptualize—a gratuity that, on the one hand, enables us to see ourselves as "unprofitable servants," and on the other imbues our practice with the vigor of gratitude. It is only an awareness of gratuity that will heal the inherent hubris of any human undertaking, however good and just. This spirituality calls for an attitude of joy in the midst of sorrow, a conviction that we can always turn to God as our Father in prayer, in the eucharist, in celebrations of everyday life, in celebrations of solidarity, or of partial triumphs.

Finally, this spirituality calls for perseverance in the spirit of a utopian hope: it calls for an act of hope that the future will be salvific. It is a spirit that drives us unswervingly toward the attainment of the unattainable, and the reconciliation of history's seemingly irreconcilables: struggle and peace, justice and forgiveness, new human beings and new structures.

2.3. Clearly, the spirituality that I have been sketching is christological. It arises in function of the Christ being rediscovered in Latin America. But it is also theologal. In other words its realization is a path to God, to the encounter with God in history. I term this spirituality "theologal" because it focuses precisely on the ultimate realities that can mediate (or block) that encounter. And I hold that their ultimacy is very radical: although they formally comprise the ultimacy to be confronted by every human being of every time and place, nevertheless, historically, they posit the ultimates of life and death in all their naked truth, and demand a response. Hence this spirituality, though specifically Christian in virtue of being christological, is basically human as well. It draws the Christian back to the basic realities and exigencies that confront human life—every human life. It forces the Christian to choose between co-responsibility and irresponsibility for a suffering humanity whose hope for life, however often it be stifled, always rises again.

The spirituality here described poses to the human spirit the questions that rise from reality itself, the questions of hope, love, and faith. Does hope really have meaning for humanity? Is it true that love is our most profound human act? Is it true that the bottommost stratum of reality is composed of good and truth? I maintain that the spirituality here described, precisely in virtue of the fact that it places the human being in contact with the reality and practice in which the physical life and death of other human beings are at stake, makes these questions inevitable and radical. Answers may vary, and the answer to the theologal problem, the problem of God, will vary accordingly.

Faced with the reality upon which this spirituality turns, it will not be unreasonable for a person to suspend judgment as to whether reality is basically good or evil, or indeed even to deny the ultimate goodness of reality. Historical justification for such an attitude is scarcely lacking. And yet some respond that reality is basically good, with or without an explicit reference to God. Even believers who practice the spirituality of liberation may not be able to put into words why they should mention God. Perhaps they will be able to say only, in the fashion of negative theology, that love is better than selfishness—that in giving their lives for love they have accomplished the most human of acts, that there is something in the deepest reaches of reality that retains the abiding promise of justice, truth, and peace, a promise that thrusts one always to the fore. In point of fact, believers do mention God, call God Father—and then let God be God, God the unfathomable mystery. The important thing is that they do so by way of an implementation of the spirituality described.

In strict logic, this spirituality should pose the greatest impediment to the acceptance of God in the presence of heinous injustice. And yet de facto it is precisely this spirituality that makes it possible to call God Jesus, and thus to experience one's own life as a journey "with God, toward God." This is the experience of the Latin American poor, and there is no point in going beyond the fact to seek an explanation. But the fact constitutes a demonstration of a further fact: that the spirituality emerging from a discipleship of Jesus in service to the reign of God for the benefit of the poor is a spirituality in the deepest sense of the word. It engages all the energies of the spirit. It responds to the gravest challenges of that spirit, and sends its greatest hopes soaring. Yes, says this spirituality to the spirit, the accomplishment of these hopes is possible.

In conclusion, let me add, if only in passing, that this theologal aspect of a spirituality of the following of Jesus is the real, concrete way in which the transcendence of Christ is accepted *in actu* by Christians of Latin America. These individuals and groups show that they believe in Jesus as the Christ not only by formulating and professing his divinity—which, by the way, they do without hesitation—but by ascribing ultimacy to discipleship of that Jesus, which is automatically to ascribe ultimacy to Jesus himself. Then they "move out" from Jesus to confront the ultimacy of their own lives and of history.

3. Application to the Churches of Europe

In the last analysis, all that I have said here can only be a challenge, as well as good news, both for those of us who are in Latin America and for European Christians. Let us face the fact: this discovery of Christ and this spirituality are real. Europeans and others often ask us what they should do—how they might develop base communities, the option for the poor, or the theology of liberation. There are no recipes. Least of all do we have any recipes, we Latin Americans, who have striven to learn to be Christians precisely within the concrete reality of Latin America, without attempting any universalizations, much less a new Christian or theological colonialism. The churches of the Third World have suffered a great deal from Christian and theological colonialisms. It is not a matter, then, of proposing, and certainly not of imposing, recipes.

However, something can be suggested to others from a point of departure in de facto experience. And so, rather than attempting to offer a finished product, either ecclesial or theological, I shall merely indicate the root of all such constructs, the "place" where the gospel will demonstrate its own creativity and flourish like a tree in a well-planned arboretum. That "place," as I have shown above, is among the poor of this world. In maintaining this correlation between the gospel and the poor, we discover Christ, we grow in spirituality, and we maintain the mystery of God as salvific. And we foster the growth of a church of the poor—something I have not discussed. The European quest for this correlation between gospel and poor is a European affair; the African quest, an African affair; and so on. I should only like to offer some suggestions that may be useful in that quest as undertaken by Europeans.

Viewing the European church as a totality, with idiosyncrasies I shall be mentioning later, the first thing that strikes me is that there are certain suppositions here, historically understandable but theologically indefensible, that must be done away with. We must put an end to the theological balderdash that Europe, having constituted the geographical center of the diffusion of the gospel, therefore continues to constitute the theological center of the faith, the church, and theology. On the historical level, we must be rid of the supposition that the European is the universal human being *simpliciter*—a proposition empirically false and theologically banal, if what is intended by it is that the faith is to be understood from a point of departure in Europeans and for Europeans, and only thereafter, in ever-broader concentric circles, for all other human beings. On the theological level, we must do away with the assumption that Europe will continue to be—if I may be allowed to speak very frankly— the privileged locus of God on the face of the earth, the locus from which God moves out to all other parts of the world, the place to stand if we would reflect on God for the whole human race, in such a way that even the European problem of God becomes the universal problem of God. As long as it is supposed, consciously or unconsciously, that European churches and European theology have a monopoly on God, little progress will be made.

And so I propose to the European churches an act of humility. I suggest that they accept that they are not purely and simply the center of the faith. Indeed, I suggest that they accept a certain silence of God in societies that focus on one-sided progress, abundance, and consumerism. I ask them not to force God's word where it is not to be heard, or presume that that word has become the perennial legacy of the European churches. This humility is a moment in the process of impoverishment. It is necessary, and it will be fruitful.

It also seems important to me to be rid of an insufficiently pluralistic attitude of acceptance (or "toleration") on the part of the European churches with respect to what is occurring in the church of Latin America—an attitude unaccompanied by a genuine openness to listen to what is transpiring there, and so to learn of its great value. As I have said, the ecclesial universality of uniformity is gone forever. Let the European churches open their ears, their heart, and their mind to other voices, other experiences, other theologies, other committed engagements, other martyrdoms, just as the Latin American churches must be open to receive whatever of the evangelical that Europe has to offer.

It seems to me that such a humility and openness will constitute indispensable conditions, in the current situation of the churches in Europe, for a rediscovery of the locus of the gospel. The positive upshot of these attitudes, where and how that locus is to be found, is a European affair, as I have said. But I do seem to see a positive upshot in the European situation as I grasp it. Europe is host to many Christian groups, groups that number priests and bishops among their members, that are making an attempt to uncover the fundamental European sin—a tragic task, but a necessary one, because it points to the world of the poor. What are the basic local and international dimensions of that sin? In asking themselves these questions, these Christian groups open themselves up to the universality of sin, and thus to the universality of the world of the poor. Then, from a grasp of this sin, they strive for their own profound conversion—a conversion that, on the one hand, supposes their genuine integration into the human world of today in virtue of a sense of co-responsibility, as human beings, for the sufferings and hopes of the impoverished majorities of this world. On the other hand, it offers a new outlook, the "perspective of the poor," which is an outlook calculated to open our eyes to the gospel.

Many Christian groups, too, resist the unquestioned ideal of a consumer society of abundance. They practice austerity as their personal protest against an unjust society and in favor of a new "civilization of poverty" (Ignacio Ellacuría). The austerity, the poverty, they practice is not a poverty of destitution, but the poverty of a communion of sisters and brothers. Such a communion cannot subsist in a society of rich and poor. Many Christian groups make a commitment to the crucial struggles of our time, the struggle for peace and the struggle for justice, in their own lands and in those of the Third World. Many European Christians develop an active solidarity with the peoples and churches of Latin America, lending their moral, economic, political, and Christian assistance, in an openness to receive what is offered them by those other peoples and churches. Such groups, organized in communities or parishes, in committees for solidarity, or in discussion groups, demonstrate admirable creativity, in liturgy and theology, in pastoral activity, and in the question of solidarity. For me, such creativity is a clear sign that the gospel has found its true place in Europe too. These groups, too, run risks, and sometimes suffer persecution of various kinds. When this happens, then these groups have encountered the gospel.

The European church no longer overwhelms the rest of the Christian world with its sheer mass, with its enormous material and intellectual resources. But it is or can be present throughout the world in a more humble and evangelical way. Many years ago, Karl Rahner described the church of the future as a "church of the diaspora." His prophecy has come true. The church will not continue to be accepted without question. Its faith will no longer be automatically received regardless of the social milieu in which it would like to be received. Rahner's conclusion was that the future of the church lies in groups of Christians possessed of a conscious, self-critical, faith. I should only like to add that "diaspora" may suggest small, withdrawn groups. But no, the European groups I have in mind are leaven. They are a phenomenon of hope.

What "the future of the European church" will be—the question asked by this round-table group—I cannot say. But from the vantage point in Latin America, I believe that the European church, as any other church, will "have a future" to the precise extent of its genuine integration into humanity as it is found today, a humanity composed of millions of suffering poor who long to live, who maintain their faith and their hope, who never leave off striving for their liberation, who, in the language of the gospel, hope and toil for the reign of God.

One sometimes hears that Latin American churches have a great advantage over European churches in that the reality of humanity appears more clearly among us, so that it is easier for us to insert ourselves into that reality. That would be a tragic advantage, surely, but as a matter of fact it is an advantage available to everyone. Each of us, Latin American or not, can accept co-responsibility for the future of this humankind composed of the poor. For anyone doing so, life recovers its meaning, indeed its joy. Now the gospel is good news again. Now the gospel is Jesus of Nazareth again. Now the life of believers becomes the following of Jesus in the world of today, nor does this discipleship any longer go hand in hand with the old ecclesiastical triumphalism: no, it is sober now, with a sobriety founded on truth. Life becomes a journey, in a profound sense; no longer do we Christians seem to have the answer to all questions. No, objectively, we now know the direction in which we are moving—toward the reign of God; and we place ourselves in the service of life.

The future of the church depends on our decision to abide by the injunction of the prophet Micah: "to do right and to love goodness, and to walk humbly with your God" (6:8), to stride to the fore without triumphalism, but also without an inferiority complex. Building the reign of God in the footsteps of Jesus, we move toward that God. In so doing, believers and their churches take up their human co-responsibility, and live the joy of their faith.

NOTES

1. This text, which I have since reworked in part, was first published as "La vida espiritual en las comunidades religiosas," *Diakonía* (Managua), 17 (April 1981), pp. 9–22. At a later date it was presented to a meeting of superiors of the Central American province of the Jesuits. Although it was written with men and women religious primarily in mind, I think it can serve as an introduction to the problematic of spirituality for all Christians who are committed to liberation.

2. This chapter was first published in *Christus* (Mexico City) (Dec. 1979–Jan. 1980), pp. 59–63. I have since reworked it in part.

3. First published in *Sal Terrae* (Santander), 72/2 (Feb. 1984), pp. 139–62.

4. First published in *Revista Latinoamericana de Teología* (San Salvador), 2 (May–Aug. 1984), pp. 195–224.

5. "Teología y espiritualidad," *Selecciones de Teología*, 13 (1974), p. 142.

6. "Significado actual de Santo Tomás de Aquino," in *Teología y mundo contemporáneo*, A. Vargas-Machuca, ed. (Madrid: Cristiandad, 1975), p. 36.

7. The subtitle *(Zur Mystik und Politik der Nachfolge)* of his work *Zeit der Orden?* (Freiburg: Herder, 1977).

8. Gustavo Gutiérrez, *Beber en su propio pozo* (Lima, Peru: CEP, 1971), p. 254.

9. See the works of Segundo Galilea, Arturo Paoli, and E. Pironio, at the beginnings of liberation theology.

10. Gustavo Gutiérrez, *A Theology of Liberation* (Maryknoll, N.Y.: Orbis, 1973), p. 203.

11. Ibid., pp. 204, 205.

12. The periodicals were *Diálogo* (Guatemala City), *Christus* (Mexico City), *Mensaje* (Santiago de Chile), *Revista Eclesiástica Brasiliera* (Petrópolis, Brazil), *Páginas* (Lima), *Estudios Centroamericanos* (San Salvador), and *SIC* (Caracas).

13. *Christus*, 529/530 (1979–1980), p. 56.

14. San José, Costa Rica: Eduardo Bonín, 1982.

15. Ibid., p. 11.

16. Ibid., p. 13

17. In his "Liberación y espiritualidad en América Latina," *Páginas* (July 1984), J. Espeja presents liberation theology in terms of spirituality, citing 223 texts of Latin American theologians. In *Vida y reflexión. Aportes de la teología de la liberación al pensamiento teológico actual* (Lima, 1983), G. Mugica treats of spirituality in terms of methodology: "El método teológico: una cuestión de espiritualidad" (pp. 21–43). He cites authors from various continents who explicitly link liberation theology with spirituality: "Exigencias de una nueva espiritualidad" (pp. 163–248). The international review *Concilium* has frequently called on Latin American theologians for articles on spirituality, martyrdom, holiness, and the like, as in the monothematic issue of March 1983. The collective work, *Conceptos fundamentales de la pastoral* (Madrid, 1983),

looked to Latin American Ignacio Ellacuría for a contribution on spirituality.

18. Ellacuría, *Conceptos fundamentales*, p. 302.

19. Gustavo Gutiérrez, "Beber en su propio pozo," *SIC* (March 1984), p. 122.

20. It would take too much time and space to compare the writings of Gutiérrez with those of all other Latin American theologians. I will mention only some writings that are more representative in the field of spirituality. (I will not cite other writings—on liberation, the poor, God, the church of the poor, Christ the liberator, and so forth— although they really express and have prepared the ground for the explicitation of spirituality, because the complete list would probably be interminable.) Among others, the following can be cited: Frei Betto, "Oração na ação, Contribuição à espiritualidade da libertação," *Suplement CEI*, 18 (Rio de Janeiro, Jan. 1977); idem, "La oración una exigencia (también) política, *Espiritualidad y liberación en América Latina*," pp. 15–26; Leonardo Boff, *La experiencia de Dios* (Bogotá, 1977); idem, "Contemplativus in liberatione," *Christus*, 529/530 (1979–1980), pp. 64–68; idem, *Via Crucis de la justicia* (Madrid: Paulinas, 1980); idem, *Vida segundo o Espírito* (Petrópolis: Vozes, 1982); Alejandro Cussianovich, "Praxis de liberación. Camino de santidad," *Diakonía*, 6 (1978), pp. 70–79; idem, "Espiritualidad cristiana y liberdadora,"*Christus*, 531 (1980), pp. 12–16; Ignacio Ellacuría, "Fe y justicia," *Christus* (Aug. 1977), pp. 26–33; (Oct. 1977), pp. 19–34; idem, "Las bienaventuranzas como carta fundacional de la Iglesia de los pobres," in *Iglesia de los pobres y organizaciones populares* (San Salvador, 1979), pp. 105–18; idem, "Espiritualidad," in *Conceptos fundamentales*; Segundo Galilea, *Espiritualidad de la liberación* (Santiago de Chile, 1974); idem, "La liberación como encuentro de la política y de la contemplación," *Concilium*, 96 (1974), pp. 313–27; idem, "La espiritualidad de la liberación como espiritualidad política," *Christus*, 499 (1977), pp. 29–32; idem, *La religiosidad popular como espiritualidad* (Madrid, 1979); idem, *Espiritualidad de la liberación segun las dienaventuranzas* (Bogotá, 1979); idem, "El rostro latinoamericano de la espiritualidad,"*Christus*, 529/530 (1979–1980), pp. 69–72; idem, *Renovación y espiritualidad* (Bogotá, 1981); J.B. Libânio, "Acción y contemplación en nuestra situación conflictiva," *CIS*, 25 (1977), pp. 57–71; idem, *Discernimento espiritual: reflexões teológico-espirituais* (São Paulo, 1977); idem, *Spiritual Discernment and Politics: Guidelines for Religious Communities* (Maryknoll, N.Y.: Orbis, 1982); Juan Hernández Pico, "El martirio hoy en América Latina," *Concilium*, 183 (1984), pp. 335–44; Pablo Richard, "La ética cristiana como espiritualidad liberdadora en la realidad eclesial de América Latina," *Cristianismo y Sociedad*, 69–70 (1981), pp. 51–59; idem, "Espiritualidad para tiempos de revolución. Teología espiritual a la luz de San Pablo," in *Espiritualidad y liberación en América Latina*, pp. 87–101; Jon Sobrino, "Espiritualidad de Jesús y de la liberación," *Christus*, 529/530 (1979–1980), pp. 59–63; idem, "Experiencia de Dios en la Iglesia de los pobres," *Cristianismo y Sociedad*, 63 (1980), pp. 87–101; idem, "Perfíl de una santidad política," *Concilium*, 183 (1983), pp. 335–44; idem, "Espiritualidad de la persecución y del martirio," *Misiones Extranjeras*, 75 (1983), pp. 315–28; idem, "Espiritualidad y liberación," *Sal Terrae*, 72 (Feb. 1984), pp. 139–62; P. Trigo, "Espiritualidad y cultura ante la modernización," *Christus*, 529/530 (1979–1980), pp. 73–77. —To these there should also be added the numerous works on the religious life and its spirituality.

21. See Boff, "Contemplativus in liberatione," p. 65; Ellacuría, *Fe y justicia*, p. 32.

22. *El Dios de la vida* (Lima, 1981), p. 6.

23. Ibid., p. 7.

24. "Contemplativus," p. 64.

25. *Espiritualidad para tiempos*, p. 87.

26. "The Church and Popular Political Organizations" (Third Pastoral Letter), Oscar Romero, *Voice of the Voiceless* (Maryknoll, N.Y.: Orbis, 1985), p. 105.

27. Ibid.

28. First published in *Concilium*, March 1983; Spanish edition, pp. 335ff.; English edition, pp. 17ff. The *Concilium* English translation is used with permission, and has been edited for inclusion in the present volume.

29. See Leonardo Boff, *La fe en la periferia del mundo* (Santander: Sal Terrae, 1981), pp. 209-62. See also the monothematic issue of *Christus*, 529 (1979-1980), on the spirituality of liberation.

30. See Ignacio Ellacuría, "Los pobres, lugar teológico en América Latina," *Diakonía*, 21 (1982), pp. 113-19, 156-59, 435-45.

31. See the pastoral letters of Archbishop Romero in *Voice of the Voiceless*, pp. 52-161; for his treatment of violence see the same volume.

32. See Juan Hernández Pico, "Martyrdom Today in Latin America: Stumbling-block, Folly, and Power of God," *Concilium*, March 1983; Jon Sobrino, *Resurrección de la verdadera Iglesia* (Santander: Sal Terrae, 1981), pp. 177-209, 243-66; idem, "Persecución a la Iglesia en Centroamérica," *Estudios Centroamericanos*, 393 (1981), pp. 645-64.

33. On the question of combatants as possible martyrs, see Pico, "Martyrdom Today," and Sobrino, *Resurrección de la verdadera Iglesia*, pp. 197ff.

34. See Ignacio Ellacuría, "El verdadero pueblo de Dios según Mons. Romero," *Estudios Centroamericanos*, 392 (1981), pp. 529-54.

35. First published in *Misiones Extranjeras*, 75 (May-June, 1983), pp. 315-28.

36. For a more detailed analysis of persecution and martyrdom in their historical reality and in their theological significance, see my works, "Persecución a la Iglesia en Centroamérica," pp. 645-64, and *Resurrección de la verdadera Iglesia*, pp. 243-66.

37. Taken from *Carta a las Iglesias* (Servicio Informativo del Centro Pastoral de la Universidad Centroamericana, San Salvador), 33 (Jan. 1983), p. 7.

38. Romero, *Voice of the Voiceless*, p. 182.

39. This second paragraph comes from Archbishop Romero's Second Pastoral Letter, ibid., p. 80.

40. First published in *Sal Terrae*, 72/10 (Oct. 1984), pp. 683-97.

41. See Ignacio Ellacuría, "Historicidad de la salvación cristiana," *Revista Latinoamericana de Teología*, 1 (1984), pp. 5-45.

42. José P. Miranda, *Marx and the Bible* (Maryknoll, N.Y.: Orbis, 1974), p. 117.

43. Joachim Jeremias, *Teología del Nuevo Testamento* (Salamanca: Sígueme, 1974), 1:122.

44. This is the basic intuition in Latin America with regard to human rights: to see them in the perspective of the right to life of the poor, and not the other way around. In terms of Christian experience, Archbishop Romero has emphasized this in his often-quoted observation: "In my country cruel death is an everyday occurrence. The poor are being murdered, campesinos are being tortured, day in, day out, with the most extreme violence. What must be defended is the minimum: God's maximum gift, life."

45. Obviously this will be applicable as well, analogously, to groups whose lives are threatened even in countries of abundance or relative abundance.

46. See, for example, various authors, *La justicia que brota de la fe* (Santander: Sal Terrae, 1983).

47. *Puebla and Beyond*, John Eagleson and Philip Scharper, eds. (Maryknoll, N.Y.: Orbis, 1979), "The Final Document," no. 1142, p. 265.

48. For an analysis of the reality of the poor, see Ignacio Ellacuría, "Las bienaventuranzas como carta fundamental de la Iglesia de los pobres," in Oscar Romero, ed., *Iglesia de los pobres y organizaciones populares* (San Salvador, 1978), pp. 105–18; idem, "Pobres y Pueblo de Dios," in *Conceptos fundamentales* (n. 18, above), pp. 786–801, 840–59; Gustavo Gutiérrez, *The Power of the Poor in History* (Maryknoll, N.Y.: Orbis, 1983).

49. Recent years have seen an abundance of Latin American reflection on this subject in relation to spirituality. See Leonardo Boff, "Contemplativus in liberatione," *Christus*, 529/530 (1979), pp. 60/62; Segundo Galilea, "El rostro latinoamericano de la espiritualidad," ibid., pp. 69–72; Juan Hernández Pico, "La oración en los procesos latinoamericanos de liberación," ibid., pp. 93–95; Gustavo Gutiérrez, *We Drink from Our Own Wells* (Maryknoll, N.Y.: Orbis, 1984); Ignacio Ellacuría, "Espiritualidad," in *Conceptos fundamentales*; Jon Sobrino, "Espiritualidad y liberación," *Sal Terrae*, 849 (Feb. 1984), pp. 139–62.

50. "Liberator God" and "God of Life" have become powerful formulas for the profession of faith in God. See Pablo Richard et al., *The Idols of Death and the God of Life* (Maryknoll, N.Y.: Orbis, 1983); Gustavo Gutiérrez, *El Dios de la vida* (Lima, Peru: CEP, 1981).

51. First published in *Iglesia Viva*, 105/106 (1983), pp. 361–77.

52. First published in *Sal Terrae*, 71 (Feb. 1983), pp. 83–93.

53. Pope Paul VI, *On Evangelization in the Modern World* (Washington, D.C.: U.S. Catholic Conference, 1976).

54. M. Hengel, *Seguimiento y carisma* (Santander: Sal Terrae, 1981), p. 128.

55. First published in *Christus*, 1983.

56. First published in *Estudios Centroamericanos*, 387/388 (Jan.-Feb. 1981), pp. 51–53. The four American missionaries were raped and murdered on Dec. 2, 1980. See Patricia Jacobsen, "God Came to El Salvador," in Martin Lange and Reinhold Iblacker, eds., *Witnesses of Hope* (Maryknoll, N.Y.: Orbis, 1981), pp. 141–53.

57. Address given to the Second Congress on Theology and Poverty, "Hope of the poor, Christian hope," held in Madrid, Sept. 5–12, 1982. First published in *Misión Abierta*, 4/5 (Nov. 1982), pp. 112–23. The final pages of the Spanish text have been omitted—passages already included in previous chapters in the present volume.

58. Text of a talk given Jan. 9, 1984, at a round table discussion, "Future of the European church? Latin America has the floor," held by the Cristianisme i Justicia Center, and published, in Catalan, in publication no. 4 of that organization, and in Spanish, in *Diakonía*, March 29, 1984, pp. 47–63.

Index

187